The Thriving Society
ON THE SOCIAL CONDITIONS OF HUMAN FLOURISHING

James R. Stoner, Jr., and Harold James, Editors

Published by the Witherspoon Institute

Copyright © 2015 by the Witherspoon Institute, Inc.

All rights reserved.

No part of this publication may be reproduced or transmitted in any form or by any means, electronic or mechanical, including photocopy, recording, or any information storage and retrieval system now known or to be invented, without permission in writing from the publisher, except by a reviewer who wishes to quote brief passages in connection with a review written for inclusion in print, broadcast, or online media.

Alicia Grimaldi, publishing director
Betsy Stokes, line editor
Margaret Trejo, text and cover design and layout
Andrew Matlack, cover artist
Printing by Thomson-Shore

Published in the United States of America by the Witherspoon Institute
16 Stockton Street, Princeton, New Jersey 08540

Library of Congress Control Number: 2015937889

ISBN 9780985108755

Printed in the United States of America

CONTENTS

	Acknowledgments	v
	Introduction *James R. Stoner, Jr., and Harold James*	vii
1	Five Pillars of a Decent and Dynamic Society *Robert P. George*	1
2	Five Pillars, Four Foundations, Three Dimensions, Two Perspectives, One Institution *John Haldane*	9
3	Caritas and Competition *Harold James*	27
4	The Person and the Parson *Roger Scruton*	37
5	The Family as First Building Block *Mark Regnerus*	49
6	Why We Need the Majesty of the Law *Harvey C. Mansfield*	67
7	Why We Respect the Dignity of Politics *James R. Stoner, Jr.*	81

Contents

8	The Vital Role of Religious Institutions *Michael O. Emerson*	97
9	The University *Candace Vogler*	107
10	Institutions of Research Vital to a Thriving Society *Sanjeev R. Kulkarni and Donald W. Landry*	119
11	Economic Sustainability *Michael D. Bordo and Harold James*	129
12	Republican Prudence: The Founders' Foreign-Policy School and Its Enduring Legacy *Paul O. Carrese and Michael Doran*	145
13	Missing Persons, Fugitive Families, and Big Brother: The Government in Relation to the Family and the Person *Gerard V. Bradley*	161
14	A Way Forward: The University *Steven Justice*	175
15	Healthcare *Jesús Fernández-Villaverde*	189
	About the Authors	205
	Index	213
	A Note on the Witherspoon Institute	225
	A Note on the Social Trends Institute	227

ACKNOWLEDGMENTS

Luis Tellez, president of the Witherspoon Institute, first conceived the idea of assembling a book of essays reflecting upon the question of what makes society thrive—indeed, of sketching in outline a thriving society—and then he recruited the authors, the editors, and the other members of the publishing team. As with many other Witherspoon projects, Carlos Cavallé was an important and supportive companion. Betsy Stokes was our patient and persistent line editor; Megan Holobowicz produced the index. Margaret Trejo designed the dust jacket and interior pages and typeset the book. Andrew Matlack created the cover art. Publicity and promotion of the entire project was entrusted to Patrick Hough, Witherspoon's executive director. Finally, if you are reading this in print, it is because Alicia Grimaldi, our publishing director, supervised the project, tirelessly ensuring that every task was completed and every detail perfected. To all of these fine people, our great thanks.

—The Editors

INTRODUCTION

Reports tell us that a majority of Americans believe the country is headed in the wrong direction. They are unhappy with the quality of our political discourse and pessimistic about their children's and grandchildren's prospects for enjoying the quality of life that they themselves have experienced. Some point fingers at those they think are at fault for our current ills, but much of their criticism is partial or superficial. Few have thought comprehensively about how modern society, with all its complexity, actually thrives.

This collection of essays by some of the most distinguished scholars of our day aims to help the thinking public understand what elements make up a society where people can flourish, to point out the reasons for some of the problems we currently experience, and to indicate several avenues for reform. We begin with Robert P. George's widely circulated essay, "Five Pillars of a Decent and Dynamic Society" (the five pillars are the person, the family, law and government, the university, and the free market), which the authors of most of the subsequent essays respond to or elaborate upon. George distinguishes a decent society (home to the first three pillars), where human beings can live moral lives and achieve a measure of happiness, from a dynamic society (which adds the latter two pillars to the first three), promising additional opportunities for individual development and promoting intellectual, economic, and social progress. Unlike those who see the choice between a decent, traditional society and a dynamic, modern society as a tragic one—supposing that the goods of tradition must be sacrificed in the course of pursuing progress or that the opportunities of modernity must be foregone if morality is to be preserved—George argues that the aims of decency and dynamism can be successfully balanced. By enabling social mobility, a dynamic society can achieve a kind of justice that traditional societies typically had to ignore. Likewise, the institutions that promote modern progress in fact depend on many of the virtues of individuals and families that decent societies aimed especially to form.

Introduction

In the spirit of George's essay, the project of explaining what makes for a thriving society is optimistic but not utopian. It is built upon the understanding that most—not all but the majority of persons—want to flourish and to help others, but cultural circumstances incline the consequences of their hopes and deeds toward good or ill, sometimes against their intention. The challenge is to chart a course for society where more people are better able to flourish, or rather, to enable a well-educated citizenry to make informed choices, individually and collectively, for themselves. Unlike some advocates of social progress, however, the authors assembled here know that it is a mistake to think we can create heaven on earth; some the world's worst atrocities have been committed under that pretense. Instead, the tone is empirical and ameliorative: observing what has value and what constitutes threat, and promoting the one while cautioning against the other. The project is ecumenical, in that its authors come from different faith traditions, have different kinds of academic expertise, take a variety of perspectives, and even hail from different countries, and also in that the society they envisage has room for many different ways of life and points of view. Recovering our society's capacity for a moral conversation is, we think, already a sign of flourishing, a positive antidote to despair.

As we mentioned, the collection begins with George's essay. Immediately following are two responses that contextualize and elaborate upon his insights. John Haldane, a moral philosopher, places George's framework in philosophical and historical context, describing his task as Hegelian. He finds four ancient foundations underlying decent societies as we have come to know them in the West—Hebraic monotheism, Christian incarnationalism, Greek aletheism, and Roman legalism—and he identifies three dimensions to moral understanding in the modern world: utilitarianism, Kantian moralism, and a focus on character or virtue. Haldane sees George's distinction between the decent and dynamic as a distinction between the premodern and the modern, or alternatively between the constitutive and the instrumental, and he concludes by wondering whether the university is best understood dynamically, as an engine for research and the increase of knowledge, or traditionally, as a place for its transmission. Economic historian Harold James reconceives George's distinction between the decent and dynamic as the distinction between compassion and competition, two intrinsic characteristics of human beings in their relations with one another. James sees value in both, and danger, too, if they are not kept in balance. Less skeptical than Haldane about the value of modern market freedom, James stresses the importance of inner conviction and its regulative effect in both economic activity and moral life.

The next essays examine in turn George's pillars. Roger Scruton offers a meditation upon the puzzle of the human person, who understands himself as a person only in relation to another but whose moral formation comes about not as a result of chance encounters but under the guidance of a moral community. Mark Regnerus, a sociologist, discusses marriage and the family, acknowledging their variance over time as the social context changes but showing as well that the consequences of family form—for better or, now often, for worse—permeate social life in many ways. Harvey C. Mansfield notes the continued "majesty of law," a traditional attribute still persisting in spite of efforts to make law wholly instrumental. James Stoner finds the dignity of politics under siege and political liberty, as a result, precarious, though the constitutional forms of American government still enable political action by those willing to embrace them.

Sociologist Michael O. Emerson writes about "The Vital Role of Religious Institutions" in the United States, providing as they do numerous volunteer services to society and constituting a seedbed of civic formation. Religion was not a separate pillar in George's framework—in a modern society that recognizes religious liberty, its social role is projected through the person—but its influence and importance appear in many of the essays. The university, founded originally by the medieval Church, is treated in its modern form by two separate essays. The first, by philosopher Candace Vogler, examines the multiple tasks undertaken by modern universities and the tensions among them. The second, by scientists Sanjeev R. Kulkarni and Donald W. Landry, focuses specifically on basic research and analyzes its vulnerability to politics and the danger of bias that vulnerability presents. Finally, Michael D. Bordo and Harold James consider the pillar of the free market in an essay on "Economic Sustainability," looking at fiscal-, monetary-, and financial-policy issues that have arisen in the wake of the recent economic crisis called the Great Recession.

The concluding set of essays are concerned with particular challenges of the present. Paul O. Carrese and Michael Doran consider the proper outlook toward foreign policy that Americans might adopt, recommending a recovery of the tradition of republican prudence, originated by George Washington and adopted by many of his successors, as preferable to today's academic theories of political realism on the one hand and liberal internationalism on the other. Society today often has an international dimension—this is certainly true for economic matters in a globalized market but also true for science and for much else in universities—but as Carrese and Doran write, "Only political institutions rooted in national identity permit the civic engagement required for a thriving society." Law professor Gerard V. Bradley presents a trenchant critique of the path of modern constitutional law regarding the family, noting its substitution of liberal ideas concerning an autonomous self for the traditional culture of personal and social formation, usually permeated by shared religious and moral ideas. Steven Justice's essay, "A Way Forward: The University," addresses some of the concerns of the earlier essays on the topic and suggests what can be done to make improvements, not by radically remaking institutions but through the work of devoted individuals within them doing their tasks especially well. Jesús Fernández-Villaverde, an economist, examines modern healthcare reform, looking critically at the Affordable Care Act but also recognizing the genuine problems it meant to address and sketching the elements of any fair, further reform.

The health of a democracy, it is often said, depends upon the education of its citizens, and it is the belief of the editors and, we think, of the authors of the essays here collected that if more Americans were given in plain language the ingredients that go into making society flourish, we would be better able to make sound choices in public life. Our aim is not advocacy of specific policies—for all that we share in our orientation toward a thriving society, we would surely find many disagreements among us were we to debate those—but the strengthening of public discourse and the widening of perspectives on public affairs. We do not think that society will ever be perfect—far from it—but we are confident that when people find compelling reasons that explain what is wrong and what can be done about it, they are more apt to act according to those reasons and work for better solutions. If reading these essays can guide that work and give readers hope for eventual success, then our aim will be accomplished.

— James R. Stoner, Jr., and Harold James

1

Five Pillars of a Decent and Dynamic Society

Robert P. George

Any healthy society, any decent society, will rest upon three pillars. The first is respect for the human person—the individual human being and his dignity. Where this pillar is in place, the formal and informal institutions of society, and the beliefs and practices of the people, will be such that every member of the human family—irrespective of race, sex, or ethnicity, to be sure, but also and equally irrespective of age, size, stage of development, or condition of dependency—is treated as a person, as a subject bearing profound, inherent, and equal worth and dignity.

A society that does not nurture respect for the human person—beginning with the child in the womb and including the mentally and physically impaired and the frail elderly—will sooner or later (probably sooner) come to regard human beings as mere cogs in the larger social wheel whose dignity and well-being may legitimately be sacrificed for the sake of collectivity. Some members of the community—those in certain development stages, for example—will come to be regarded as disposable, and others—those in certain conditions of dependency, for example—will come to be viewed as intolerably burdensome, as useless eaters, as "better off dead," as *lebensunwerten Lebens*.

In its most extreme modern forms, the totalitarian regime reduces the individual to the status of an instrument to serve the ends of the fascist state or the future communist utopia. When liberal democratic regimes go awry, it is often because a utilitarian ethic reduces the human person to a means rather than an end to which other things, including the systems and institutions of law, education, and the economy, are means. The abortion license against which we struggle today is dressed up by its defenders in the language of individual and even natural rights—and there can be no doubt that the acceptance of abortion is partly the fruit of me-generation liberal ideology—a corruption (and burlesque) of liberal political philosophy in its classical form. But more fundamentally, it is underwritten by a utilitarian ethic that, in the end, vaporizes the very idea of natural rights, treating it (in Jeremy Bentham's famously dismissive words) as "nonsense upon stilts."

In cultures where religious fanaticism has taken hold, the dignity of the individual is typically sacrificed for the sake of tragically misbegotten theological ideas and goals. By contrast, a liberal democratic ethos, where it is uncorrupted by utilitarianism or me-generation expressive individualism, supports the dignity of the human person by giving witness to basic human rights and liberties. Where a healthy religious life flourishes, faith in God provides a grounding for the dignity and inviolability of the human person by, for example, proposing an understanding of each and every member of the human family (even those of different faiths or no faith) as persons made in the image and likeness of the divine Author of our lives and liberties.

The second pillar of any decent society is the institution of the family. It is indispensable. The family, based on the marital commitment of husband and wife, is the original and best ministry of health, education, and welfare. Although no family is perfect, no institution matches the healthy family in its capacity to transmit to each new generation the understandings and traits of character—the values and virtues—upon which the success of every other institution of society, from law and government to education and business, vitally depends.[1]

Where families fail to form, or many break down, the effective transmission of the virtues of honesty, civility, self-restraint, concern for the welfare of others, justice, compassion, and personal responsibility is imperiled. Without these virtues, respect for the dignity of the human person, the first pillar of a decent society, will be undermined and sooner or later, lost. For even the most laudable formal institutions cannot uphold respect for human dignity where people do not have the virtues that make that respect a reality and give it vitality in actual social practices. Respect for the dignity of the human being requires more than formally sound institutions; it also requires a cultural ethos in which people act from conviction to treat one another as human beings should be treated: with respect, civility, justice, and compassion.

The best legal and political institutions ever devised are of little value where selfishness, contempt for others, dishonesty, injustice, and other types of immorality and irresponsibility flourish. Indeed, the effective working of governmental institutions themselves depends upon most people most of the time obeying the law out of a sense of moral obligation and not merely out of fear of detection and punishment. And perhaps it goes without saying that the success of business and a market-based economic system depends on there being reasonably virtuous, trustworthy, law-abiding, promise-keeping people to serve as workers, managers, lenders, regulators, and payers of bills for goods and services. It is within the institution of a healthy family that these traits are born.

The third pillar of any decent society is a fair and effective system of law and government. This is necessary because none of us is perfectly virtuous all the time, and some people will be deterred from wrongdoing only by the threat of punishment. More importantly, contemporary philosophers of law tell us the law coordinates human behavior for the sake of achieving common goals—the common good—especially in dealing with the complexities of modern life. Even if all of us were perfectly virtuous all of the time, we would still need a system of laws (considered as a scheme of authoritatively stipulated coordination norms) to accomplish many of our common ends (safely transporting ourselves on the streets, to take a simple and obvious example).

The success of business firms and the economy as a whole depends vitally on a fair and effective system and set of institutions for the administration of justice. We need judges skilled in the craft of law and free of corruption. We need to be able to rely on courts to settle disputes, including disputes between parties who are both in good faith, and to enforce contracts and other agreements and enforce them in a timely manner. Indeed, the knowledge that contracts will be enforced is usually sufficient to ensure that courts will not actually be called on to enforce them. A sociological fact of which we can be certain is this: Where there is no reliable system of the administration of justice—no confidence that the courts will hold people to their obligations under the law—business will not flourish, and everyone in the society will suffer.

A society can, in my opinion, be a decent one even if it is not a dynamic one, if the three pillars are healthy and therefore functioning in a mutually supportive way. Now, conservatives of a certain stripe believe that a truly decent society cannot be a dynamic one. Dynamism, they believe, causes instability that undermines the pillars of a decent society. So some conservatives in old Europe and even the United States opposed not only industrialism but the very idea of a commercial society, fearing that commercial economies inevitably produce consumerist and acquisitive materialist attitudes that corrode the foundations of decency. And some, such as some Amish communities in the United States, reject education for their children beyond what is necessary to master reading, writing, and arithmetic, on the grounds that higher education leads to worldliness and apostasy and undermines religious faith and moral virtue.

Although a decent society need not be a dynamic one (as the Amish example shows), dynamism need not erode decency. A dynamic society need not be one in which consumerism and materialism become rife or where moral and spiritual values disappear. Indeed, dynamism can play a positive moral role and, I would venture to say, almost certainly will play such a role—where what makes it possible is sufficient to sustain it over the long term.

That is, I realize, a rather cryptic comment, so let me explain what I mean. To do that, I will have to offer some thoughts on what in fact makes social dynamism possible.

There are two pillars of social dynamism: First, there are institutions of research and education in which the frontiers of knowledge across the humanities, social sciences, and natural sciences are pushed back and through which knowledge is transmitted to students and disseminated to the public at large. Second, there are business firms and associated organizations and economic institutions by and through which wealth is generated, widely distributed, and preserved.

We can think of universities and business firms, together with respect for the dignity of the human person, the institution of the family, and the system of law and government, as the five pillars of decent and dynamic societies. The university and the business firm depend in various ways for their well-being on the well-being of the others, and they can help to support the others in turn. At the same time, of course, ideologies and practices hostile to the pillars of a decent society can manifest themselves in higher education and in business, and these institutions can erode the social values on which they themselves depend not only for their own integrity but for their long-term survival.

It is all too easy to take the pillars for granted. So it is important to remember that each of them has come under attack from different angles and forces. Operating from within universities, persons and movements hostile to one or the other of these pillars, usually preaching or acting in the name of high ideals of one sort or another, have gone on the attack.

Attacks on business and the very idea of the market economy and economic freedom coming from the academic world are, of course, well-known. Students are sometimes taught to hold business, and especially businesspeople, in contempt as heartless exploiters driven by greed. In my own days as a student, these attacks were often made explicitly in the name of Marxism. One notices less of that after the collapse of the Soviet empire, but the attacks themselves have abated little. Needless to say, where businesses behave unethically, they play into the stereotypes of the enemies of the market system and facilitate their effort to smear business and the free market for the sake of transferring greater control of the economy to government.

Similarly, attacks on the family, and particularly on the institution of marriage on which the family is built, are common in the academy. The line here is that the family, at least as traditionally constituted and understood, is a patriarchal and exploitative institution that oppresses women and imposes on people forms of sexual restraint that are psychologically damaging and inhibiting of the free expression of their personality. As has become clear in the past decade and a half, there is a profound threat to the family here, one against which we must fight with all our energy and will. It is difficult to think of any item on the domestic agenda that is more critical today than the defense of marriage as the union of husband and wife and the effort to renew and rebuild the marriage culture.

What has also become clear is that the threats to the family (and to the sanctity of human life) are at the same time and necessarily threats to religious freedom and to religion itself—at least where the religions in question stand up and speak out for conjugal marriage and the rights of the child in the womb. From the point of view of those seeking to redefine marriage and to protect and advance what they regard as the right to abortion, the taming of religion—and the stigmatization and marginalization of religions that refuse to be tamed—is a moral imperative. It is therefore not surprising to see that they are increasingly open in saying that they do not see disputes about sex and marriage and abortion and euthanasia as honest disagreements among reasonable people of goodwill. They are, rather, battles between the forces of "reason" and "enlightenment" on the one side, and those of "ignorance" and "bigotry" on the other. Their opponents are to be treated just as racists are treated—since they are the equivalent of racists. That doesn't necessarily mean imprisoning them or fining them for expressing unacceptable opinions—though "hate crimes" laws in certain jurisdictions raise the specter of precisely such abuses—but it does mean using antidiscrimination laws and other legal instruments to stigmatize them, marginalize them, and impose upon them and their institutions various forms of social and even civil disability, with few if any meaningful protections for religious liberty and the rights of conscience.

Some will counsel that commercial businesses and businesspeople "have no horse in this race." They will say that these are moral, cultural, and religious disputes about which businesspeople and people concerned with economic freedom need not trouble themselves. The reality is that the ideological movements that today seek, for example, to redefine marriage and abolish its normativity for romantic relations and the rearing of children are the same movements that seek to undermine the market-based economic system and replace it with statist control of vast areas of economic life. Moreover, the rise of ideologies hostile to marriage and the family has had a measurable social impact, and its costs are counted in ruined relationships, damaged lives, and all that follows in the social sphere from these personal catastrophes. In many poorer places in the United States, and I believe this is true in many other countries, families are simply failing to form, and marriage is disappearing or coming to be regarded as an optional "lifestyle choice"—one among various ways of conducting relationships and having and rearing children. Out-of-wedlock birthrates are very high, with the negative consequences being borne less by the affluent than by those in the poorest and most vulnerable sectors of society.

In 1965, Daniel Patrick Moynihan, a Harvard professor who was then working in the administration of President Lyndon Johnson, shocked Americans by reporting findings that the out-of-wedlock birthrate among African Americans in the United States had reached nearly 25 percent. He warned that the phenomenon of boys and girls being raised without fathers in poorer communities would result in social pathologies that would severely harm those most in need of the supports of solid family life. His predictions were all too quickly verified. The widespread failure of family formation portended disastrous social consequences of delinquency, despair, violence, drug abuse, and crime and incarceration. A snowball effect resulted in the further growth of the out-of-wedlock birthrate. It is now more than 70 percent among African Americans. It is worth noting that at the time of Moynihan's report, the out-of-wedlock birthrate for the population as a whole was almost 6 percent. Today, that rate is more than 40 percent.

The economic consequences of these developments are evident. Consider the need of business to have available to it a responsible and capable workforce. Business cannot manufacture honest, hardworking people to employ. Nor can government create them by law. Businesses and governments depend on there being many such people, but they must rely on the family, assisted by religious communities and other institutions of civil society, to produce them. So business has a stake—a massive stake—in the long-term health of the family. It should avoid doing anything to undermine the family, and it should do what it can where it can to strengthen the institution.

As an advocate of dynamic societies, I believe in the market economy and the free-enterprise system. I particularly value the social mobility that economic dynamism makes possible. Indeed, I am a beneficiary of that social mobility. A bit over a hundred years ago, my immigrant grandfathers—one from southern Italy, the other from Syria—were coal miners. Neither had so much as remotely considered the possibility of attending a university; as a practical economic matter, such a thing was simply out of the question. At that time, Woodrow Wilson, the future president of the United States, was the McCormick Professor of Jurisprudence at Princeton University. Today, just two generations forward, I, the grandson of those immigrant coal miners, am the McCormick Professor of Jurisprudence at Princeton University. And what is truly remarkable is that my story is completely unremarkable. It is not that I'm great; it's that we have a great system—one that enables people to rise from humble beginnings and develop their talents. My story, or something quite like it, is the story of millions of Americans. Perhaps it goes without saying that this kind of upward mobility is not common in corporatist or socialist economic systems, but it is very common in market-based, free-enterprise economies.

Having said that, I should note that I am not a supporter of the laissez-faire doctrine embraced by strict libertarians. I believe that law and government do have important and, indeed, indispensable roles to play in regulating enterprises for the sake of protecting public health, safety, and morals; preventing exploitation and abuse; and promoting fair, competitive circumstances of exchange. But these roles are compatible, I would insist, with the ideal of limited government and with the principle of subsidiarity. According to subsidiarity, government must respect individual initiative to the extent reasonably possible and avoid violating the autonomy and usurping the authority of families, religious communities, and other institutions of civil society that play a primary role in building character and transmitting virtues.

But having said *that*, I would warn that limited government—considered as an ideal as vital to business as to the family—cannot be maintained where the marriage culture collapses and families fail to form or easily dissolve. Where these things happen, the health, education, and welfare functions of the family will have to be undertaken by someone, or some institution, and that will sooner or later be the government. To deal with pressing social problems, bureaucracies will grow and with them, the tax burden. Moreover, the growth of crime and other pathologies where family breakdown is rampant will result in the need for more extensive policing and incarceration and, again, increased taxes to pay for these government services. If we want limited government, as we should, and a level of taxation that is not unduly burdensome, we need healthy institutions of civil society, beginning with a flourishing marriage culture supporting family formation and preservation.

Advocates of the market economy, and supporters of marriage and the family, have common opponents in hard-left socialism, the entitlement mentality, and the statist ideologies that provide their intellectual underpinnings. But the uniting of advocates of limited government and economic freedom on the one hand and supporters of marriage and the family on the other is not, and must not be regarded as, a mere marriage of convenience. The reason they have common enemies is that they have common principles: respect for the human person, which grounds our commitment to individual liberty and the right to economic freedom and other essential civil liberties; belief in personal responsibility, which is a precondition of the possibility and moral desirability of individual liberty in any domain; recognition of subsidiarity as the basis for effective but truly limited government and for the integrity of the institutions of civil society that mediate between the individual and the centralized power of the state; respect for the rule of law; and recognition of the vital role played by the family and by religious institutions that support the character-forming functions of the family in the flourishing of any decent and dynamic society.

The point has been made by past Republican vice-presidential nominee Congressman Paul Ryan:

> A "libertarian" who wants limited government should embrace the means to his freedom: thriving mediating institutions that create the moral preconditions for economic markets and choice. A "social

issues" conservative with a zeal for righteousness should insist on a free market economy to supply the material needs for families, schools, and churches that inspire moral and spiritual life. In a nutshell, the notion of separating the social from the economic issues is a false choice. They stem from the same root. A prosperous moral community is a prerequisite for a just and ordered society, and the idea that either side of this current divide can exist independently is a mirage.[2]

The two greatest institutions ever devised for lifting people out of poverty and enabling them to live in dignity are the market economy and the institution of marriage. These institutions will, in the end, stand or fall together. Contemporary statist ideologues have contempt for both of these institutions, and they fully understand the connection between them. We who believe in the market and in the family should see the connection no less clearly.

NOTES

1. The family is typically assisted in carrying out its indispensable functions by other institutions of civil society that mediate between the person and the state and help in the project of forming character and transmitting virtues. First among these are the institutions of religion. In modern societies, schools are also important contributors. So are voluntary associations of all sorts, from service organizations such as the Boy Scouts to mutual-aid societies of every description. Of course, to do their jobs properly, these institutions themselves must be in good shape, especially from the moral vantage point. Otherwise, they become part of the problem, not the solution.
2. Hudson Institute event speech, June 2009.

2

Five Pillars, Four Foundations, Three Dimensions, Two Perspectives, One Institution[1]

John Haldane

In his essay, "Five Pillars of a Decent and Dynamic Society," which forms the text of a widely delivered lecture,[2] Robert P. George distinguishes between *decency* and *dynamism* as societal attributes and identifies several evaluative and structural supports of each of these. Decency, he claims, requires (1) respect for the human person, (2) the flourishing of the family (as built around heterosexual marriage and parenting), and (3) justice in the making and upholding of law. Beyond this, social dynamism is held to depend chiefly upon two further factors: (a) institutions of higher education and research and (b) businesses that produce goods and provide services.

Here I switched from numbers to letters for two reasons. First, because George maintains that a society can be decent without being dynamic, i.e., it can flourish morally without a higher education sector and without engaging in commercial production and exchange. Second, because he seems to regard these latter supports as being of a different sort than the first three pillars, inasmuch as they are not themselves intrinsically ordered to the human good—or at least they are not so directly and intimately connected to it.

At the same time, however, George argues that there is an important relationship between the two sets of pillars, since each supports the other. The broad character of this support differs in each direction: the first three provide specific moral content and orientation to the latter, while the second two may encourage general independence of thought and action and thereby limit the tendencies of secular statist ideologies or religious fanaticism to constrain or assault the human person, the family, and the institutions of law and government.

Further, George encourages defenders of the pillars of decency and advocates of the pillars of dynamism to be aware that attacks on each have tended to come from the same left-liberal quarters. He also claims that so far as Western societies are concerned, a major source of such attacks has been *academia*. If this is correct, then there are two main kinds of threat to decency and dynamism: first, various specific assaults upon and corruptions of the values represented by the three moral pillars; and second, the deployment of the power and prestige of one of the institutional pillars to undermine others.

While his essay offers some analysis and argument, its style and purpose are more rhetorical than dialectical. It gives little space to considering counterpositions or to anticipating and responding to objections and replies. Nor does it elaborate on the content of or the grounds for the favored conceptions of human dignity, family, and justice. Instead it seeks to remind its audience of important values to which it assumes they already subscribe, pointing to connections between these goods and social institutions, and thereby establishing a commonality of moral and political interests, all with the ultimate aim of persuading and motivating readers to take up the defense of marriage, the family, and limited government.

In saying the general argument is primarily and even avowedly rhetorical, I do not mean to criticize it on that account. On the contrary, I would say that it is a common and serious fault of academics when writing on social affairs that they either fail to address the interests and values of a general audience—pursuing instead abstract formulations and fabricated scenarios—and so are unable to persuade and motivate them, or else they mask what is essentially advocacy and even propaganda with an opaque veneer of academic analysis. George, by contrast, is undisguisedly an advocate and proceeds from what he takes to be shared commitments, via an account of their interdependence, to encourage the recognition of specific threats to them.

My interest is in locating these issues and exploring the ways in which they may be argued over within other contexts: firstly, that of the philosophy of social critique; secondly, that of the (four) cultural foundations of Western civilization; thirdly, that of the three dimensions of the structure of moral reasoning; fourthly, that of two contrasting outlooks; and fifthly, that of institutionally embodied higher education. The treatment of these elements will be brief but I hope sufficient to suggest further ways of engaging with arguments of the sort George presents.

SOCIAL PRACTICE AND SOCIAL PHILOSOPHY

While the ethical writings of Plato and Aristotle[3] are foundational for Western moral, social, and political philosophy and remain among the most important resources for thinking about questions of value, conduct, and policy, the most significant work by a great philosopher on the nature of the very endeavor of social philosophy may be Hegel's *Elements of the Philosophy of Right*, first published in

1820.[4] While Hegel does not repudiate the idea of natural law as it was developed by the Greeks and their medieval followers, he argues that what is required for freedom in the modern age is the existence of positive law and of the legal or constitutional state.

According to Hegel, property, contract, family, economic activity, and political life all depend for their protection upon the structure and operation of law, and since human freedom is realized in relation to these institutions, without law we cannot genuinely be free, either from external coercion or from internal compulsion. This is an important argument, developed at great length in *Elements*, where Hegel proceeds through three stages of social consciousness, from *abstract right* to *morality* to *ethical life*—within the last of which he locates family, civil society, and the state itself. While his argumentation is complex and is often expressed in terms of his speculative theory of the nature of mind or spirit (*geist*), the general form is recognizably Aristotelian: identifying action as behavior directed toward an end conceived of as good and arguing that human nature is realized progressively through forms of social life. Moreover, the conclusion is a strengthened version of George's case for the necessity of the third pillar of a decent society, namely, "a fair and effective system of law and government."

Hegel's work also shows a way that common goods are not only *common goals*, in the sense of ends that individuals and groups might converge upon, but common in respect to being intrinsically interpersonal: goods that are only available in and through community. Among the goods of family life, for example, some are instrumental, but others are constitutive: the having and raising of children, the care of elderly adults, preparation and participation of a family meal or other common work or leisure activity. These all provide opportunities for forms of shared benefit that are not aggregations of individual goods. The common good is only participated in through the course of the common activity and cannot be possessed independently of it.

These are important features of Hegel's argument, and they are certainly congenial to George's own case, but I mentioned that *Elements* is especially significant for what it has to say about the nature of reflection on forms of social life. Having said in the preface that the task of philosophy is "to apprehend what is," Hegel adds, "As far as the individual is concerned, each individual is a child of his time; thus philosophy, too, is its own time comprehended in thoughts."[5] From this general "historicist" premise, he draws a striking conclusion about moral philosophy in particular:

> A further word on the subject of *issuing instructions* on how the world ought to be: philosophy at any rate always comes too late to perform

this function.... When philosophy paints its grey in grey, a shape of life has grown old, and it cannot be rejuvenated, but only recognized by the grey in grey of philosophy.[6]

To understand this, we need to note that Hegel is focusing on the ambitions of normative philosophy: that which proposes ends of action. The tasks of science are description, explanation, and prediction. So far as it may be directed to human behavior, science may tell us what we *do*, what we *could* do, and perhaps even what we *would* do, but it cannot tell us what we *should* do. So while the gathering of empirical data and the forming of theories may be relevant to answering the question of what ought to be (done), science cannot of itself determine an answer. For that, we need moral insight and moral reasoning. But what Hegel says next suggests that moral argument is itself powerless, since it comes "too late" in the day to have practical effect.

Without entering into details, I propose the following interpretation and resolution of the seeming paradox: Forms of human life are shaped and directed toward various ends not by philosophical reflection but by tacit recognition of the good and by ordinary reasoning about its attainment. This is a historical process, and the practice of human life is historically embedded and transformed. Reflective philosophy may provide an abstract description and critique of these forms of life and of the logic of moral argument, but the specific content of the human good is given in and is only available through historically evolved institutions and practices. When philosophy says what "ought to be," it is reflecting on what has already been identified and adopted through the lived experience of past generations. What "always comes too late" on the scene is not first-order moral reasoning but philosophical argument.

This is a deep and challenging thought. Though at least in my interpretation, part of it harmonizes with previously expressed ideas, such as that of Aristotle when he writes that practice and not theory is the key to acquiring virtue.[7] Consider also Thomas Aquinas's observation that as well as being an object of philosophical analysis and argumentation, the human good is primarily an object of "connatural" knowledge, i.e., the kind of intuitive understanding that an ordinary person might have of the good of justice or of chastity by themselves being unreflectively (which is not to say ignorantly) just or chaste.[8] Again it chimes with the (Edmund) Burkean idea that there is a form of practical knowledge prior to—and more deeply rooted, wide-ranging, and reliable than that afforded by—abstract reflection: inherited wisdom. Burke writes, for example, of the practice of asserting basic liberties as entailed inheritances from forefathers:

> This policy appears to me to be the result of profound reflection; or rather the happy effect of following nature, which is wisdom without

reflection, and above it. A spirit of innovation is generally the result of a selfish temper and confined views. People will not look forward to posterity, who never look backward to their ancestors.[9]

These considerations may serve to validate moral reasoning antecedent to philosophical analysis and argumentation, but what of the idea that the latter comes "too late" to teach the world what it ought to be, for by that point, "a shape of life has grown old, and it cannot be rejuvenated, but only recognized by the grey in grey of philosophy"?

This concern was in Karl Marx's mind in the early 1840s, when he wrote *Critique of Hegel's Philosophy of Right* less than a quarter century after its publication, and he concluded his *Theses on Feuerbach* in 1845, with the sentence, "The philosophers have only interpreted the world, in various ways; the point is to change it." This closing, however, is ambiguous, for it can be read either as an endorsement of Hegel's analysis, thus enjoining those who wish to change the world to reject or set aside philosophy for that purpose, or else as an injunction to rethink the task of philosophy along practical and not just interpretative or critical lines. The latter is the more plausible reading and is required if one thinks that Marx is, or thought of himself as being, a philosopher. It does not, however, resolve the substantive questions of whether social philosophy can only function as a critical observer of society and not an agent within it and whether, even when operating only critically, it is dealing with a form of life that cannot be restored. The latter possibility would certainly be bad news for George, who wishes to think philosophically about society in the service of rejuvenating the social forms he views as having come under attack and having been weakened to some significant extent.

Some social conservatives do give the impression that their work is and can only be that of confirming the death of the thing they loved, lamenting its passing and perhaps preserving its memory in a spirit of tragic loss. At times the English philosopher Roger Scruton seems to represent such a position, begin- ning one particularly wistful work by quoting an adjoining sentence of Hegel's Preface:

> " 'The Owl of Minerva spreads its wings only with the gathering of the dusk.' Hegel's words ring true of every form of human life: it is only at the end of things that we begin to understand them. And understanding them we know they are lost."[10]

Elsewhere, however, Scruton stands in criticism of nostalgia as loss, as when writing about T.S. Eliot:

> "Like Burke, Eliot recognized the distinction between a back- ward-looking nostalgia, which is but another form of modern

sentimentality, and a genuine tradition, which grants us the courage and the vision with which to live in the modern world."[11]

The suggestion, reinforced in a subsequent essay celebrating the ideas of the German economist Wilhelm Röpke, is that there is a form of "positive" nostalgia—a longing to return—which is to be judged rational according to where it is one aims to return and to the feasibility of getting there (perhaps by rebuilding what was damaged).[12] Scruton's favored course is toward "localisation," by which he hopes to see a restoration of moral community; but two aspects of this are likely to concern George. First, the direction is proposed as "a solution to the market-induced disorders of modern society." Second, it seems to involve turning one's back on the wider society, giving it up as a bad lot. As regards the former, George is liable to view the analysis of the problem as a version of a position he wishes to reject, as when he writes, "Conservatives of a certain stripe believe that a truly decent society cannot be a dynamic one. Dynamism, they believe, causes instability that undermines the pillars of a decent society . . . fearing that commercial economies inevitably produce consumerist and acquisitive materialist attitudes that corrode the foundations of decency."

Additionally, George, or we, may regard the "localist" solution as analogous to the position of a protestant sect that only seeks salvation for its members rather than, as in the Catholic and apostolic tradition, seeking salvation for all. The relation between moral health and spiritual redemption is an interesting and difficult issue in moral theology and not for discussion here (though Scruton as, like Eliot, an Anglo-Catholic and George and I as Roman Catholics can hardly be indifferent to it). But the analogy of disposition remains relevant, for when George speaks of "a decent and dynamic society," he is not thinking of or recommending a return to local communities. His aspiration is at least national and arguably hemispherical, if not universal.

For what it is worth, I am at least agnostic about George's claim that commercial business, the market economy, and free enterprise share common principles with supporters of traditional marriage and the family—especially when it comes to the recognition of the role of religious institutions, though there may be alliances of convenience between businesses and churches in resisting state incursion. Some members of businesses are of course members of churches, and some who are not may yet concur with aspects of moral traditionalism, but these are contingent connections, and it is neither ignorant nor prejudiced to suspect that the market has been a significant cause, be it a secondary one, of the erosion of traditional morality. That said, and assuming that as well as being critical after the fact, philosophy can be practically effective in rejuvenating or undermining a form of life, I turn to the cultural and intellectual foundations of that traditional morality and, following this, to its logical structure.

FOUR FOUNDATIONS

What is the source of the idea of a decent society as George characterizes it—including respect for the dignity of the person, the role of male-female monogamous marriage and the associated family, and the institutions of fair law and government?

In human affairs, sources are always multifactorial; nothing human is simple, and nothing complex is the product of a single cause. Ideas and diseases, plenitude and paucity, terrain and trade all make their contribution along with many other causes and conditions. But in contrast, if not exactly in contradiction, to Hegel, I want to urge (in relation to the establishment and development of Western society and civilization) the claim of four certain fundamental systems of ideas operating not as mere *recapitulations* of historical phenomena but as *causes* of them: Hebraic monotheism, Christian incarnationalism, Greek aletheism, and Roman legalism.

Setting aside the practice of contemporary encyclopedists to avoid charges of cultural alienation and discrimination through a liberal use of the term "monotheism," it is evident that the first monotheists in the common understanding of the expression were the Israelites, the immediate descendants of Abraham, his son Isaac, and his grandson Jacob. The foundation of Judaic monotheism is the calling of Abraham and the resulting covenant, rendered in *Genesis* and *Exodus* as follows:

> I will make you into a great nation,
> and I will bless you;
> I will make your name great,
> and you will be a blessing.
> I will bless those who bless you,
> and whoever curses you I will curse;
> and all peoples on earth
> will be blessed through you
> (Genesis 12: 2–3, NIV).

> I shall take you as my own people, and I will be your God.
> Then you will know that I am the Lord your God,

who brought you out from under the yoke of the Egyptians
(Exodus 6: 7, NIV).

The actual and presupposed content and its implications are clear enough. There is one God, cause and sustainer of every other thing and state, Who ordains the course of cosmic history to His own purpose. This God elected, and then enters into covenant with, His chosen people. This relationship excludes ideas of local deities and overrides human kingdoms and principalities. There is only one King and one kingdom: God and His creation. Out of this divine source and its gratuitous concern for the people of the initial covenant—marked by their liberation from slavery in Egypt—there is given a second Mosaic covenant containing, among other laws and provisions, the Decalogue. All but the fourth and fifth commandment of this (keeping the Sabbath holy and honoring one's parents) are prohibitions (a fact of philosophical significance, or so shall I suggest later). Thus is established the idea of *one God, one law, one people*.

Judaism, however, was a tribal religion, and the covenants were restricted to that population. Yet in the passage I have quoted and more explicitly elsewhere within Hebrew scripture, there is mention of the rest of humanity, of God's plan for it and of a mediational role of the Jewish people in that plan. Thus in Isaiah 49: 5–6, we read,

> And now the Lord says—
> he who formed me in the womb to be his servant
> to bring Jacob back to him
> and gather Israel to himself,
> for I am honored in the eyes of the Lord
> and my God has been my strength—
> he says:
> "It is too small a thing for you to be my servant
> to restore the tribes of Jacob
> and bring back those of Israel I have kept.
> I will also make you a light for the Gentiles,
> that my salvation may reach to the ends of the earth" (NIV).

These passages are referred to by Luke, following the narrative of Jesus's birth and presentation at the temple. There Simeon, who we are told "is an upright and devout man [who] looked forward to the restoration of Israel," takes the infant Jesus in his arms and blesses God, saying,

> "Sovereign Lord, as you have promised,
> you may now dismiss your servant in peace.

For my eyes have seen your salvation,
which you have prepared in the sight of all nations:
a light for revelation to the Gentiles,
and the glory of your people Israel" (Luke 2: 29–32, NIV).

In salvation theology, the incarnation of the Son of God in the person of Jesus of Nazareth serves three purposes: first, restoring the repeatedly breached covenant between the Lord of Abraham and the people of Israel; second, making atonement to the Father for the sins of humanity more generally; and third, initiating a new covenant between God and all mankind through which humanity may be saved. So far as present matters are concerned, the point is to note that Christianity preserves and extends the idea of providential monotheism and moral command: *one God, one law, all people*.

Returning to philosophy and to a period perhaps a century or so after the writing of Isaiah, we find in Greek culture a move away from mythic and heroic poetry as modes of explanation of the world and of human nature, and toward speculative and practical theorizing. Two moments in this movement toward philosophy are relevant: first, the attempts in the sixth century among the pre-Socratics to answer such fundamental questions as where everything comes from, whether reality is many or one, and whether what happens is accidental or necessary—and if necessary, whether this is due to force or reason. The second moment comes in the following century, with a shift in talk of virtue (*arête*) from martial contexts to political and educational ones and with the development of itinerant teachers of self-styled virtue, the Sophists. Of relevance to the present context is what emerges next by way of reaction and response to pre-Socratic speculation and Sophistic practical philosophy.

Each of these two moments gave rise to certain internal tensions. In the first case, for example, there was the recognition of change alongside the assertion of permanence in the subject(s) of change—also the acknowledging of the manyness of things while recognizing unifying commonalities among them. In the second case, there was balancing of the idea that there are answers to the question, "What ought one to do?" with the thought that these answers are not, and perhaps cannot be, universally applicable. The great move forward into rigorous and systematic dialectical inquiry was achieved in three rapidly successive leaps performed by Socrates, Plato, and Aristotle. Of course the differences between them are many and complex, but I beg leave to abstract from these differences and proceed to their shared commitments. They assert that reality is intelligible, being under the governance of reason, and that human conduct is likewise answerable to standards that are not of our own making, singly or socially, but are derived from the ordered nature of the real. In short, and analogously to the writers of Hebrew and

Christian scripture, they assert the reality of Mind as a principle of cosmic order, the objectivity and unity of truth as a proper measure of correctness in thought, and the good as a proper ground of human law: *one reality, one truth, one moral foundation.*

I turn last to the inheritors from the Greeks of the mantle of reason and civilization. Roman religion was polytheistic and syncretistic, attributes generally denigrated in Hebrew scripture. Prior to the Jewish war leading to the destruction of the temple in Jerusalem, Jews in Rome and across the empire were generally tolerated, though their dietary laws and disavowal of temple imagery were viewed as odd. Subsequent to the war, however, attitudes changed: Jerusalem was brought under direct Roman rule and colonized, Jews were barred from the city, and the Temple was maintained in ruination. In the early period, Christians were barely distinguished from other Jewish groups. But soon they were differentiated, deemed "atheists" for not sacrificing to or celebrating Roman deities, and made subjects of particular persecution. By stages, of course, converts were won, and Christian influence grew—reaching the period of Constantine's conversion in the early fourth century, by which time Christianity was the dominant religion in the empire, then being adopted as the state religion in 380.

Through this period, Roman philosophy, which drew from the Greek schools, oriented itself more to the practical than the speculative. In particular, it influenced Roman thought about law—which had developed in prior centuries out of a religion-oriented form of civil law, applying only to Roman citizens—ushering in a form of comprehensive legal theorizing. While Plato and Aristotle both concerned themselves with forms of constitution and the role of law in maintaining order, neither developed a science of law: a systematic articulation of first and derived secondary principles. That, however, is exactly what the Romans did, applying Greek ideas to develop in the first two and a half centuries of the Common Era what came later to be known as classical Roman Law. Within this are elements of *jus civile* (citizen law) applicable to Roman citizens and *jus gentium* (law of peoples) applicable to foreigners in their relations with citizens. These corresponded to various statuses, such as that of a Roman citizen (*status civitatis*) and that of one who lived under the laws of another authority (*alieni iurus*). An important element of Roman jurisprudence was the objectivity and universality of natural or true law expressed by Cicero in a famous passage of *De Re Publica* III, 22:

> There is a true law [*vera lex*], right reason [*recta ratio*]—which is in accordance with nature [*naturae congruens*], applies to all [*diffusa in omnes*], and is unchangeable [*constans*] and [*sempiterna*]. By its commands this law summons men to the performance of their duties; by

its prohibitions it restrains them from doing wrong.... It will not lay down one rule at Rome and another at Athens, nor will it be one rule today and another tomorrow. But there will be one law, eternal and unchangeable, binding at all times upon all peoples; and there will be, as it were, one common master and ruler of men, namely God [*magister et imperator omnium Deus*], who is the author of this law.

By "God," Cicero means something closer to the Greek idea of an overarching cosmic mind than to either the pantheon of Greek popular religion and the related Roman idea of personal deities, or the Judeo-Christian notion of a supreme personal God. But by stages, his notion would be brought into alignment with the monotheistic conception, through a synthesis begun by the Church fathers, realized most fully in the thought of the medievals, and then presented most prominently and effectively in the work of Aquinas, in whom one can see Hebraic monotheism, Greek aletheism, Christian incarnationalism, and Roman legalism fully integrated. Even so, one can hear in Cicero's words something close to an echo of a formula stated above: *one universal reason, one truth, one humanity, one law*.

THREE DIMENSIONS

In considering, then, George's three pillars of a decent society (and what supports them), one may then be led to identify a more extensive, historically developed normative ground comprised of four foundational elements: two religious and two broadly philosophical. These were subsequently fused into a normative philosophical-cum-theological anthropology, out of which developed the "modern" notions of the dignity of the person, the value of marriage and the family, and the need for just law and government.

George presupposes the rationality of moral thought in his essay and elsewhere has explored the general character of this,[13] but it may be useful to say something here about the structure of moral thinking as I see it. Mine is somewhat different from George's approach but compatible with it. The prevailing dimension of moral decision-making in the West remains that of utilitarianism: looking to determine which among the range of available courses in a given situation would produce the greatest utility (factoring into the choice of action the relative probabilities of realizing the various outcomes). Beginning with Jeremy Bentham and John Stuart Mill, utility was identified first with pleasure, then with happiness, and later by others with either preference satisfaction or welfare. There is an evident oscillation here between subjective and objective conditions, explicable by a concern to avoid two problems: first, that mere pleasure or satisfaction are themselves open to evaluation as good or bad, depending upon their objects, and second, that happiness and welfare are contested notions and seemingly immeasurable. More to the point, however, is the concern that utilitarianism instrumentalizes individuals by treating their state as simply a component of overall utility and warranting harm and destruction for the sake of the general good. In recognition of this, it became increasingly common from the 1970s onward to observe that even where the promotion of welfare is at issue, there are constraints in its pursuit arising from requirements of justice and respect for rights. Mill had written, "Happiness is the only thing desirable, as an end, all other things being desirable as means to that end." But the fact is that we recognize, even where we choose to override, other kinds of value the desirability of which is not as means to happiness.

In reaction to utilitarianism, some have returned to a kind of Kantianism that ties moral value and requirement to the imperative to act only in ways that can rationally be universalized and never to treat others or oneself solely as means. At a less formal level, the Kantian idea of respect for persons lies behind the rise of concern in various sectors for securing consent in the collection of personal, sensitive information. But if utilitarianism is problematic in neglecting the integrity of the individual, neo-Kantianism seems at risk for neglecting the demands of welfare and failing to allow for legitimate paternalism. An important lesson from the debates between advocates of consequentialism and of deontology is, I suggest, the need to recognize the inadequacy of one-dimensional moral thinking, in its deliverances on particular issues but more importantly, in its failure to recognize the plurality and incommensurability of kinds of moral considerations. Furthermore, in addition to there being considerations deriving from the desirability of attaining human goods, and others deriving from demands of justice and respect, there are also considerations relating to motivation and character. Mill himself recognizes this:

> It really is of importance, not only what men do, but also what manner of men they are that do it. Among the works of man, which human life is rightly employed in perfecting and beautifying, the first in importance surely is man himself... desires and impulses are as much a part of a perfect human being, as beliefs and restraints.[14]

This third dimension of moral thinking (motivation and character) corresponds to the category of virtue. For Mill as for Kant, there is something of this sort to be acknowledged, but in each case their one-dimensionalism means that they reduce virtue's value to that of acting in accord with their favored norm: the good (utility) and the right (duty), respectively. To the contrary, I believe, as I think

Mill's own observation suggests, we recognize *character* as a distinct kind of moral factor. And there is a further feature to note, which also indicates the need to bring diverse considerations into play: when thinking about the good (and here it will be sufficient to take the case of human well-being), it is necessary to distinguish between *promoting* that good and *protecting* it. There is an asymmetry involved in the recognition of the value of the human good, namely, that one may not violate it in one case for the sake of promoting it in another. The expression *primum non nocere* ("first, do no harm") has gained currency in medical ethics, where it is often interpreted as "Avoid doing more harm than good." The deeper notion is that in acting for the good, one's dominant attitude and source of constraint is to respect and protect it.

Returning to George's three pillars of decency, the relevance of the foregoing is that it serves to illuminate: firstly, the idea that "every member of the human family . . . [should be] treated as a person, as a subject bearing profound, inherent, and equal worth and dignity," and secondly and derivatively, the case for protecting and promoting the integrity of family life and justice in the framing and administration of law.

TWO PERSPECTIVES

George's claims about the nature of and conditions for a decent and dynamic society are not presented on the basis of historical analysis and argumentation and are addressed to contemporary audiences with the aim of influencing future policy. In considering them, however, I think it is possible to recognize a duality of viewpoints.

On the one hand, there is an evocation of "conservative" moral values: human dignity, traditional marriage and family, and just law and government. On the other, there is the invocation of the benefits of the market economy and free enterprise. I have indicated that the latter seem to me more instrumental than constitutive of the human good, and also that there is some reason for agnosticism about their actual effect as regards the production or maintenance of a decent society. I suggest, however, that the two sets of claims and values divide to some extent between two different perspectives: a premodern view of humanity and of nature more widely as a locus of purposes and meanings, and a modern view of human life as dynamic behavior representable in terms of the exercise of instrumental rationality deployed in the production and distribution of objects and activities.

My point here is not one of opposition but rather the suggestion that there might be a case for bringing the dynamic within the scope of the decent, not contingently but constitutively. The key to this would be an analysis of the good of productive labor. This is an important theme of nineteenth-century writings in response to industrialization and alienation, not only in the writings of Marx and of English socialists such as John Ruskin and William Morris, but in Papal statements as well. Most famously, in the encyclical "*Rerum Novarum*," Leo XIII connects the rights and responsibilities of work to the defense of the institutions of ownership and private property, the natural right and purpose of marriage, and the true society of the family.[15]

More needs to be said in defense of the pillars of decency, about how recognition of these pillars poses a challenge to the "modern" view of nature as consisting only of extrinsic qualities of matter/energy. To speak meaningfully of the intrinsic value of all human persons, of the proper nature of marriage, of the purposive good of the family, and of the obligations of justice, we have to recognize that we are seeing nature as a place of meanings, values, and goals and judging these qualitatively in light of a broader idea of reality than is represented by science. This is not a burden but an opportunity, since it is clear enough that, other than when under the influence of various forms of skepticism, materialism, and nihilism, people do see human life in terms of intrinsic goods and evils.

ONE INSTITUTION

Finally, I complete the countdown by turning to the fourth of George's pillars, the first of those upon which he takes dynamism to rest, namely, universities. Since he uses this term having previously referred to "institutions of research and education," I take it he intends the two elements to be conjoined, as is now common. On the other hand, when he speaks of attacks upon the other pillars and especially the attack on business and the market economy as "coming from the academic world," I am sure he means to include liberal arts and other tertiary colleges, as well as universities, within academia. I raise this matter not out of pedantry but because historically, universities were not thought of as institutions of research and education but as places of teaching and learning. The research university—where undergraduates may be accommodated but are seen as constituting the first level of an institution, the highest purpose of which is inquiry directed toward discovery and the acquisition and transmission of new knowledge—is a recent invention. Moreover even as the seeds of it were being sown, others sought to uproot and discard them. To cite only the most famous of the nineteenth-century writers on the nature and purposes of universities, John Henry Newman writes as follows in the preface to his *Idea of a University*:

> The view taken of a University in these Discourses is the following: That it is a place of *teaching* universal *knowledge*. This implies that

its object is, on the one hand, intellectual, not moral; and, on the other, that it is the diffusion and extension of knowledge rather than the advancement. If its object were scientific and philosophical discovery, I do not see why a University should have students; if religious training, I do not see how it can be the seat of literature and science.[16]

This is not the occasion to embark on a discussion of the function of universities and their relation to higher education and scientific research,[17] but it is relevant to note that there may be a connection between the dramatic expansion of the university sector in the West (including its aspiration to conduct research) and the development of challenges to traditional understandings of the human person, marriage and the family, and law and government.

Of course, any serious intellectual examination of existing concepts and practices must be open to the possibility of finding them flawed and perhaps harmful (and to making public these findings—such things matter and should be addressed, and intellectual virtue demands that purported discoveries be subjected to the rigorous critique of one's fellow scholars). That said, there are liable to be consequences in shifting from the Newmanian idea of the university academic as a teacher whose scholarship is in the service of understanding better the things he teaches (what Newman's near contemporary Mathew Arnold described as "the best which has been thought and said in the world")[18] to the idea of the academic as one who challenges existing conceptions, breaks through the carapace of settled understandings, and reveals new truths. It is not, of course, necessary that research be revolutionary with respect to existing understandings, but there are psychological and market motivations toward novelty. Add to these the expansion of participation in higher education and the popularization of "ideas." What results is an impetus to render the novel challenging, subversive, progressive, and advantageous to the elevation of researchers' interests.

Such, however, is the economic and social position of academics. And so great are the demands imposed on their time by the effort to maintain the practice of discovery that their lifestyles are increasingly distant from the common forms of life. Here I am conscious of moving toward thoughts suggested by Marx in his *Contribution to the Critique of Political Economy* (written after his *Critique of Hegel's Philosophy of Right*) and by the French philosopher Julien Benda, author in 1927 of *La Trahison des Clercs* (*The Treason of the Learned*). While rejecting Marx's belief in the materialist conception of history, one may yet see truth in his claim that the ideas and values of a person or an institution cannot be considered independently of their material conditions. As he wrote,

> The social structure and the state are continually evolving out of the life-processes of definite individuals, however, of these individuals, not

as they may appear in their own or other people's imagination, but as they actually are, i.e., as they act, produce materially, and hence as they work under definite material limits, presuppositions and conditions.[19]

Benda's targets were French and German nationalist intellectuals of the late-nineteenth and early-twentieth centuries who had abandoned disinterested study in favor of political interest. The phenomenon he identified is more general and as likely to afflict "leftists" and "liberals" as "rightists" and "conservatives." Significantly, Benda's recommendation for countering the tendencies he challenged was to return to the study of classical civilization and of the universalism of traditional Christianity. In short, and in my formulation, to orient intellectual activity toward the fourfold foundation upon which rest the three pillars of human dignity, family, and law. To do so in the present day would not preclude humanities academics engaging in research, but it might serve to induce a greater sense of humility and an awareness of the possibility adverted to by Burke that a spirit of innovation is generally the result of confined views. It might also encourage renewed reflection on Newman's identification of the university as a place for *teaching* universal *knowledge*. He chose to emphasize the words "teaching" and "knowledge," but in the present context, I would also emphasize "universal," meaning by it what pertains to human nature and to the realization of the human good, particularly as that is recognized, respected, and fostered in morally decent societies.

NOTES

1. Written while in residence at the University of Notre Dame, Center for Ethics and Culture as the 2013–14 Mary Ann Remick Senior Visiting Fellow. I am very grateful to the director of the Center, Carter Snead, and to the Remick Fellowship for the opportunity to work on this and other projects.
2. An earlier version of the text is available at http://jp2alf.org.au/wp-content/uploads/2012/08/JP-II-Australian-Leaders-Forum-August-2012-.pdf.
3. Most important, of course, are Plato's *Republic* and *Laws*, and Aristotle's *Nicomachean Ethics* and *Politics*.
4. G.W.F. Hegel, *Elements of the Philosophy of Right*, ed. Allen W. Wood, trans. H.B. Nisbet (Cambridge, England: Cambridge University Press, 1991).
5. Ibid., 21.
6. Ibid., 23.
7. See *Nicomachean Ethics*, book II.
8. See *Summa Theologiae* II, II, q. 45, a. 2: "Rightness of judgment is twofold: first, on account of perfect use of reason, secondly, on account of a certain connaturality with the subject about which one has to judge. Thus, about matters of chastity, a man after

inquiring with his reason forms a right judgment, if he has learnt the science of morals [*scientiam moralem*], while one who has the virtue of chastity judges of such matters by a kind of connaturality [*connaturalitatem*]."

9. Edmund Burke, *Reflections on the Revolution in France* in *Select Works of Edmund Burke* (Indianapolis, IN: Liberty Fund, 1999), part I, sec. 39.
10. Roger Scruton, *England: An Elegy* (London, England: Continuum, 2006), vii.
11. Roger Scruton, "T.S. Eliot as Conservative Mentor," *Intercollegiate Review*, orientation issue (2008): 65–75, p. 67.
12. See Roger Scruton, "The Journey Home," *Intercollegiate Review* 44 (Spring 2009): 31–39, p. 38.
13. See Robert P. George, *In Defense of Natural Law* (Oxford, England: Oxford University Press, 1999).
14. John Stuart Mill, *On Liberty*, chap. III, sec. 4.
15. See Leo XIII, "*Rerum Novarum*: Rights and Duties of Capital and Labor" (Vatican: 1891).
16. John Henry Newman, *The Idea of a University* (London, England: Longmans, Green & Co, 1907).
17. For discussion of these matters, see John Haldane, "The Future of the University," *American Catholic Philosophical Quarterly* 87 (Fall 2013): 731–749.
18. See Matthew Arnold, *Culture and Anarchy*, originally published in London, England: 1869. Quotation from the preface, added later.
19. Karl Marx, *The German Ideology*, part 1 ("Feuerbach"), under "First Premises of Materialist Method."

3

Caritas and Competition

Harold James

A striking development of political language has been the expulsion or purgation of God—of invocations of the divine. This is a relatively recent process, over the last fifty years, and it is not explicable in terms simply of an inexorable process of secularization. A better explanation lies in a process of progressive buildup of expectations within people about a whole range of institutions—most prominently the state, the public sector, and the government. When these expectations are disappointed, the disappointment leads to more demands. When demands cannot be met, the result is disenchantment with the political process and with society at large.

This change has occurred on both sides of the Atlantic. In Europe, the transformation has probably been the most dramatic. Take the way in which the idea of Europe was articulated. At moments of crisis—1848, 1945, or 1989, when political collapse, existential angst, and an explosion of the imagination occurred—the answer, "Europe," was held out in a remarkably consistent way. From Victor Hugo (1849):

> The day will come when we will see these two vast groups, the United States of America and the United States of Europe, face to face, stretching out a hand over the oceans, exchanging their products, their trade, their industries, their arts, their genius, clearing the globe, colonizing the deserts, improving creation under the eye of the Creator, and together combining, for the good of all, those two infinite forces, the fraternity of men and the power of God![1]

From Winston Churchill (1946): "This noble continent.... It is the fountain of Christian faith and Christian ethics.... If Europe were once united in the sharing of its common inheritance, there would be no limit to the happiness, to the prosperity and glory which its three or four hundred million people would enjoy."[2]

From Vaclav Havel (1996): "freedom and responsibility are two sides of the same coin and that freedom is thinkable only when it is based on a sense of responsibility toward an authority that transcends us."[3]

Such language has simply disappeared in the middle of Europe's most recent crisis. Why? Briefly put, Europeans were too complacent that they had all the right institutions that were needed to deal with any eventuality. They had lost a sense of humility, of the fragility of human achievements, but also a sense of the power and creativity that is inherent in human capacity.

The same process is occurring in the United States, where the key constitutional principle of religious neutrality (no established religion) is increasingly retranslated into an aggressive secularism that both limits public forms of religious expression and is so all-embracingly tolerant that it holds religion up to ridicule.

I

The departure point for constructive thinking about a better society must lie in reflection on what it is to be human. Dignity, the recognition of the uniquely human, requires a respect of autonomy and of freedom. Giving dignity allows humans to choose; they choose because they feel themselves to have autonomy. We also know from experimental psychology that humans who are deprived of respect make bad and foolish and destructive choices.

Humans interact best in a society that provides them with a framework of laws or rules to guide their interaction. This framework will only appear as just if it is universally applicable, and in an impartial (blind) way; laws that have idiosyncrasies and apply to some people or groups rather than to all are no longer general laws and are often referred to as private laws, or "privileges." The profusion of privileges undermines the authority of law, whose enforcement is ultimately the task of government.

Do such general considerations require revision or updating because of the pace of social and economic change? In modern society, the provision of a general, stable legal framework poses more and more challenges. The range of new or growing threats to security and well-being—from climate change, from terrorism, from rogue states, from sophisticated criminal operations—calls for a protective response. We also recognize the enhanced importance of personal choice in responding to a world in which the nature of work is being transformed by the application of technology—a process that first reduced the amount of work required in the production of food, then in manufacturing, and is now also revolutionizing the provision of services.

The provision of government in particular is subject to tremendous ever-growing demand, where the nature of the demand may limit and constrain the effectiveness of the government response. We are used to the idea of government stepping in to solve collective-action problems or deal with market failures, but what happens when there is no adequate solution? That rarely discredits the call for government and collective action. On the contrary, it often produces a demand for an intensification, for a more extensive set of interventions. And government ratchets itself up in a perpetual spiral of constraint and compulsion.

That is why the framework within which we think about government and what it does matters so much. The structure of the law reflects a spirit that animates it and enables those subject to the law to see that it is a reflection of their own deep needs and interests (that they consent to it). The problem is that the proliferation of value norms in modern society has led to an individualization of preference formation, and in consequence, it is hard for many to believe that there is one genuinely universal law to which they can assent and which they thus recognize as their own will.

II

I would propose that what makes society both decent and dynamic depends on two human capacities and their development. First, a notion of sympathy or compassion, an ability to put oneself mentally in the place of another being and to reflect on what it would mean to be him or her. There is an exclusive version of this kind of action: We lose ourselves in another and are completely absorbed in romantic love. But there is also a wider and inclusive version: The Christian tradition recognizes this when we think of finding Christ in one another.

The great Abrahamic faiths recognize eating in common as a way of establishing a community. Christians treat the divine provision of manna in the desert (Exodus 16) and the miracle of the loaves and the fishes as an anticipation of the sacrament of communion. Many scholars suggest that the Last Supper is related to the Jewish Passover meal. The Quran also gives a substantial significance to manna.

Secondly, human beings are competitive and seek preeminence. That makes for ingenuity, then technical advancement, then the provision of a more satisfactory base for human flourishing. Religions live organizationally on the competitive principle—as against each other, but also internally (think of the rivalry of Dominicans and Franciscans). But they also encourage people to see it as their duty to develop their capacities, to excel, and even to measure themselves against others (for instance, in the parable of the talents).[4]

The most direct and obvious effect of competition is that it produces a better, more reliable, and at the same time cheaper supply of goods, whose quality increases as suppliers compete with each other to sell to consumers. The larger the market is, the more transportation (itself competitive) opens up other markets, the more competitive it all becomes, and the greater the benefits. Competition thus contributes in a straightforward way to the fulfillment of human needs. By contrast, planned methods, however ingeniously executed, encounter bottlenecks, which are not overcome, because the decision-makers at the bottleneck have no motivation or incentive to take corrective action.

Competition also has been seen as an ingenious way of inculcating virtue. Adam Smith appears to have made this argument when he reflected upon self-interest and in parallel, evolved a partial theory of good or virtuous behavior. The passage about tradesmen's motives is probably the best-known and most-quoted sentence of the *Wealth of Nations*: "It is not from the benevolence of the butcher, the brewer, or the baker, that we expect our dinner, but from their regard to their own interest."[5] But Smith had also, in a separate work, made the complementary argument, "When the greater part of the people are merchants, they always bring probity and punctuality into fashion, and these are the principal virtues of commercial nations."[6]

The way in which competition limits the capacity for vicious behavior is strictly prudential. A merchant who tries to abuse a dominant market position to eliminate rivals is likely to take on liabilities and bets that are irrational and that in the end undermine his position. In Thomas Hardy's *Mayor of Casterbridge*, there is a beautiful example of this, when the mayor, Michael Henchard, sets out to build up a large, speculative position against his younger and more dynamic rival. In the end, he succeeds only in destroying himself. Prudence, not virtue, should have limited his wish to engage in that fight.

Some religious figures saw a paradox in the way their doctrine urged excellence. John Wesley put it like this, in a famous passage that Max Weber made the key to his interpretations in his *Protestant Ethic and the Spirit of Capitalism*:

> "Religion must necessarily produce both industry and frugality, and these cannot but produce riches. But as riches increase, so will pride, anger, and love of the world in all its branches. . . . Is there no way to prevent this—this continual decay of true religion? We ought not to prevent people from being diligent and frugal; *we must exhort all Christians to gain all they can, and to save all they can; that is, in effect, to grow rich.*"[7]

The "decay of true religion," or what Weber called disenchantment, thus followed an inexorable logic.

There is a solution to the Wesley/Weber dilemma. Each of the two desirable intrinsic characteristics of the human personality, caritas and competition, has its obverse that develops when the two features do not work in balance with each other. Competition unmitigated by communality or caritas turns into a war of all against all. It is driven by a different characteristic, frequently described as a vice: envy. However, solidarity without any competition to perform—and to actually demonstrate solidarity—becomes inactivity. Again, we often refer to this sort of behavior by using the language of vices: in this instance, sloth or indolence. Monasteries—set up to realize the ultimate Christian life—in practice often became alternately centers of envy (in which monks resented each other) or sloth.

It is the capacities for love and for excelling that make humans worthy of respect. At the same time, we generalize this sense of dignity and insist that even human beings who in their current state represent these capacities poorly still deserve exactly the same respect. Why? We think like that because we are aware of potential: the potential that lies within an infant (or of course an unborn child) and also within the dignity of the aged—the potential for suffering and sickness that exists within all of us. Humans develop, and that is also a constituent part of their dignity.

III

The vision of development or ripening is profoundly unfamiliar to the two currents of thought that have dominated a great deal of modern debate. For most of the twentieth century, the most powerful prevalent belief was a faith in mechanisms that offered to coordinate development on a large scale and promised to give a more efficient coordination than the chance outcome of the interactions of myriads of individuals responding to each other and to each other's needs and wishes. Planners have liked the idea of a central state rationalizing and directing the course of human progress and eliminating wasteful and unnecessary competition that seems to stand in the way of cooperation and coordination. They take on a critique of the market and of the principle of competition.

Social conservatives often express a skepticism of the market, and of competition, for a different reason: because it is destabilizing and tends to undermine traditions. They see in traditional institutions a key to social cohesion. They think of marketing as seducing and purveying false information rather than educating about real needs that had not been previously envisaged. They point out the dangers of materialism, excessive consumption, ostentation, and luxury, while economic liberals like to show how marketing can persuade people to brush and floss their teeth, maintain cleaner and more attractive homes, pursue better education, and in other words, take steps that most hold to be generally desirable.

Markets do not necessarily promote any particular set of values; they do not generate progressivism automatically, any more than they lead to an entrenchment of traditional values. That is why both tendencies emphasize the need to tame, dominate, or restrain market mechanisms through some other institutions. Progressivists (the planners) think usually in terms of a state that can formulate a coherent plan. Conservatives by contrast think about the nation, professional associations, cultural institutions, or (most frequently) the family. For Edmund Burke, for instance, it was the family that "grafts benevolence even upon avarice."[8]

Against the planners, and against the social conservatives and traditionalists, economic and political liberals dislike government-imposed conformity, because it stifles initiative and also undermines the ability of those subject to the law to see the law as ultimately an expression of not only their own interest but their own will. If laws are commanding me to act in a way that I hold to be absurd or undignified, I lose my respect for the law.

The freedom to experiment and to innovate—and to serve others—will be inhibited by the imposition of laws and regulations that attempt to micromanage social and economic interactions. It is impossible to define laws like this in a generally valid way; they become examples of particular laws, or privileges. There are grey areas—such as laws on decency/indecency—where it is better to err on the liberal side, because of the bad consequences of imposing restrictions from the state. Those consequences include delegating to state agents enforcement capacities that easily become arbitrary.

At the same time, economic liberals need to recognize that pure liberty can be terrible and destructive—if it is not accompanied by a principle of sympathy. The thinkers of the European Enlightenment were very clear on this issue. We see it in the way that Adam Smith prepared the idea of sympathy as the dominant theme of the *Theory of Moral Sentiments* before he expanded the economic analysis in his *Wealth of Nations*. One of the highest reflections of this approach is offered by Mozart in *Don Giovanni*: The hero is a powerfully charismatic figure—an innovative, dynamic champion of liberty. (Consider the first act finale with the insistent and maniacal repetition of *"Viva la libertà."*) But without sympathy, the energy is ultimately destructive.

The unique feature of the human position—and an essential aspect of the dignified nature of man—is that compassion, and also love, cannot be compelled. Compassion involves the emotional ability to put oneself in someone else's position—to make the imaginative leap that is needed to generate a Kantian code of ethic. Love means going much further, forgetting or abandoning the idea of a separate self, as the sense of being an individual is lost in the contemplation of a common bond with the other.

These sentiments of compassion and love must come from within, not be a product of external laws. John Henry Newman provided a beautiful depiction of how persuasion to the truth should work, in a sermon in which he contrasted the fiery denunciations of Girolamo Savanarola (for whom he nevertheless had much sympathy) with the quiet persistence of St. Philip Neri. As Newman put it, "The Almighty displayed His presence to Elias on Mount Horeb. 'The Lord was not in the wind,' nor 'in the earthquake,' nor 'in the fire;' but after the fire came 'the whisper of a gentle air.'"[9] Or, as it is famously worded by Bible translators (and in the hymn of John Greenleaf Whittier), the "still, small voice."

Something of the one-sided veneration of institutions for their own sake, which is inherent to the social-conservative position, comes across very strikingly when Robert P. George discusses the firm and the family as, respectively, pillars of a dynamic and a decent society. I do not believe that we should think of an institution, the family or the firm or the university (any more than say, a hospital or a prison), as having this centrality *as such*. Institutions of higher learning can be inspirational, but they can also be deeply dysfunctional. What is important is the extent to which they potentially offer a way of developing dispositions and behavioral traits.

The family is—as George correctly presents it—a way of learning virtues that are indispensible to the health of a society at large. It is a microcosm that prepares for other-oriented action on a larger scale. This view is ubiquitous in classical thought, and it has been articulated very powerfully in other traditions. The Confucian classic *Dà Xu*é (*The Great Learning*) puts the case as follows:

> The ancients who wished to illustrate illustrious virtue throughout the world, first ordered well their own States. Wishing to order well their states, they first regulated their families. Wishing to regulate their families, they first cultivated their persons. Wishing to cultivate their persons, they first rectified their hearts. Wishing to rectify their hearts, they first sought to be sincere in their thoughts. Wishing to be sincere in their thoughts, they first extended to the utmost of their knowledge. Such extension of knowledge lay in the investigation of things.

A modern analyst concludes: "*Ideally speaking*, it is in the bosom of the family that the individual learns to act in terms of virtuous motives as ends in themselves rather than as means to ulterior ends."[10]

Families and firms are by no means always good; they can be dysfunctional, divisive, corroding. We judge them, I think, by the extent to which they adequately reflect the human characteristics of compassion and of competition. Economists hold that firms are usually abusive when they have monopoly positions—in other words, when they are not constrained by competition.

That view probably applies to the family also: Families that are dominated by one person, in which there is no mutual compromise based on the idea of "losing" oneself, are tyrannical. We should not get into the position of, for instance, justifying Islamic family law as an alternative to the law of the secular state, even though many Islamic families represent models of compassion and caring.

There is a risk of a vicious cycle of challenge and response, in which we observe the decay of institutions that for good reasons we venerate and then call on the state and the law to act more vigorously and more comprehensively to protect them. Such action rarely arrests the process of decline, and it overestimates the ability of the law and of coercion to enforce norms. In that process, there is a risk that the authority of the state is gradually eroded (in the same way that the authority of the state is undermined when it gets into the details of economic management).

IV

Only a comprehensive approach in which we recognize the limits of external discipline and the importance of the inner conviction can usefully illuminate the discussion of the great social issues of our age. Inequality is rising—and makes it more difficult for us to be compassionate or to realize caritas. Pope Francis rightly condemns the "globalization of indifference."[11]

The causes of the relatively recent rise in inequalities in almost every industrial society (despite tax systems that aim at redistribution) are complex, but they include inadequate innovation (which tends to privilege inherited wealth positions) as well as policies that accidentally or inadvertently increase inequality (as both monetary and fiscal policies after the Great Recession have done). An important driver is also the disintegration of traditional families and the erosion of marriage in poorer households, giving rise to a cycle of underachievement and deprivation. That social disintegration is harder to deal with through conventional policy mechanisms. Inequality, surprisingly, has not been well-addressed by attempts to counteract it through fiscal policy. Economic growth and dynamism—as described in the celebrated recent book by Thomas Piketty[12]—and a generally more certain (and hence better) policy can discourage that inequality that makes it harder to realize our basic human attributes.

The dynamics of interactions with others—unlike state compulsion—do not force us to be better. They rather inspire us. What ultimately is the source of that inspiration? We might—indeed we should—like to think that it is the God whom the logic of disenchantment has been pushing out of public debate.

NOTES

1. Victor Hugo, *Douze Discours* (Paris, France: Librairie Nouvelle, 1851).
2. Winston Churchill, speech in Zurich (September 19, 1946), Churchill Society, www.churchill-society-london.org.uk/astonish.html.
3. Vaclav Havel, "The Hope for Europe," *New York Review of Books* 43 (June 20, 1996): 38.
4. See Matthew 25: 14–30.
5. Adam Smith, *An Inquiry into the Nature and Causes of the Wealth of Nations* (Chicago, IL: University of Chicago Press, 1976), 18.
6. Adam Smith, *Lectures on Justice, Police, Revenue and Arms: Delivered in the University of Glasgow* (Oxford, England: Clarendon Press, 1896), 255. Many modern authors move between the "butcher" passage and the "probity and punctuality" passage rather seamlessly. See, for instance, Jerry Z. Muller, *Adam Smith in His Time and Ours: Designing the Decent Society* (Princeton, NJ: Princeton University Press, 1995), 132; Peter J. Dougherty, *Who's Afraid of Adam Smith: How the Market Got Its Soul* (New York: John Wiley, 2003), 11; Yuval Levin, "Recovering the Case for Capitalism," *National Affairs* 3 (Spring 2010): 121–136, pp. 126–127.
7. John Wesley, as quoted in Max Weber, *The Protestant Ethic and the Spirit of Capitalism* (New York: Routledge, 2001), 118–119.
8. Edmund Burke, "Reflections on the Revolution in France," pp. 1–250 in Iain Hampsher-Monk (ed.), *Burke: Revolutionary Writings* (Cambridge, England: Cambridge University Press, 2014), 52. See also Jerry Z. Muller, *The Mind and the Market: Capitalism in Modern European Thought* (New York: Knopf, 2002), 393.
9. John Henry Newman, Cardinal, *Sermons Preached on Various Occasions* (London, England: Burns & Oates, 1881), 218.
10. Benjamin I. Schwartz (1985), as quoted in Yongjin Zhang, "The Idea of Order in Ancient Chinese Political Thought: A Wightian Exploration," *International Affairs* 90 (January 2014): 167–183, p. 180. See also Zhao Tingyang, "A Political World Philosophy in Terms of All-under-heaven (Tian-xia)," *Diogenes* 56 (February 2009): 5–18, p. 13.
11. First mentioned in a homily on July 8, 2013.
12. See Thomas Piketty, *Capital in the Twenty-First Century* (Cambridge, MA: Harvard University Press, 2014).

4

The Person and the Parson

Roger Scruton

The term "persona" comes to us from the Roman and Etruscan theater, where it denoted the mask worn by the actor and therefore represented the character whom the actor portrayed. The term was borrowed by Roman law to describe any entity that has judiciable rights and duties. That includes corporate entities and other more abstract constructions. The primary examples of legal persons, however, on which all other personae depend, were, for Roman law as for our law, adult human beings, whose legal personality is the direct consequence of their ability to make free and accountable choices.

The term was borrowed again by early Christian theologians in order to explain the doctrine of the Trinity by distinguishing the three persons of God. Discussions of the Trinity led to the view that personhood belongs to the essence of whatever possesses it, and the sixth-century philosopher Boethius took this as his cue in defining the essential nature of the human being. For Boethius, the human person is "an individual substance of a rational nature." That definition was adopted by Thomas Aquinas and remained in place until the Enlightenment, when two great philosophers—John Locke and Immanuel Kant—saw fit to re-examine the whole idea and untangle its philosophical complexities.

For Locke, *person* is a "forensic" term—one that is used to "appropriate actions and their merit" or, as we might rather say, to impute actions and responsibilities to an individual, as in a court of law.[1] For Kant, as for Boethius and Aquinas, the concept contains the secret of the human condition. In Kant's view, however, it is not the idea of "individual substance" but that of our "rational nature" that is the crux. Persons are distinguished from all other objects by their reason and therefore by the "transcendental freedom" upon which the exercise of reason depends. As a consequence of this freedom, the human person is subject to the categorical imperative, which obliges him to treat every person, himself included, as an end in himself. Locke raised the unsolved, and in my view unsolvable, question of personal identity. Kant initiated the philosophical tradition that runs through

Friedrich Schiller, Friedrich Schelling, Johann Fichte, and Georg Hegel, which sees the subject—the self-conscious I—as the heart of the moral order. This tradition has gone through many subsequent reforms and amendments, to enter modern debates in the existentialism of Jean-Paul Sartre, the "personalism" of Max Scheler and Karol Wojtyła, and the discussions of freedom and justice in analytical philosophy.

Looking back across that historical landscape, we see the evolution of the concept of the person as part of the self-understanding of Western civilization and as a crucial factor in the emergence of the modern world. The concept began in the theater, passed to the law, was picked up by theology and then by philosophy, and finally was embedded in the social and political norms of the modern world. Almost everyone makes use of the concept when endeavoring to describe what is distinctive of the human condition and the constraints on how human beings should be treated. When we refer to human rights, human dignity, what we owe to each other, and such fundamental values as freedom, justice, and the rule of law, we are making use (directly or indirectly) of the concept of the person, which provides the shared perspective from which we address virtually all such issues. Human communities are communities of persons, and this is the point of agreement from which our disagreements begin.

Precisely because it is so widely accepted as foundational, however, the idea of the person has been detached from the history that gave rise to it and presented in purely abstract terms, as a rational construct that is not dependent on any specific experience of community. This movement toward abstraction is vividly apparent in the writings of Kant, and it was one of the aspects of the Kantian philosophy that subsequent idealists, Hegel especially, strove to overcome. But I do not think that Hegel's lesson has been learned, and we find ourselves today with a deeply conflicted idea of the person upon which we nevertheless rely as the premise of our collective decision-making.

The conflicts are immediately apparent in the sphere of human rights. For libertarians, human rights are freedoms, which must be protected by the state in order to safeguard the sovereignty of the individual. For socialists, human rights are claims, which must be satisfied by the state in order to offer a viable and dignified life to all its citizens.[2] Libertarians defend individual freedom against the state; socialists defend the state against individual freedom. We see this vividly in the current disputes over education and healthcare, with libertarians arguing for choice and socialists arguing for equal provision, something that only the state can attempt, and then only by removing choices from the active, the ambitious, and the strong.

If we look again at the history of the "person" idea, we see that this conflict was all but inevitable. As it evolved, the concept of the person became caught up in the unceasing intellectual conflict between individualists and communitarians. The concept was required to embrace both individual sovereignty and political community. Persons know in their hearts that they are pulled in both directions, that they value individual liberty as the *sine qua non* of consensual government, and that they also value community, as the soil in which liberty grows. Jean-Jacques Rousseau's fantasy that we are "born free" ought to have no weight for us today, now that we have seen what results from the attempt to put it into practice, and the knowledge that we *become* free reminds us of all the other aspects of human communities that must be in place if real individual freedom is to emerge among them.

For those and related reasons, getting clear about the concept of the person is, for our generation, an intellectual priority. Countless secular philosophies lean upon the idea. Those who build a universal political doctrine on the foundation of human rights are in need of a theory that tells them which rights belong to our nature—our nature as persons—and which are the product of convention. That theory will be a theory of the person. Marxists who found their critique of bourgeois society on the idea of exploitation and the dignity of labor rely on the view that there is a fulfilled and free relation between people that the capitalist system suppresses. That view demands a theory of the person. Theists see the goal of human life as the knowledge and love of a personal God, whose presence is revealed in the natural order. We can make sense of that view only if we have a theory of the person. Left-liberals see political order as a mechanism for reconciling individual freedom with "social justice." That idea too depends on a theory of the person. The allegedly Kantian philosophy of the person assumed by John Rawls in his defense of the redistributive state is used by Robert Nozick to attack it. In every area of political conflict today, we find the concept of the person at the center of the dispute yet treated as a mere abstraction, with little or no attention to its social and historical context.

We see this problem surfacing in the difficult social issues of our time. If the defining feature of the human person is the freedom to make autonomous choices, then libertarians will argue that governments and civil associations have no right to interfere with those choices, save on the ground proposed by John Stuart Mill, of protecting others from harm.[3] We move quickly from that position to a defense of pornography as free speech, of no-fault divorce as a contractual right, of gay marriage as a lifestyle choice, and of teenage promiscuity as a practice run for later commitments. If the defining feature of the human person is, rather, the life in a community of mutual aid, then communitarians will argue that we must constrain antisocial lifestyles and provide for a compassionate society in which caring is an institutional fact. We then move quickly to a defense of redistribution, of ideological vetting of textbooks, of laws forbidding "hate speech" and free association, of a moratorium on prayers in the classroom and Christmas festivities in the public square. Usually there is very little consistency here. In my experience, the same person will use libertarian arguments to justify pornography and promiscuous sex and communitarian arguments to justify redistributive taxation, hate-speech laws, and the expulsion of Christianity from the public square. All those policies satisfy a need to repudiate the old social order of the settled Christian community, in which marriage, children, church, and security were the primary social goals and all of life enjoyed the vague but inclusive blessing of the resident parson. It is as though the concept of the person has turned against the civilization that gave rise to it, flashing its chameleon tongue at all our cherished customs. But with what authority, we do not really know.

The conflicting accounts of the person to which I have just alluded arise because people have taken the concept out of context, seeking to define it in abstract terms and without reference to the way in which personhood is a way of *becoming*, not just a way of being. Libertarians emphasize freedom but give us no real account of the origins of freedom or its metaphysical basis. Communitarians emphasize social dependence but fail to explore the difference between the groupings of animals and those of free beings, whose associations are founded in contract and consent and whose social fulfillment comes only in the mutual recognition of their individual autonomy.

What we should recognize, I believe, is the origin of personality in the I-You encounter. The point has been made poetically by Martin Buber, in his celebrated book *Ich und Du*, and analytically by Stephen Darwall in *The Second Person Standpoint*, but we owe the underlying insight to Hegel's *Phenomenology of Spirit*.[4] Personal relations are a *calling to account*. I give reasons to you and ask for reasons in return. I explain myself through describing what the world means in my perspective. I am answerable to you for what I say and do, and you likewise to me. It is not that these features of our condition flow from our transcendental freedom, as Kant would put it. They are *what freedom consists in*. Giving each other reasons, holding each other to account, praising, blaming, and negotiating, working for the other's acceptance and being in turn influenced to accept—these are all moments in an ongoing dialogue in which each of us aims his or her attention not to the body of the other but to the first-person perspective that shines in it.

To put it in Hegel's way, we are subjects for each other, not objects, and the subject-to-subject encounter is one of mutual recognition, in which each acknowledges the other's autonomy and also holds the other responsible for what he is and does. My freedom is not an uncaused eruption into the world of human events; it is a product of my social condition, and it brings with it the full burden of accountability to the other and the recognition that his voice has just as much authority as mine.

If this is so, then we should conclude that the libertarian and the communitarian are both equally one-sided. Freedom and accountability are coextensive in the human agent. And the I-You dialogue through which we address each other involves a search for reasons that have weight for you as much as for me. There is, at the heart of the human community, the common pursuit of reasons that will be valid for all of us. Next time you have a quarrel with someone, you can test this out. You will find that you seek to justify yourself with reasons that the other will accept, whose validity does not depend on the particular desires that distinguish you but on matters which lie rooted in your shared human nature and shared social circumstances. Freedom and community are linked by their very nature, and the truly free being is always taking account of others in order to coordinate his presence with theirs.

That kind of freedom is, in everyday life, a disjointed and improvised thing, of course. Our lives and desires are not always properly harmonized with those who depend on them, and full coordination is more an ideal than a fact. Nevertheless we can approximate to that ideal and give symbolic form to it in art. Indeed the social nature of individual freedom is never more clearly conveyed than by dancers, when they consciously lift their bodies above the world of cause and effect and place them in a realm where every movement has a shared reason and a shared meaning and not just a physical cause. I don't say that every dance is like that. But in its highest form, dancing creates a community of persons whose movements are movements of the I, movements with a reason, where *my* reason is *you*. Schiller noticed this and gave the following somewhat Kantian description of what we now know as Scottish country dancing (but which he described as "English"):

> The first law of gentility is: *have consideration for the freedom of others*, The second; *show your freedom*. The correct fulfillment of both is an infinitely difficult problem, but gentility always requires it relentlessly, and it alone makes the cosmopolitan person. I know of no more fitting image for the ideal of beautiful relations than the well danced and multiply convoluted English dance. The spectator in the gallery sees countless movements which cross each other colorfully and change their direction willfully but *never collide*. Everything has been arranged so that the first has already made room for the second before he arrives, everything comes together so skillfully and yet so artlessly that both seem merely to be following their own mind while never impeding the other. This is the most fitting picture of a maintained personal freedom, which respects the freedom of others.[5]

The important point here is that individual freedom and social coordination come into being together, and the sight of their coincidence is the most persuasive confirmation available to us that they are, deep down, one and the same. If you are not persuaded by Schiller's example, then a glance at the YouTube records of Fred

Astaire and Ginger Rogers, or the miraculous Nicholas Brothers, will surely convince you of this.

It is not that we begin life as animals and then *become* persons. It is rather that personhood, which is an essential part of the human condition, is also a form of becoming. It is a potential wrapped within us from the outset, and it gradually unfolds through encounters with others as we respond to them I-to-I, each taking responsibility for his own actions, emotions, and desires. We should see the life of the person as rooted in the community of others, growing into autonomy and independence, flowering in the moments of love and commitment, and bearing fruit, in due course, in the next generation.

But this means that things can go wrong as well as right. The libertarian view that sees personhood as a kind of universal premise from which society is derived by an invisible hand, assumes that we possess full and capable autonomy from the outset, that we are, in Rousseau's words, "born free." If personhood is a form of *becoming*, however, that develops through relations with others, then it can be stunted, distorted, turned against itself by the circumstances of its growth. Parents know this, and children feel it. Yet it is often misunderstood, and not only by libertarians. Democracy supposes that we are all developed persons, bound in networks of mutual trust and accountability. But maybe this is no longer so. Our society is in the grip of forces that influence what we become and that discourage the "gentility" praised by Schiller. Many of the most fundamental relations through which we encounter other people are now veiled by narcissism. We shield ourselves behind soft barriers of false sentiment so as to cushion the impact of others' demands on us and to secure our retreat. This is especially so in the matter of sex, and I shall venture some remarks about this topic, since it shows why persons cannot be prized from their context in the libertarian way and still retain their nature as beings in relation with their kind.

In the past, children were prepared for the impact of sex through the inculcation of what were then seen as virtues—modesty, chastity, and shame.[6] Religion played an important part in this *éducation sentimentale*, and it was the parson rather than the schoolteacher who was the leading authority. This was one important illustration of a general truth, which is that religious obedience exists in part because of its function in personal development. Religious education is of course directed toward a right relation with God. But that means a right relation with other persons and therefore the growing exercise of responsibility toward both self and other. Fully formed persons are those whose promises are worth what they ask for them and whose commitments endure. And this is part of what godliness consists in.

The parson has lost this role, which has been ceded to the classroom teacher, construed usually as a servant of the state. Modern sex education assumes that attitudes such as shame and guilt are unhealthy—costs that cannot be outweighed by the benefits of the enduring passions that they favor. Hence we should strive to free ourselves from these hangovers and learn to engage in sexual activity in full awareness that it is in essence no more guilty than eating or drinking—a psychological benefit that need have no psychological cost. Much modern sex education is therefore designed as a therapy for guilt and shame, a way of getting young people to accept their sexual urges and to find ways to express them without feeling bad about it. What makes people feel bad, it is suggested, is the "judgmental" attitude prevalent in the surrounding culture, which young people interiorize, so that they accuse themselves in the very moment of sexual release. Moral progress means freeing ourselves from this internal judgment, learning to express our sexuality freely, and overcoming the irrational guilt that stems from others and not from our true inner selves. And we can see in that belief another version of the "born free" fallacy that we find in Rousseau.[7]

The parson might have agreed that we must find ways to express our sexual desires without guilt and shame. But he would have added that guilt and shame are often justified and that what they demand of us is not therapy in order to remove them but right conduct in order that they should not occur. And that raises the question of what right conduct might be and how it could be taught to the young. This is where a deeper understanding of context is required. And the context is that of childhood and adolescence, where we slowly shape ourselves as persons by interacting with those who truly care for us so as to acquire the virtues needed for our own flourishing.

According to Aristotle (whose works precede the full evolution-of-the-person idea), this process of moral development depends on example and imitation, whereby we rescue our states of mind from animal appetite and incorporate them into the life of reason. What was an instinctive reaction then becomes a responsible choice. Consider courage: a virtue of considerable importance for Aristotle. Courage enables us to surmount the animal instincts of fear and rage in order to do what is right and honorable, even in the midst of danger. Courage should not be confused with the instinctive aggression of the cornered animal. True, soldiers on the front line respond to an attack on their comrades by joining with them in the fight, and this response is also exhibited by pack animals. However, the soldier who rushes to share the danger of his comrades is not just obeying an instinct. He has a motive, and not just an urge, to join the battle; that motive is honor and duty toward his fellows, and shame at letting them down. Such a motive can prevail over fear and dread only because the soldier also has the virtue that enables him to act upon it. And in acting from this motive of honor, the soldier is acting for *others* and from a conception of how he looks in others' eyes. In short, he acts from a full, free, personal involvement in his predicament, conscious that he is judged for what he does, aiming at a good which he understands in personal terms. The function of the virtues is precisely to replace the animal with the person as the center of our activity, to ensure that our actions stem from our own accountability and self-conception and that they cement the relations of dependency and commitment on which our lives depend.

Exactly similar things should be said of sexual desire.[8] This is rooted in instincts that we share with the other animals, and when one person pursues another, it may at times not look so very different from the encounter of stallion and mare in a field. However, just as in the case of the soldier, the person who responds to this instinct also stands in judgment upon it. Is it right or wrong to respond? And when he responds, it is from a judgment that this is the right person, that in doing this thing, he is—in her eyes—not demeaning himself but gaining acceptance, just as she is in his. There is a reciprocity of glances involved, a gradual accommodation, as consent is woven into the very fabric of the desire, so that when they finally give way to it, the desire has become an expression of something other than instinct.

There is a remarkable feature of the I-You encounter that should be noticed at this point. By our use of the word *I*, we create a new center of being: We set the body aside, as it were, replace the organism with the self, and present to others a target of their interest that is reserved. It must be made to sally forth in order to treat with those who address it. Others enter into dialogue with this thing called *I* and see it as standing in its sovereign arena, both part of the physical world and also situated on its very edge. In a person, desire is therefore recentered, self-attributed to the I, so as to become part of the interpersonal dialogue. It is transmuted into another state of mind altogether, to become an interpersonal emotion in which subject and object confront each other, I-to-I.

In describing sexual desire, we are describing *John's* desire for *Mary*, or *Jane's* desire for *Bill*. And the people themselves will not merely describe their desires but will also experience them, as *my* desire for *you*. "I want you" is not a figure of speech but the true expression of what I feel. And here the pronouns identify that very center of free and responsible choice, which constitutes the interpersonal reality of each of us. I want you as the free being that you are, and your freedom is wrapped up in the thing I want—the thing that you identify in the first person when you engage with me I-to-I. In popular culture, love songs are therefore elaborations of the second-person pronoun: "All the Things You Are," "I've Got You Under My Skin," etc.

Sex, so conceived, involves treating the other as a free subject and enjoying the mutual arousal that is possible only through that reciprocal interest in each other as self-conscious and free. The other may refuse to cooperate, may turn away in disgust, may act in ways that elicit shame and humiliation. (That is why you have to be ready for it, and one reason why it is such an injustice to inflict sexual relations on children.) In the face of this risk, people are tempted to retreat from the direct forms of sexual desire and take refuge in fantasy objects—objects that cannot damage or threaten you, that cannot withhold consent since they cannot give it, that are without the capacity to embarrass or shame the one who makes use of them.

Such objects are provided by pornography, in which there is no real object of desire, but only a fantasy, and no real subject, since there is nothing ventured of the self. Like all cost-free forms of pleasure, porn is habit-forming. It bypasses the streams and valleys of arousal, where the self is always at risk from the other and so motivated to give itself freely if at all. The short-circuiting mechanism here is also depersonalizing. It installs the habit of viewing sex as something external to the human personality, to relationship, and to the arena of free encounters. Sex is reduced to the sexual organs, which are, one might imagine, glued onto the body like cutouts in a child's anatomy lesson. To think that this alteration of perception can occur—and its habit become fully established—without damage to the capacity to be a person or to incorporate sexual pleasure into the narrative of personal love is to make a large and naïve assumption about the ability of the mind to compartmentalize. Indeed psychologists and psychotherapists are increasingly encountering the damage done by porn, not to relationships only but to the very capacity to engage in them.[9]

The individualist defense of porn is like the collectivist approach to sex education: It is defending something that destroys the social topsoil in which the seed of personhood is planted. Only stunted growths will come from these things, as from all other forms of child abuse. And I have dwelt on the issue of sex because, to my mind, it illustrates the threat presented by modern habits to the proper growth of personality. We are entering a condition in which the emergence of the fully fledged person, bound to a community in which love and commitment are the norm, is no longer guaranteed. We are witnessing the emergence of an atomized world of short-term desires and appetites, where people are only nominally accountable to each other.

Hence the "depersonalization" that we witness in our contemporary attitudes to sex we also witness elsewhere in the culture. The suggestive passage from Schiller reminds us of what dancing has since become. For the most part, young people now dance *at*, but not *with*, each other.[10] Look at popular entertainment in its current forms, and you will find a kind of atrophy of the person, celebrated and iconized in film, music, and advertisement. The human form is stripped of its personal and sociable attributes and presented as a raw, youthful, and essentially unfinished product. This is not a biological but a cultural phenomenon, a loss of the carefully nurtured sense, inherited from the long attempt at civilization, that what we essentially are is also what we become through our social endorsement. Personhood is not an all-or-nothing attribute that is granted absolutely, as the libertarians assume. Nor is it granted to us as members of the herd, the pack, or the hunter-gatherer clan. Personhood is a process; it can flourish and decline. It can find fulfillment and satisfaction, and all the greatest efforts of the human community—in art, politics, and religion—are devoted to enhancing it.

If we understand things aright, therefore, we will be disposed to reject the assumption, so widespread in moral and political debates today, that the world can be created anew, that we enjoy unlimited freedom to remake our institutions, customs, and natural circumstances, and that we can do so and still enjoy the fruits of personality. We are persons by nature, sure. But that nature is also a *dunamis*, a potential for growth, flourishing, and fulfillment. To develop fully as persons, we need the virtues that transfer our motives from the animal to the personal center of our being—the virtues that put us in charge of our passions. These virtues are not available outside a tightly woven social context. Without socially endorsed forms of education, without families and spheres of mutual love, without the disciplined approach to *eros* and the mutuality of courtship, our social emotions are not fully re-centered in the *I*. Human beings find their fulfillment in mutual love and self-giving, but they get to this point via a long path of self-development, in which imitation, obedience, and self-control are necessary moments. This is not a hard point to understand, once we see the development of personality in the terms suggested by Aristotle. But it is a hard thing to practice. Nevertheless, when we understand things rightly, we can begin to turn back, to pick up the process where it was left off before the individualists and the collectivists tried to replace the tried-and-proven forms of moral education with their nostrums for the future of mankind. We might then strive to put virtue and good habits back where they belong, in the place now occupied by fun and thrills.

NOTES

1. See John Locke, "Of Identity and Diversity," *An Essay Concerning Human Understanding* (1690).
2. For the distinction here, see Wesley N. Hohfeld, "Fundamental Legal Conceptions as Applied in Judicial Reasoning," *Yale Law Journal* 23 (1913).
3. See John Stuart Mill, *On Liberty* (1859).
4. See Martin Buber, *I and Thou*, tr. Ronald Gregor Smith (Edinburgh, Scotland: T&T Clark, 1937); Stephen Darwall, *The Second-Person Standpoint: Morality, Respect, and Accountability* (Cambridge, MA: Harvard University Press, 2006); Georg W.F. Hegel, *The Phenomenology of Spirit*, tr. A.V. Miller (Oxford, England: Oxford University Press, 1977).

5. Friedrich Schiller, "Kallias or Concerning Beauty: Letters to Gottfried Körner (1793)," pp. 145–183 in J.M. Bernstein, ed., *Classic and Romantic German Aesthetics* (Cambridge, England: Cambridge University Press, 2003), 173–174.
6. See Max Scheler, "Über Scham und Schamgefühl" (1913), *Schriften aus dem Nachlass*, vol. 1 (Frankfurt, Germany: 1955).
7. I have given an account of this fallacy in *The Uses of Pessimism* (New York: Oxford University Press, 2010), ch. 3.
8. In what follows, I draw on the argument of my *Sexual Desire: A Philosophical Investigation* (New York: Free Press, 1986).
9. See the journal *Sexual Addiction & Compulsivity* for cases.
10. See my "Soul Music," *The American,* online magazine (February 27, 2010).

5

The Family as First Building Block

Mark Regnerus

Social scientists of the family have until fairly recently noted the comparative stability and social benefits of the two-parent (opposite-sex) married household, when contrasted to single parents, adoptive parents, cohabiting couples, and ex-spouses sharing child custody. Two well-published sociologists noted as recently as 1994 that if they were asked to design a system that would make sure children's basic needs get met, they "would probably come up with something quite similar to the two-parent family ideal."[1] Why? Because it has it all, they asserted: access to the time and resources of two adults, a system of checks and balances for quality parenting, and—importantly—two biological connections to the child, heightening the "likelihood that the parents would identify with the child and be willing to sacrifice for that child, and it would reduce the likelihood that either parent would abuse the child."[2]

While the empirical evidence in favor of this statement has diminished little since 1994, the resolve to publicly acknowledge it has receded among professional social scientists. By now it should be obvious that the family—and marriage in particular—is under a great deal of popular and political scrutiny. There is a tug-of-war in the social sciences over what we *know* with confidence about the contemporary family, which has not shifted a great deal, and what can be said about it (and who can say it).

But while scholarly norms, language, and state and federal family law can shift with remarkable speed—as they have in the West over a few short decades—the data collected from thousands of regular people who are living, or have lived, in all manner of household structures and family experiences have not changed nearly so fast. The empirical evidence still documents the pivotal importance of family stability and well-being in social life. Where we see children and young adults flourishing best, we're apt to see stable families as well. The family remains the first building block—necessary but not sufficient—in any large, decent, dynamic, and sustainable social order.

IS THE FAMILY A SOCIAL CONSTRUCTION?

Much is made of the socially constructed nature of the family. Indeed, calling a social practice or pattern "socially constructed" is a popular theme in contemporary sociology, and to wit, it has some merit. Most aspects of social life, and the institutions within or under which we live, are social constructions, by which we mean that people made them and that for them to continue, we must remake and reinforce them regularly. But calling the family *simply* a social construction is often an effort to undermine the reality of the thing so constructed and to suggest that its structure and functions could be radically different or not exist at all. This is the product of a *strong* social constructionism that is amateurish to assert, one that treats institutions—like the family, religion, or education—as arbitrary and as tractable as a taste or preference.

But there is something to be said for the socially constructed nature of the family, insofar as we are referring to the historical malleability of its expressions across the centuries and in different cultures. The contemporary nuclear family of the West—parents and children under the same roof—looks different from families in other times and in other locales, especially the common absence of multiple generations within or near the household, as well as other matrilocal or patrilocal practices. And yet there are common and permanent characteristics of the family. There is a structure to it that is historically reliable and that—when functioning competently—cannot be topped in its ability to accomplish six key tasks:

- economic production,
- reproduction,
- socialization of children,
- recreation,
- sexual control, and
- care of the sick and aged.

This is what families historically *do*: they make things, reproduce themselves (sexually), socialize their children, do things together, guard sexual access to family members—sometimes very tightly, while in other settings quite carelessly—and they take care of ill or aging family members. Historically these functions varied little, even as we recall or witness examples of individuals—and even whole communities—that seemed more or less adept at each of these. For example, contemporary Americans often outsource the care of elderly family members due to necessity (such as employment obligations) or excessive expense. While plenty of families prioritize shared evening meals, other families seldom do so. Some parents oversee their adolescent children's dating activities carefully—or curb them altogether—while other parents show little interest in discerning their youths' romantic and sexual activities. Some outsourcing—like sending children to day care (outsourcing socialization)—can and may be uneventful in its immediate consequences, while other outsourcing—like IVF or surrogacy (reproduction) or paying little attention to the romantic lives of one's adolescent children (sexual control)—is commonly perceived as far more problematic and risky.

Other hallmarks of the family are increasingly in question. Marriage, long the bedrock foundation of the family, is caught up in significant cultural conflict, with little evidence this will subside soon. Older concerns about the divorce revolution have given way to new concerns about how many adults are now delaying marriage or avoiding it altogether. Marriage rates continue to drop precipitously among young adults ages 25 to 34—the historic "sweet spot" for marrying—according to the American Community Survey (census) data (see Figure 1). Between 2000 and 2012, the share of young adults ages 25 to 34 who reported being married declined 13 percentage points, from 55 percent to 42 percent. During the same period, the percentage who have never been married increased sharply, from 34 percent to 49 percent. Thus in a rather remarkably short period of time, the

Figure 1: Percentages of Young Adults (Ages 25–34) Married and Never Married, by Year

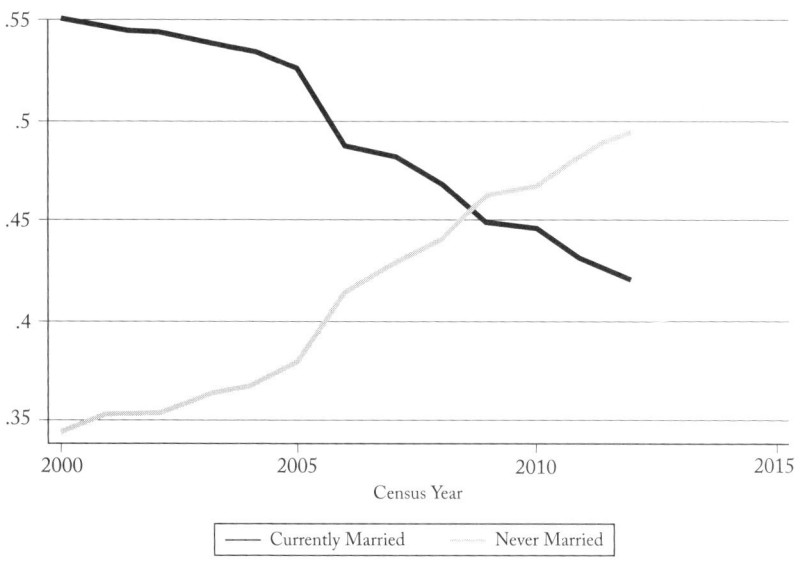

Source: American Community Survey

share of young adults in the United States who have never been married now well exceeds those who are married.

Alongside this flight from marriage is the legal and political debate about the *structure* of the marital union itself. Is marriage socially constructed to such an extent that its basic structure is malleable, subject to collective will? Can a marriage be comprised of two men or two women? Few believed so prior to thirty years ago, and only in the past ten years has majority opinion in European countries asserted so. Americans remain divided on the matter, while its legal system seems keen on affirming the new malleability in the structure of marriage as it shifts toward a greater and greater focus on the individual apart from social constraints and arrangements.

Georg Simmel, early sociologist and forerunner of social network analysis, wrote extensively about the nature of the dyad, including the structure of marriage, which—he asserted—is anchored in sexual intercourse, an act that is "alone . . . common to all historically known forms of marriage, while perhaps no other characteristic can be found without exceptions."[3] While attempting to discern his thoughts on the very modern matter of same-sex marriage would be anachronistic, his comments on marriage suggest its structure is important and may not be so pliable as many think:

> In regard to its content, and interest, as well as to its formal organization, this most personal relation of all is taken over and directed by entirely super-personal, historical-social authority. This inclusion of traditional elements profoundly contrasts marriage with friendship and similar relations, in which individual freedom is permitted much more play. Marriage, essentially, allows only acceptance or rejection, but not modification. . . . Although each of the two spouses is confronted by only the other, at least partially he also feels as he does when confronted by a collectivity; as the mere bearer of a super-individual structure whose nature and norms are independent of him, although he is an organic part of it.[4]

This is exactly how sociologist Christian Smith describes the reality of institutions that are subject to social construction but are not themselves *arbitrary* in their manifestations.[5] Some facets endure. In other words, while any of us may choose not to form marriages or families—indeed, we may openly resist the forms of both presented to us—we are not capable of socially constructing them out of existence.

THE FAMILY AND SOCIAL CHANGE

While the family can readily survive shifting functions, historically variable manifestations, and perhaps even activists seeking to "construct" different visions of the family, how it has fared more recently in the wake of technological change deserves closer scrutiny. Writing well before the era of widely utilized contraception, Simmel noted the tight link between love, marriage, and reproduction: "Passion seeks to tear down the borders of the ego and to absorb 'I' and 'thou' in one another. But it is not they which become a unit: rather, a *new* unit emerges, the child."[6]

But today's children no longer follow the marital union in such a predictable and timely sequence. Talk of "starting a family" (that is, having children) is nearly ubiquitous today, denoting the control over fertility so widely utilized and cognitively taken for granted. It is this—more than anything else—that has made possible the *strong* social constructionist talk about marriage, relationships, and fertility today. "Effective contraception," social theorist Anthony Giddens wrote in 1992,

> meant more than an increased capability of limiting pregnancy. In combination with the other influences affecting family size . . . it signaled a deep transition in personal life. For women—and, in a partly different sense, for men also—sexuality became malleable, open to being shaped in diverse ways, and a potential "property" of the individual. . . . Now that conception can be artificially produced, rather than only artificially inhibited, sexuality is at last fully autonomous.[7]

Fully autonomous: that is, separated from embeddedness in strong (or even romantic) relationships. The "individual freedom" of which Simmel wrote as reflecting friendship more than marriage is now "permitted much more play" in sexual relationships, including marriage. Giddens asserts that more change should be expected to follow: "Once there is a new terminology for understanding sexuality, ideas, concepts and theories couched in these terms seep into social life itself, and help reorder it."[8]

What Westerners have witnessed over the past several decades, then, is *not* the social construction of marriage or family simply toward different plausible ends as a product of political will, but the reality of technology-driven social change, which brings about new social structures, which then act back upon the phenomena that gave rise to them. Following Smith's model, a conceptual model of the emergence of social change in marriage and family appears in Figure 2. It counters simplistic, reductionistic explanations like "social construction," "the right side of history," "liberation," or "the triumph of rights and freedom over ignorance and bigotry" for new variations in the structure of socially sanctioned intimate relationships (including the decoupling of sex from committed relationships and the altered meaning and structure of marriage). The numerous boxes displayed in the

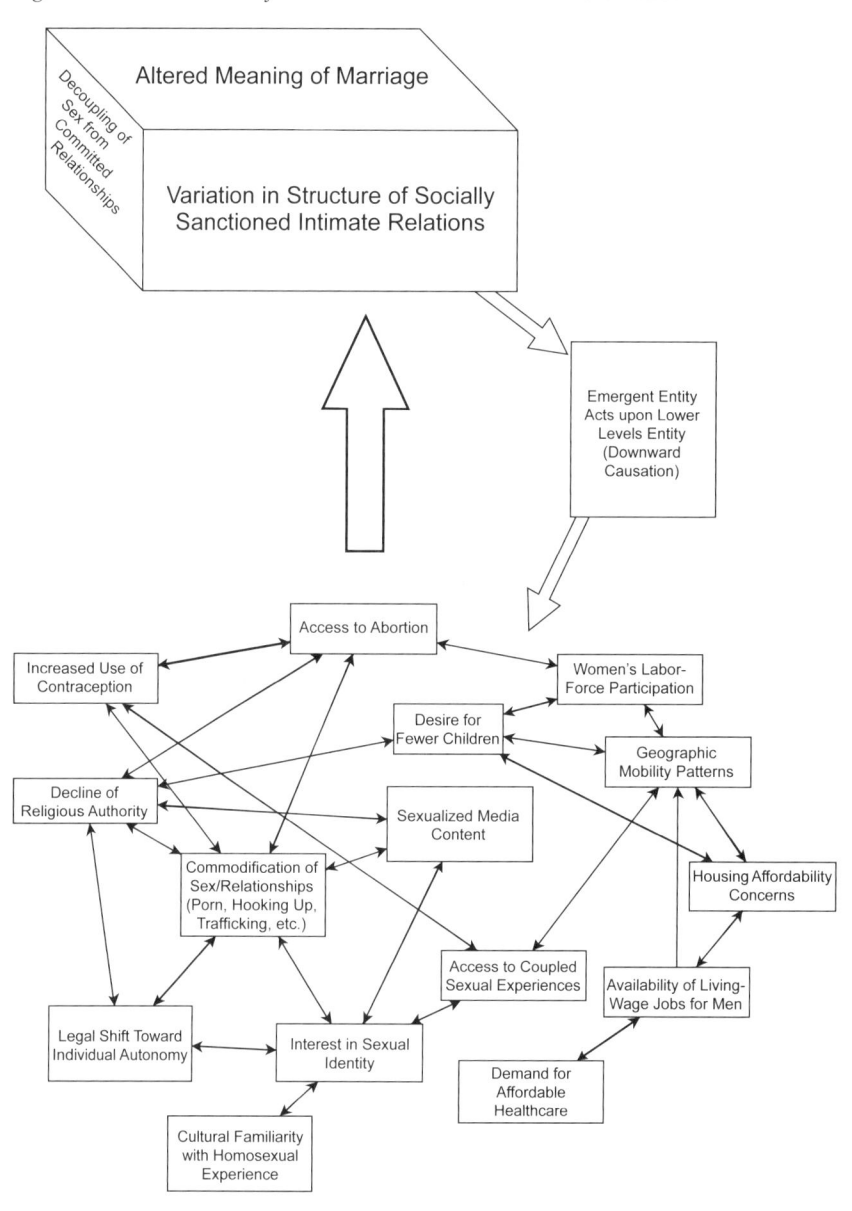

Figure 2: Interaction of Major Social Shifts and Relational Redefinition

bottom half of Figure 2 are each important component parts of social realities that concern family and marriage today. Many are interrelated, meaning change in one can affect the other. For example, "Desire for Fewer Children" is associated with "Women's Labor-force Participation." The same is true for "Access to Abortion" and "Decline of Religious Authority"—the two are associated.[9]

In what Giddens calls a "double hermeneutic," when we discern and name some change in the social world—unlike in the natural world—we're not only classifying the change (that is, noting it), but we're allowing it, actively or passively, to act back upon the social world, altering how people then must navigate it.[10] Sociologist James Hunter agrees about naming such social shifts, asserting that culture change is a work of legitimation and delegitimation, of naming one thing normal and right and its competition deviant, stupid, inferior, ridiculous, or just plain wrong.[11] At bottom, he asserts, culture is the power of "legitimate naming," a move which, when successful, penetrates the structure of our imagination, the frameworks for how people think and converse, the words they use, the arguments they permit each other to make, and their perceptions of what ought to constitute normal reality. This is certainly a significant form of power.

Neither the power to name nor the wielding of that power hinges on an individual's abilities to discern such social change (though many are cognizant of its outlines). One need not discern the shift in meaning of marriage in order for it to affect his cognitive frameworks around relationships as well as his own relationship behaviors. Nor do we need to understand the decoupling of sex from committed relationships for it to have causally affected our demand for contraception and abortion. These things will happen, and have happened, regardless of our naming it.

This new idea—malleability in socially sanctioned intimate relationships—alters other entities as well, including the emerging same-sex marriage movement and the rumblings of interest in other permutations of sexual relationships. In step with Giddens, Hunter, and Smith, this significant social shift in family now acts back upon those entities from which it arose, fostering still more change of note:

- still greater legal shifts toward individual autonomy and choice in family law,
- greater cultural familiarity with homosexual expression and diverse sexual identities,
- decline in religious authority (and rise in concerns about religious freedom), and
- greater mobility (and an increase in homogeneous communities).[12]

Thus while same-sex marriage activists have long asserted that expanding marriage rights to include two men or two women need not alter how marriage is practiced among others, such a claim is shortsighted and ignores the reality of how social change works. Same-sex marriage does not *only* add access; it also acts back upon the entities from which it sprang. Thus there will not likely be two kinds of marriage, but rather one—marriage not rooted in biological and sexual difference and serving to protect women and/or children but rather rooted in the malleability of intimate relationships made possible by the technological severance of sexual expression from predictable reproduction. Any given community need not endorse same-sex marriage for it to feel the influence—described earlier—of this shift in the structure of marriage that is already well-advanced.

Its development—as well as its resistance—is not a simple matter. Friends of same-sex marriage ought not reduce the voices behind its resistance to simple prejudice against progress, convenient and therapeutic though that may seem. Nor should its foes account for their resistance using simplistic narratives of "cultural degradation." The conceptual model is intended to convey the situation's complexity as well as the powers of the new social reality that has emerged.

As an example of such powers, consider the decoupling of sex from committed relationships: Figure 2 suggests it not only arose in part as a result of widespread contraceptive use, women's rising labor-force participation and career orientation, and less availability of living-wage jobs for men (making fewer men "marriageable"), but it now *acts back upon* this complex of entities, prompting, among other things,

- demand for abortion (due in part to standard failure rates in an era of elevated contraceptive use and increased sexual activity),
- demand for affordable housing and healthcare (given the rise in solitary living and the reduction in resources once accessed through marriage), and
- the general commodification of sex and relationships (apparent in sexualized media content, the normative use of "hooking up" language, a rise in human trafficking, etc.).

The conceptual model is intended not only to visualize the emergence of significant social change in the domain of family and sexuality, but also to hint at the consilience of factors that are often treated as conceptually independent. In reality, they are rarely so. Perspectives on abortion, sex, fertility, marriage, and religion—as well as affordable housing and even healthcare—often appear to hang together precisely because they are interconnected in reality, bound together by their direct or indirect ties to the family change displayed by the three-dimensional box of Figure 2. Thus, for example, pro-choice activists are more often favorable toward same-sex marriage, positive about universal healthcare, supportive of the legal turn toward individual rights, and unconcerned about religious-freedom issues, not because there are only two broad options (to be for or against all of these), but because to them, the entities involved *are* all related. They see a desirable social change in family and sexual relationships whose consequences—like increased individual vulnerability to market phenomena—must be managed (by wider access to community provisions such as health insurance, abortion, unemployment compensation, etc.). The opposite is true among pro-life activists, who commonly perceive in these social, legal, and legislative priorities a decisive turn away from the nuclear family, which they hold to be the source of much individual as well as social and economic good.

Thus when sociologist Eric Klinenberg popularly documents the recent surge in solitary living, it is easy to concur with him that Western society did *not* have a model for large numbers of people living alone until quite recently.[13] The social changes around family—and their resultant cognitive, economic, and socially structured realities—that would be necessary to support this shift in household-living patterns had not yet taken place. Klinenberg attributes the rise in living alone to the rise in women's opportunities, among other things. I do not disagree but only counsel that these two social phenomena—living alone and women's opportunities—are components (and thereafter, altered products) of the shift in meaning and structure of marriage and intimate relationships. Klinenberg notes that social observers expected the recent Great Recession to shrink the living-alone population, and yet this did not happen. And, he suspects, it will not happen. I agree, given what's occurring. There is simply too much demand for solitary living, together with factors that foster such demand. Associated interests include personal inexperience with large families, affordable housing and healthcare, mobility, women's employment, and the vagaries of men's marriageability. In other words, for solitary-living patterns to decline, we would have to witness *far* more than simple economic downturn but rather more dramatic structural shifts that disproportionately affect women's opportunities. I see little evidence of that currently.

DO CHILDREN THRIVE IN EMERGENT FAMILY FORMS?

As the variation in the meaning and structure of marriage and other intimate relationships widens, it is worth wondering if there are intergenerational costs to these notable shifts that are difficult to ameliorate or manage. Giddens concurs, cautioning that "it would certainly not be right to suppose that childhood has remained unaffected" by the new realities in parental romantic relationships.[14]

Indeed, families anchored by stably intact, married parents *are* becoming rarer, as the conceptual model detailed above would predict and as U.S. Census Bureau data bear out. Does this matter? Yes. In their study titled "The Puzzle of Monogamous Marriage," a team of an economist and a psychologist, an anthropologist, and an environmental scientist painstakingly detail the long-term social benefits of monogamy and marriage for many public outcomes, including those of children.[15] The authors note, among other things, the significance of a biological connection:

> Living in the same household with genetically unrelated adults is the *single biggest risk factor* for abuse, neglect and homicide of children. Stepmothers are 2.4 times more likely to kill their stepchildren than birth mothers, and children living with an unrelated parent are between 15 and 77 times more likely to die "accidentally."[16]

One should not read such statements as a general indictment of stepparenting, since most stepparenting arrangements are peaceable. The social science, however, remains clear that—on average—genetic unrelatedness is a higher risk to children then relatedness. Data analysis from the 2011 New Family Structures Study (NFSS)[17] reveals far more than just information about what it was like to have a parent who had had a same-sex relationship, although it can do that, with limitations.[18] An unsung narrative in the NFSS data, outlined briefly below, is the persistently impressive results that are more apt to be displayed among respondents whose parents were and remained married—either up to the present or until the death of one of them—when compared with the lives of young adults, who had quite different things to report about their household experiences while growing up. Table 1 documents consistent advantages, across fifty outcome measures, enjoyed by young adults who report having witnessed the stable marriage of their parents. (Their parents' marital happiness, however, was not evaluated.) As you can see, not all of the measures are different between the two groups. That is to be expected. But across different types of measures, the benefits of having grown up with a married biological mother and father who are still together (or else one or both have since passed away) are obvious.

Out of fifty outcomes, on only two do we see numeric equivalence or respondents from nonbiological families performing better (or in a more sociable direction) than respondents who grew up in their biological families. And out of fifty outcomes, forty—or 80 percent—display statistically significant between-group differences, meaning that there are genuine distinctions between adult children who grew up in intact, biological families and those who did not. (These forty outcomes are bolded in the table.)

Table 1: Outcome Differences between Stably Intact Biological Families and All Other Household Types

Data source: NFSS, adults ages 18–39
(Bold indicates between-group difference is significant at p<0.05.)

Outcome Measure The respondent . . .	All Others	Intact Biological Families
has ever had an abortion.	15%	11%
was ever forced to have sex.	16%	8%
was ever touched sexually by an adult caregiver or parent.	15%	6%
ever cheated while married.	22%	14%
ever had a sexually transmitted infection.	17%	12%
views porn weekly.	15%	16%
has ever been in jail.	22%	11%
has ever been convicted of a crime.	17%	11%
has ever used illegal drugs (not marijuana).	25%	17%
has used marijuana in the past year.	25%	18%
smokes daily.	17%	11%
has ever had problems because of drinking.	13%	9%
drank with the intent to get drunk any time in the past year.	44%	38%
drinks with the intent to get drunk weekly.	9%	9%
has often thought that his/her current romantic relationship was in trouble.	37%	25%
has discussed ending his/her current romantic relationship several/numerous times.	24%	12%
has broken up several/numerous times with his/her current romantic partner.	14%	7%
has ever had problems with close relationships.	15%	12%
has thought about leaving his/her spouse/partner in the past 12 months.	33%	20%
has thought seriously about committing suicide in the past 12 months.	8%	4%

(continued)

Table 1: Outcome Differences between Stably Intact Biological Families and All Other Household Types *(continued)*

Outcome Measure The respondent...	All Others	Intact Biological Families
has received counseling/therapy for an anxiety-related condition.	8%	3%
is very unhappy with life.	4%	1%
was not physically active in the previous week.	20%	13%
receives less than 6 hours of sleep on a regular night.	15%	12%
reports poor/fair physical health.	15%	8%
reports having a bad temper.	29%	17%
is obese (BMI>35).	17%	8%
has been diagnosed with hypertension.	14%	10%
has been diagnosed with diabetes/high blood sugar.	7%	3%
agrees that "I don't feel like I can depend on my family."	20%	10%
did not work last week.	41%	29%
has debt (other than mortgage) greater than $50,000.	9%	15%
has been without health insurance for the past 12 months.	36%	25%
currently receives public assistance.	28%	10%
doesn't have enough money to pay bills on time.	18%	10%
watches more than three hours of TV (continuously) daily.	14%	5%
spends over 2 hours (continuously) on social networks daily.	20%	14%
spends over 2 hours playing video games daily.	15%	10%

Outcome Measure The respondent...	All Others	Intact Biological Families
watches more than 2 hours of TV a day.	51%	37%
voted in 2008.	52%	56%
considers it very important to maintain his/her relationships with siblings.	63%	70%
is currently married.	38%	44%
is very happy with life.	32%	43%
has been physically active in the last 24 hours.	45%	47%
reports excellent or very good physical health.	47%	62%
owns a home.	42%	53%
attends church weekly or more often.	19%	26%
considers that his/her current job is achieving respondent's career goals or preparing the respondent to do so.	49%	67%
has a household income of more than $50,000.	41%	60%
agrees that "My childhood years were happy."	63%	82%

For example, only 11 percent of young adults from biological families reported ever having been in jail, half the rate (22 percent) of those from non–biologically intact households. Double the number of the latter reported thinking seriously about suicide within the past twelve months (8 versus 4 percent), breaking up several or numerous times with their current partner (14 versus 7 percent), or agreeing that they don't feel like they can depend on their family (20 versus 10 percent). Twenty-eight percent reported current receipt of public assistance, compared to 10 percent of respondents who grew up in their biological families. Whereas 63 percent of young adults from non–biologically intact households agreed that their childhood years were happy, the same is true of 82 percent of respondents from biological families. Differences appear as well among a variety of sexual-behavior measures, as well as drug use, relationship concerns, media usage, religious activities, employment, and income. Other outcomes display little difference of note, including alcohol use, physical activity, voting behavior, and sleep habits. To be sure, some of the distinctions are not profound, comprising a few percentage-point differences. Yet many are.

Space does not permit a more thorough evaluation of these outcomes or the drawing of finer distinctions in household structure or experience here, as I did in my November 2012 article in *Social Science Research*.[19] As that analysis made clear, not all forms of "diminished kinship" in household structure and experience (grouped together in Table 1 as "all others") appear to have been equally problematic in the lives of the respondents. A stable parental relationship (even if nonbiological) is far preferable to an unstable household displaying multiple transitions and parental romantic relationships.

This is not a claim about the malicious intentions of particular types of family systems but rather the simple observation that *kinship matters*: to be stably rooted in your married mother and father's household is to foster the greatest chance at lifelong flourishing. It's not necessary, of course. It just has the best odds. It is with some irony that we hear of airplane manufacturers spending billions in research and development in order to achieve fuel-efficiency gains of a few percentage points, while the human social and economic efficiencies of stably intact families are *obvious* but largely ignored or explained away. Parental marriage, parent-child biological kinship, and stability each matter for kids—including after they've become adults—and are goods to be *recognized* even when they cannot be *realized*.

I do not plumb the depths of why exactly children from stably intact, married households seem to perform better. The NFSS data is not longitudinal and not conducive to making strong claims about parenting influences. Social scientists, equipped with a near-innate skepticism about cross-sectional data, may raise the question of social selectivity. That is, are the differences *really* about the effects of parental marriage and the intact family, or is there something to say for the *kind* of people who tend to marry, have children, and stay together? This is a reasonable concern, one that cannot be ruled out here. Yet, selectivity concerns raise the question of just how "the kind of people who tend to marry and stay together" are *themselves* formed. There's a likely answer: by their own experience of stable family life. (To be sure, we witness considerable resilience among those who have not experienced such stability and yet find ways to resurrect it in their own lives. And we see vulnerability, too, when the products of stable families do not exhibit stability themselves.)

Henrich and his fellow authors prefer an *ecological* explanation in their meticulous account of the benefits of monogamy and marriage for children (and for adults):

> We predict that imposing monogamous marriage reduces male reproductive competition and suppresses intra-sexual competition, which shrinks the size of the pool of low-status, risk-oriented, unmarried men. These effects result in (i) lower rates of crime, personal abuse, intra-household conflict and fertility, and (ii) greater parental investment (especially male), economic productivity (gross domestic product [GDP] per capita) and female equality.[20]

Although the NFSS is not poised to test ecological models like this one, recent research into mating markets reinforces the perceptiveness of such an account.[21]

THE FAMILY, THE STATE, AND THE FUTURE

Both inside and outside the academy, however, many believe the West can survive—even thrive—without relying on the support of stable, biological families. Stability, it is believed, can be generated in other meaningful ways or its benefits replaced by other means or sources. This is certainly a gamble, one with high stakes. Social conservatives tend not to be interested in taking such a leap of faith when the data on the long-term benefits of the intact biological family are so consistent. Indeed, social conservatives are often (but certainly not always) economic conservatives because of their tacit or explicit fondness for "subsidiarity." Subsidiarity is not—as some might perceive it—a declaration of radical independence and individualism. Rather, it is a reflection of *inter*dependence and a hierarchy of social responsibility, beginning with the family—the level at which very many of the challenges of life are best met. And yet it is obvious that many persons live in fractured families. The brokenness common to the human experience isn't best remediated by subsidies or a generous state, however, but by love. At the bottom of healthy, productive, good societies is interpersonal love. And familial love is the first and most natural love, not easily replaced—or equaled in scope and responsibility—by friendships, let alone associations or "assigned casework" forms of care. When families become incapable of providing such love, care, and assistance—and this happens with regularity—it devolves to other persons, other families, and to society to provide for their needs. However, "society" ought not be equated with the state, as is often the assumption in a modern world increasingly bereft of vibrant mediating institutions (e.g., congregations, aid associations, unions, and civic organizations).

Nevertheless, the state has a role to play in a thriving society. It is responsible for care and provision in the absence of more immediate and local options. Simply put, some problems cannot be tackled at the local level. The state, however, ought not be neutral on the relationship and family-form choices of its citizens, for it cannot be neutral without economic and social consequences, given that the biologically intact, stably married household remains both the best and cheapest source of provision, care, love, and socialization of children. All other solutions are *concessions* to be made in the absence of the ideal. This principle is at the heart of why so-called family conservatives are also often fiscal conservatives, because they have made personal sacrifices so that their family members—sons, daughters, spouses, and parents—are cared for, covered, protected, and assisted, and they rebel at the mandate that resources they earn in order to accomplish these very things ought to be widely shared (via taxation) with those who, by their own or others' choices, are not in a position to receive the care of a family. In that case, social conservatives are apt to *sympathize* but are less likely to *empathize*, because, they figure, that's what families are for. They take care of each other and sometimes others as well, following the logic of subsidiarity. This does not appear sustainable, although the timetable for the depletion of social, emotional, and economic "capital" long accrued by the sacrifices—and difficult lives, no doubt—of so many stably married households is anything but clear. As more families fail—and as the legal shift in family law toward favoring adults' personal wishes continues unabated—subsidiarity as a principle is threatened and seems increasingly untenable. There is political pressure to make more commitments to meet the needs of persons no longer interconnected by marriage or family. This all makes sense and is in keeping with the conceptual model of family change depicted in Figure 2.

But a good society seeks to discourage broken kinship ties and continues to struggle over how to manage those that are unavoidable. It does *not* respond by simply declaring biological bonds to be irrelevant or such brokenness only imagined or discrimination in family and sexual choices unfair. Brokenness, after all, costs. It costs time and money and emotional resources from extended families—the most optimal source for help—as well as from communities, caseworkers, public-health clinics, mental-health counselors, criminal-justice systems, and the public that underwrites these. In addition to material resources and efforts, however, the genuine amelioration of brokenness commonly requires love (not something in which social scientists normally traffic, or even typically acknowledge in research).

Few question that the family is one of the oldest institutions in the human community or that it is important for human flourishing. But its status as "first building block" is certainly up for grabs. The cultural turning away from the biological family in the academy and the legal community is remarkable. Even while the evidence for its strengths is incontrovertible, and the costs borne by communities in its absence obvious, it is increasingly politically unpalatable to go to bat for the nuclear family while the pitched battle over the emergence of new family forms and meanings rages on.

NOTES

1. Sara McLanahan and Gary Sandefur, *Growing Up with a Single Parent: What Hurts, What Helps* (Cambridge, MA: Harvard University Press, 1994), 38.
2. Ibid.
3. Kurt H. Wolff, *The Sociology of Georg Simmel* (New York: Simon and Schuster, 1950), 131 (note 10).
4. Ibid., 130.
5. Christian Smith, *What Is a Person? Rethinking Humanity, Social Life, and the Moral Good from the Person Up* (Chicago, IL: University of Chicago Press, 2010).
6. Wolff, *Sociology of Simmel*, 128.
7. Anthony Giddens, *The Transformation of Intimacy: Sexuality, Love and Eroticism in Modern Societies* (Redwood City, CA: Stanford University Press, 1993), 27.
8. Ibid., 28.
9. The model depicted in Figure 2 is not interested in explaining how such things like the desire for fewer children came about or why living-wage jobs for men have receded—important topics though these are.
10. Although critical realists like Smith (2010) do a fine job explaining the reality of *emergence*, which is admittedly a challenging phenomenon to satisfactorily describe, I do not believe that understanding it is necessary to explain the social changes witnessed in the domain of family over the past several decades. Nevertheless, the type of emergence of which Smith speaks is characterized by the development of structured norms and social facts that themselves then act causally back upon those "entities" that together gave rise to them. Such a process is hardly uniform, nor are its consequences certain, since other forces are at work as well.
11. See James Davison Hunter, *To Change the World: The Irony, Tragedy, and Possibility of Christianity in the Late Modern World* (New York: Oxford University Press, 2010).
12. Bill Bishop discusses this at length in his book *The Big Sort: Why the Clustering of Likeminded America Is Tearing Us Apart* (New York: Houghton Mifflin, 2008).
13. See Eric Klinenberg, *Going Solo: The Extraordinary Rise and Surprising Appeal of Living Alone* (New York: Penguin, 2012). Klinenberg writes that before 1950, living alone comprised about 10 percent of households, mostly men, and mostly in the rural West. Today, it's 28 percent of households, and mostly in cities. In Manhattan, where he lives, every second household has a solitary occupant.

14. Giddens, *Transformation of Intimacy*, 98.
15. Joseph Henrich, Robert Boyd, and Peter J. Richerson, "The Puzzle of Monogamous Marriage," *Philosophical Transactions of the Royal Society, B: Biological Sciences* 367 (March 2012): 657–669.
16. Ibid., 665.
17. The NFSS interviewed just under three thousand adults ages 18–39 and asked batteries of questions, including a calendar of household occupants, details about relationships with parents and parental figures, and many contemporary outcomes.
18. See Mark Regnerus, "How Different Are the Adult Children of Parents Who Have Same-Sex Relationships? Findings from the New Family Structures Study," *Social Science Research* 41 (July 2012): 752–770; Mark Regnerus, "Parental Same-Sex Relationships, Family Instability, and Subsequent Life Outcomes for Adult Children: Answering Critics of the New Family Structures Study with Additional Analyses," *Social Science Research* 41 (November 2012): 1367–1377.
19. Regnerus, "Parental Same-Sex Relationships." See previous note.
20. Henrich, Boyd, and Richerson, "The Puzzle of Monogamous Marriage," 658.
21. See Mark Regnerus and Jeremy Uecker, *Premarital Sex in America: How Young Americans Meet, Mate, and Think about Marrying* (New York: Oxford University Press, 2011).

6

Why We Need the Majesty of the Law[1]

Harvey C. Mansfield

The notion of *majesty* in the law may seem disagreeably obsolete to us in our time, living as we do in the style of democratic informality. But it is not lost, as one may see from the title of Justice Sandra Day O'Connor's memoirs.[2] In this chapter, I mean to call upon what is awesome and venerable in the law, as I think the good justice did as well. My inquiry relates to the third pillar of Robert P. George's foundation for a thriving society, the one that requires "a fair and effective system of law and government." The majesty of the law justifies and ennobles the functions of deterrence and coordination needed for such a government.

MAJESTY AND LEGAL REALISM

I shall speak of why "the law" is a whole, why the law necessarily has certain defects, and why it deserves respect as a whole despite them. Our law is human law, but it looks upward to a higher realm of the intelligible and the divine. The law can never be perfect, yet it is wrong to consider it as a mere instrument of human will. I shall proceed to this conclusion by arguing from fundamental facts we usually take for granted.

Informality is not an accidental feature of our democracy, insofar as everything in our lives is held open to change in the hope of reform, and too much stuffy dignity seems to give support to the status quo and to stand in the way of reform. We are still attached to the formality of procedure and the solemnity of judicial garb designed to maintain respect for the law. We do not need regal magnificence in our judges, but we do require republican assurances that public justice is serious business. Above all, any appearance that the law can be toyed with, that it can be circumvented by private approach or by interested calculation, is to be avoided. What happens behind the scenes in the enacting and executing of the law, we still believe, must stay behind the scenes, with compelled respect for its public face.

Against this intimation of majesty practiced in our time is the movement of thought known as "legal realism." I will argue that majesty is good and that legal realism is inadequate. Legal realism is not all wrong, but the view that it is enough is all wrong.

Legal realism has several modes, each of which might be described more precisely than I will do here. They all declare that something other than law, and more powerful than law, is the cause of law. The "realism" consists in seeing through the pretentious, showy appearances of law and establishing the fact of this more powerful force. Once established, that fact must not be covered up in order to accommodate the moral consciences of those who are hopeful and naïve about the law; it must be published, taught, and spread. Legal realism is expected to bring good to society by its inventors, who have quickly become, if they were not from the first, its advocates. It asserts that our law will be better if through clear thinking, we dispense with its irrational majesty.

This realism is really idealism. In the old days, when philosophy was young, the pre-Socratic philosophers thought that laws are made for the convenience of rulers and that nothing good was to be expected from politics. They thought *that* was realism. In America by contrast, advocates of legal realism have arisen from the Progressive tradition, joined now by libertarian conservatives, who claim public good will result from their public unmasking of law. Despite the fact (as they maintain) that no one aims at the public good, they believe it does exist; Socrates was right about that.

The sort of thinking our legal realists recommend can be seen in the famous prisoner's dilemma, which is the essence of game theory (the most fashionable mode of legal realism). The prisoner's dilemma posits a situation in which a prisoner must choose between defecting from a fellow prisoner and cooperating with him. In the scenario, we are not told whether the prisoner is guilty. We do not know whether the law he may or may not have violated deserves to be respected. But notwithstanding the nonjudgmental language of "defecting" (rather than betraying), the example is not as neutral as it seems. One's sympathies are unjustifiably enlisted on the side of the prisoner by the adoption of his point of view. From the standpoint of the law, the prisoner who cooperates with a fellow prisoner is defecting from the law instead of cooperating with it by confessing, as is his duty. The example, typical of game theory as a whole, substitutes calculation for duty and is actually about how to evade the law if it is advantageous to do so.

It is not unreasonable to question the coherence of such allegedly neutral strategizing. Suppose the prisoners are murderers. Shouldn't people believe that two murderers, if they don't confess themselves, should at least accuse each other? Strangely, murderers say that to accuse a guilty comrade is to "rat him out." The phrase expresses a noble disdain toward betrayal, a nobility to which murderers are not entitled. Yet even pseudo-nobility might get in the way of calculation. It will be objected that respect for the law is due only when the law seems good to us. But if this were correct, people would simply do what is good for them, harmony would result, and there would be no need for law. It seems that law needs to seem good even when it may not be; it needs, as we say, legitimacy. Does legitimacy require majesty to give it authority?

GOLD AND STONES

I have been speaking so far of "the law," as if law were one whole. Even we in pluralistic America use that expression. A whole such as an animal organism has parts with a definite order, each with its functional contribution to the whole. But the law is a whole without articulated parts. It is a whole of a peculiar kind, in which every law carries the wholeness of law. Yet the law consists of laws, each of them applicable by itself and not necessarily coherent with the others. Law is composed of laws, but every law is the law; disobey one, and you have disobeyed "the law." You cannot plead that you obey most all other laws; one hunded-percent obedience is required.

One could compare law as a whole with stone and also with gold. When you cut a stone, you get stones, each *a* stone now, a whole on its own. Law is a whole that when cut into parts is no less of a whole than before it was cut. For every law is a cut as well as a whole. But when you cut gold, you get *some* gold, not a gold; this is called the partitive construction. Some gold is part of all gold but not a whole on its own. It is as if the whole of gold wanted to hold on to its wholeness, jealous of any new whole. The law is like both stone and gold, divisible into parts yet with each part reflecting the status or dignity of the whole. Law is also common, like stone, and precious, like gold.[3]

POSITIVE AND NATURAL LAW

For example, take a law against jaywalking. This law makes a cut, distinguishing the legal from the illegal way of crossing a street. Yet the whole remains in the reason why this law was "cut"—why was the law passed? With this law, a community shows its concern for the well-being of its citizens (though not necessarily tender concern, since vehicular accidents cause not just human suffering but public expense). And why such a concern? These are not just any bodies being protected, but human bodies. Human bodies have minds, possibly souls. The bodies of dogs, cats, and deer are not as valuable as these bodies, and besides, they are not capable of obeying a law against jaywalking. The law against jaywalking protects citizens from death. It therefore assumes that death is bad and life is good. Is that true? And how do we know? Add up all the implications of this law, and you see that a comprehensive whole is assumed to be true by the law, one that gives a special status to human beings (among other questionable assertions).

A law is therefore a cutting and an inclusion. A cut is the result of a decision of what should be legal and what illegal. This reminds us of the positivist theory of law or of the notion of sovereignty. In this theory, law is made law by its efficient cause, by the positive or sovereign power to decide. But there must be some reason for the cut, some justification, and the necessity for a reason compels us to include in our consideration all the things that surround the cut. As we have seen in the example of jaywalking, we would have to go as far as to establish the order of nature, detailing what is man's as well as what is above and below man. We could not omit the question of the existence of God as possible governor or creator of the whole that is nature. Is the law against jaywalking consistent with the startling findings of modern physics that challenge the idea of the "order of nature"? "Jaywalking" itself contains a metaphorical sense of human waywardness outside the rules—or is it better to say, of being on one's own, improving on the rules? Now we have arrived at the theory of natural law, rival to positivist law, which says that law is a rational determination of what is naturally and thus truly right. The law is determined by its rationality—the formal cause—and by its purpose, the final cause.

Unfortunately it seems difficult to choose between the two theories, because both seem to be true, but only up to a point, and not so that either can dispose of the other. It seems true that law is an arbitrary decision that could have been otherwise than it was; consider the various conflicting laws in different countries and at different times, or conflicting proposals by different parties in the same time and place. Think of Obamacare,[4] now much disputed. Yet these decisions are choices made for a reason, not arbitrary whims of fate. The reason for a law may be stated in a preamble (or prelude) that moves toward a statement of aspiration concerning the whole. Think of the (partial) title of the "Affordable Care Act." Observe all that stems from the word "affordable," meaning within (rather than beyond) our means. It speaks to the limits of human attainments. And what about "care"? It raises the question, "Does God take care of us, or does He leave us unprotected so that we must scramble to do so on our own?" Similarly, the welfare state is translated in French as *l'État-providence*. Does that mean that law is made in consonance with God's providence or to substitute for it? Here we have a fleeting glimpse of the majesty of the law, but does that law reflect God's majesty or substitute for it? One should not believe the answer does not matter, but either way, law has or needs majesty—perhaps all the more if it wants to do without God or the divine.

These are not questions that citizens or even professionals such as lawyers, judges, policemen, and professors of law habitually think about. They take the majesty of the law for granted, believing that because law professionals are not mere instruments of powerful rulers, they deserve the respect they habitually receive. They are not on the level of cunning, strategizing criminals like the players of game theory! They are something higher. So there must *be* something higher, and this, whatever it is, is on the side of the law. That is the working presumption.

PROCRUSTES AND CONSISTENCY

The law, however, is not simply good, as the notion of natural law seems to require. "The law" consists of the laws of any city or state, however contradictory they may be. But since the law is a whole, it tries for consistency and insists on generality. It is a brave overstatement, Procrustean in character. Procrustes was a host who fit his guests to the beds he had, cutting off their limbs if they were too long, stretching them out if too short. The law is Procrustean but with an easy conscience; it doesn't have a sense of proportion in its parts—all of them being laws that are equally law.

For example, does the law on jaywalking apply to the police? The late James Q. Wilson, in an excellent book with a superlative title, *Varieties of Police Behavior*, contrasted the behavior of the Oakland, California, police department with that of other police departments, in this regard.[5] It happened that the parking lot of the Oakland department was located across the street from the department, so that policemen had either to walk a distance and cross at the corner, or jaywalk.[6] Under the watchful eye of some graduate student, it was seen that in Oakland, the police took the trouble to obey the law. Elsewhere the police, with more discretion, would be more relaxed and excuse themselves from a law they did not enforce on others. This small difference was the sign of grander contrast between one department preferring to "go by the book," and another ignoring the law when convenient or efficient to do so. One can see reason in both ways, and the most reason when both are combined. But they cannot easily be combined, because the spirit of each is antithetical to the other. It is just because law wants to be consistent that it must be arbitrary and Procrustean.

Any time that a legislator makes a law, he makes a cut between something declared legal and something illegal. As we have seen, in making a cut, he makes a whole. But he usually does so unwittingly, thinking only of jaywalking and forgetting the further implications. If he tried to take into account these implications, however, he would need to have great scientific, philosophical, or superhuman knowledge. He has no time for this sort of study, and meanwhile, jaywalking is a present evil. So he has to make a stab at it, looking ahead to the consequences he can foresee and at the same time meeting a present need. This is something like a professor's opening lecture in a course; to begin, he needs to look inexactly at the end. The preamble to a law states its purpose quickly and tendentiously, introducing the law proper, which by itself is not argument but command. But one could also say that the law *is* the preamble by itself, because it includes by implication all those things that are suggestively set forth in the preamble. The trouble is that it is easier to change the professor's opening lecture than to change the law. The professor simply admits that his first statement was tentative or even wrong, but the law cannot say that. Every change of law implies a new whole, different from the one implied by the previous law, requiring a new explanation replacing the old one. But the very arbitrariness of the law makes it difficult to admit its arbitrariness. The old law, after all, was no less *the law* than is the new one, and the new one is no more so than the old.

LOWER THE HORIZON

Modern political science had a cure for this arbitrariness in the law. It was to lower the horizon of law so that it covered only minimum human necessities, for example, bodily security. Law would no longer claim to comprehend the whole of human life, or what you do with your secure body. The law would merely free the citizen to do what he pleased, having satisfied the demands of his and others' security of body. The soul and its requirements would no longer be part of the law. It would be necessary, then, to *prevent* the law from including these larger matters, in order to make it a whole of itself. From this lowering of horizon comes the modern theory of sovereignty, which sacrifices the nobility and beauty of the law for the power of the legislator. In keeping with this theory, a "separation of powers" ensures that power is safely confined to a necessary minimum while simultaneously contrived to do the job with energy. Once the problem is defined as one of power—power made both safe and capable—the rational element in law is ignored, and cutting no longer implies including. So the theory of sovereignty admits the necessity of arbitrariness in the law—even makes a point of it—but then reduces it by confining law to matters of the body, like jaywalking, that people can see the reason for and can agree on, as opposed to more disputable questions regarding the soul. Then it becomes more appropriate to speak of *laws*—"settled standing laws," in the plural—than of *the law* as if it were a whole, though that phrase continues to be used.[7]

If "the law" somehow seems to express something useful, then perhaps the whole of the law can be understood as a "system," meaning a network of conceptually related items. One could make a whole out of all the human necessities, with the necessities of the soul abstracted, and call the result "empirical political theory." The necessities of the soul, reflecting the human desire to do better than the minimum, to demand justice and stand up for it, to seek excellence rather than mediocrity, beauty rather than dullness, greatness rather than pettiness—would be left open, unconnected to the necessities of the body. A society could change its beliefs and practices without touching its laws on the minimum necessities. Having no whole, it could change without changing the whole; it could experiment harmlessly, risking only bloodless revolutions. It would take three or four centuries of evolution and experiment after the invention of modern political science, but at the end, we could call this result "pragmatism." Pragmatism was the theory of the Progressives, who were also patrons of legal realism. The spirit of pragmatism was stated well by Franklin D. Roosevelt in a speech on May 22, 1932, at Oglethorpe University, before he became President: "The country needs and, unless I mistake its temper, the country demands bold, persistent experimentation. It is common sense to take a method and try it: If it fails, admit it frankly and try another. But above all, try something."[8] It is remarkable that this almost desperate demand for ingenuity could be considered "common sense" (what happened to "look before you leap"?) and connected to a theory known as "legal realism."

It would seem that the real realism is illegal, as Machiavelli said: "And because there cannot be good laws where there are not good arms, and where there are good arms there must be good laws, I shall leave out the reasoning on laws and speak of arms."[9] Of course arms are not enough; he also speaks of conquering by fraud so as to maintain the "majesty" of the prince.[10] So "law schools" would still be needed, in Machiavelli's considered view, as a branch of the military schools.

What people used to call majesty was reverence or veneration for the prince or the law. Majesty could be calculated in the ways that Machiavelli shows us, but obviously, it cannot appear unmasked as calculated. A sense that there is a noble or divine source of law is necessary, in addition to its goodness or utility. As Max Weber implied in his clumsy way—by both affirming and denying the legitimacy conferred by reason—the law must have legitimacy through charisma, even when it is rational. What the people hold to be good comes more from what they think to be a good source than from a self-interested calculation. The source used to be *vox dei*; now, it is *vox populi* or "our Fathers." Abraham Lincoln referred to the founders as "fathers" to give them authority as spokesmen of, and to, the people.[11]

THE SOURCE OF LAW

The law needs a good source, not just good content. Having a good content will not by itself get the law respected and obeyed. The good content would have to be appreciated by those to whom it applies, but they may not understand its goodness or may interpret it in their own favor when the law frustrates them. Even when the law is confined to minimum necessities that one might think universally appreciable, such as the law against murder, one might be confronted with honor killing as justifiable homicide. And merely to explain why murder is limited to fellow human beings requires an appeal to the specialness of human life. One must make this appeal to a higher order, the order of nature that permits us to make laws to guide our own lives. Human beings did not make their own capacity to make, after all. Now we are on the verge of dangerous territory, where superhuman merges into the divine. But let us leave it unsaid whether God is a person or the personification of an impersonal order. One can speak of "the divine" as did the ancient philosophers, or of "Nature's God" as does the Declaration of Independence, and still retain the sense of the sacredness of human life. One certainly cannot retain that sense under the aegis of pragmatism.

Thus the law—despite being a whole that confers on each particular law the importance of "the law"—has a higher and lower content. How to define "higher" and "lower"? We can listen briefly to those who want to rationalize our lives with their clever schemes. They think highly of "reason"; reason is or ought to be in charge. The human being is one who can control himself by reason and control others by manipulating or "nudging" their subrational tendencies (subrational means "below reason").

Let us then call law facilitating the use of reason the higher part, and law dealing with ways in which reason is necessarily and deplorably constrained the lower part. A lawyer could pick apart the distinction, but let it refer to the difference between facilitating and constraining the freedom of our reason: a law providing support for education, for instance, versus one against burglary. This distinction is something like the older conception of "higher law" that used to be spoken of in law schools. The trouble with it is that it detracts from the wholeness of law and thus from the legality of the lower law, and thus from the majesty of law as such. In America, the higher law is constitutional law, a definite source, which does indeed detract from the majesty of ordinary law, particularly when frequently appealed to. Still, constitutional law bestows favor as well as frown.

A related difficulty is the triviality of many laws and regulations. The noble city of Cambridge should not be so concerned with specifying exactly when its citizens place their trash bags (as opposed to their trash barrels) out for collection, one feels. The law must deal with small matters, but when it does so, it gives the full weight of "the law" to measures that do not deserve it.[12] I doubt there is any solution to this problem, but it does show further why the goodness of the law in content is not sufficient to secure its respect. Only the goodness of the source can keep the law whole as it needs to be—not what it *is* so much as where it comes from. To say "where it comes from" gives access to "the divine" in law, the higher source that promises the rule of the higher good. I earlier made shift to identify the higher good, reason, by looking at the order of nature presupposed by the pragmatists, for to understand the law, it is necessary to consider its goodness in content, not only in source. How otherwise would one learn that the source is in fact good? But "the good" is too general and too particular, too difficult and too easy, for human society to understand.

Society needs a law that is good because it has a good origin—because it is *ours* as well as good. This origin may be God or may be persons outside the law, but it has the form of law, the form of a certain whole, that makes law its own cause. To be its own cause, law must be a whole. To be a whole, the law must have a whole community in view. But the whole community includes both the wise and the unwise, the former more capable of discerning and the latter less capable but more powerful. How can a whole be made out of this division? "The good" and "nature," when considered simply and without reference to what is ours, become too divisive when they are distinguished, as they must be, from the folly of the many. Goodness is needed, but together with harmony, so as to make a whole of a community. The folly of the many must be taken into account and included in the whole. In practice, of course, the wise and the unwise are found in both of our political parties, and the harmony each party seeks reaches only for a winning majority that will represent the whole. And of course there is such a thing as the folly of those who are supposed wise. In sum, the goodness of a community needs to be compromised in order to keep it, in fact, a community, but in its law, the community cannot afford to admit a compromise. If it did, it would fracture the respect for its law as a whole and thus defeat the compromise.

A common source provides the necessary mix, though admittedly at the cost of consistency; some difficulties must be glossed over. The U.S. Senate, for example, is a democratized aristocratic institution with a democratic composition and an aristocratic function. It is impressive that such a mix could be thought up and put across, both a resounding departure from the republican tradition of an aristocratic senate and a quieter bow to it. We seem to have moved from God as the source to the founding of a regime that cares for the whole of a free country. The constitutional convention used to be lauded as an assembly of demigods or heroes. Progressives cannot abide this designation, as it does not include them, and now one hears it less frequently, at least among the sophisticated. The consequence is an indecent scramble for appropriate titles for their majesties, the replacement demigods.

ABIDING BY THE LAW

The law does not depend so much on an opinion that it is legitimate, as with Weber's types of legitimacy, as it does on plain law-abidingness. With any opinion of what is just, people must be taught to obey the law—the law as a whole, not the legitimate law as a distinction within it. Human beings have by nature the capacity to make laws and to live by them, but only after a primary education in obedience, which they also need by nature. For some reason it is natural, in the lower sense of our nature, to resist the law as well as to resist reason, or in general, to resist what is good for you. Parents know these facts and try to cope with them. The law needs education in obeying the law—any and all laws. The temptation to pick and choose must be firmly resisted. It's true that Progressives try to make their children into little Progressives, thus endorsing their rebellions against authority, including the authority of Progressive parents. But there are limits even to pragmatism, which one can either anticipate or discover.

That humans resist the law is the main reason in practice why the law must appear as a whole, without having the consistency in reason that would commend it to a philosopher. The law does not address philosophers, those who are convinced by reason and only by reason. It does not agree with Machiavelli that "it is good to reason about everything."[13] As a whole, the law has an answer for everything—or for everything it needs, which is very extensive. The law must be inculcated in the young and repeated to those of the old who forget. This is elementary education in the virtues, particularly the virtue of justice. You learn to follow the rules by playing the game. Even our liberal law requires education in courage when it drafts soldiers and teaches military discipline. It requires moderation in not driving when drunk and the minimal wisdom of learning to read bureaucratic prose so as to fill out forms correctly. These are the first virtues, dealing with our resistance to reason during the transition from the life of unreason to reasonable maturity, from low to high but guided by the high.

Not having the savvy of a law professor, my view from the outside tells me that law professors greatly underestimate the importance and the difficulty of moral education against unreason. Education in the law is preceded by education in obeying the law. No other professional school needs to have its students arrive with an education in its subject learned as toddlers. From this fact we see that the law has priority and is inescapable. Living outside the law is nothing but living on the wrong side of the law. The law with its blind spots may not always see you, but it always has its eye on you. If you think this is not the case in a free society, ask an illegal immigrant. Legal realists believe that as social scientists, they can live harmlessly and even respectably outside the law as if they had no stake in it. They are like illegal immigrants, except that they do not understand themselves and are not understood as such. Our society allows them this confusion and includes them under the protection of the law they obey but, as social scientists, do not respect.

Reasons given to children in early stages should be reasons for obedience. Later on, they can learn that even unreasonable laws must be obeyed. Authority needs an authoritarian beginning, not necessarily with spanking but with firmness. Reason comes when the laws are seen to embody principles and the person of the authority fades into the background (obedience being no longer merely on his say-so). This beginning education is needed just as much in our free society, if not more so, than in an authoritarian one, where no one is ever left to guide himself. It is what we do, often without realizing it.

Education in obeying the law is supplemented by enforcement of the law. The law decides not only who should be educated and how but also who goes to jail and for what. It is not enough for us to talk of virtue; we also have to consider the less pretty topic of vice and punishment for it. It seems to question the majesty of the law that it can send human beings with their natural dignity to jail, greatly curtailing their natural freedom. But in this the law protects their dignity by holding them personally responsible for their misdeeds, Immanuel Kant tells us.[14] In any case, the police need the power that goes with majesty, and they do everything they can to preserve it. They need the power to overawe possible miscreants and to make such people fear—to attract their attention. Of course this fear is in good part expressed in their calculation, but calculation out of fear rather than calm consideration.

THE SOUL AND MODERATE RESPONSIBILITY

I have one more base to touch. We need to know about the soul—or the psyche, if using the Greek word makes people feel better. The ancient philosophers have all the answers, but they do not have the solutions that we like. The subject of the soul arises from the question always asked about punishment. Is it for deterrence or for vindication, or for some mix of the two? Deterrence by itself says nothing about the moral responsibility of the malefactor; it just wants to prevent him from doing the deed again. Under that principle, a wife-murderer might be paroled if one were sure he wouldn't commit the crime again, and a bicycle thief could be executed if he showed himself to be incorrigible. The gravity of the crime committed is not relevant, only prevention of the next crime.

Why, in the view of deterrence, is moral responsibility not in question? It is because the crime was committed through mistake; the criminal did what he thought was right but wasn't. It was a mistake of intellectual virtue, not of moral virtue: He was living in a bad neighborhood, or he did not have a healthy family environment, etc. The criminal did not know what he was doing. Don't get angry in such cases—but also, don't show mercy; prevention is the goal. You cannot say that murder or capital punishment is wrong because human life is sacred, for under the assumption that sin is ignorance, nothing is unquestionable or beyond reason, and nothing is sacred. In this difficulty, you cannot have recourse to God suddenly when you need Him. For those who live by reason alone cannot have one argument that uses the sacred to justify human rights and a contrary one denying it to explain, for instance, human evolution.

The trouble with moral responsibility by itself, practically speaking, is that it insists too much on vindicating justice in the least detail, never letting go, vengefully crossing the boundary between just punishment and cruelty. Another trouble is that one cannot use punishment prudently, taking account of circumstances that aggravate or palliate and times that call for action or quiet. Moral responsibility assumes, contrary to deterrence, that you knew or should have known that what you were doing was wrong. Your crime was voluntary. You have a soul that permits you to choose what you do, as you very well know whenever you begin some action. So don't say you didn't know what you were doing; just find out the law, and follow it. If it's complicated, buy yourself the services of a clever lawyer. In the end, it is clear we need both moral responsibility *and* deterrence, but also that the two theories are contrary to each other. We have encountered this difficulty before; the law demands an impossible mix of arguments. It is indeed a whole, but by the force of compromise of the moral with the intellectual. We want moral responsibility, but we also want to be able to guide it prudently, with judgment.

This compromise of contraries is invisible to legal realism. Legal realism wants to be rational even more than it wants to be realistic—much more, in fact. It wants everything to be calculated so that the morality of actions disappears into incentives and disincentives. Therefore it doesn't get angry. But how can one be realistic about the law if one does not recognize the anger that people feel at a crime? How is it realistic not to see that this anger must be both expressed and controlled? The solemnity of a judge, arising from the majesty of the law, honors both the accusation and the defense, because it respects the seriousness of both sides. A judge could not be impartial, or seen as impartial, if he were not, as representative of the law, above both parties—and this is again partaking of majesty. Legal realism addresses the motives of the parties, seeing them as self-interested rather than exposing their intellectual mistakes (as Socrates would have done). It exists in a limbo between philosophy and morality, and with understanding of neither.

What is needed is a philosophical understanding of both. Men have souls that cause them to move into action and also to pause and reflect. Why do we need to act rather than merely think? Because our souls are encased in bodies, each of them private and individual, with individual interests. But we also have the capacity to rise above our interests and reflect, even to feel shame. The majesty of the law helps us do this. It is both moral and intellectual and with both their contrary qualities. The majesty of the law is not an obsolete irrationality but the prime feature of the phenomenon of law. It is necessary in our time as in all times. It serves to give expression to our moral outrage but also to control it precisely, in the interest of our common humanity. At the same time, it requires us to reflect on what enables us to rise to that level and on what justifies our sense of the sacredness or specialness of mankind.

NOTES

1. This chapter is based on my article, "On the Majesty of the Law," *Harvard Journal of Law and Public Policy* 36 (Winter 2013): 117–129.
2. See Sandra Day O'Connor, *The Majesty of the Law: Reflections of a Supreme Court Justice* (New York: Random House, 2003).
3. See Plato, *Minos,* 313a–b.
4. Patient Protection and Affordable Care Act, public law 111-148 (March 23, 2010), 124 stat. 119.
5. See James Q. Wilson, *Varieties of Police Behavior: The Management of Law and Order in Eight Communities* (Cambridge, MA: Harvard University Press, 1968), 12.
6. Ibid., 180.
7. See John Locke, *Two Treatises of Government*, 2:137, 143.
8. Franklin D. Roosevelt, *Address at Oglethorpe University* (May 22, 1932).
9. Niccolò Machiavelli, *The Prince,* ch. 12.
10. See ibid., ch. 21 (end).
11. See Abraham Lincoln, "Gettysburg Address."
12. See Plato, *Laws*, 788a–c.
13. Niccolò Machiavelli, *Discourses on Livy*, 1.18.1.
14. See Immanuel Kant, *The Metaphysics of Morals*; *The Universal Doctrine of Right*, 6:331–337.

7

Why We Respect the Dignity of Politics

James R. Stoner, Jr.

A decent and dynamic society accords respect to political activities and to the choice of a career in politics, and it needs to do so for that society to thrive. This might seem obvious, but in fact today, politics is often held in low repute or, alternatively, looked upon as a mode of personal fulfillment. Both attitudes breed contempt for the day-to-day activities of citizens and politicians involved in the making of law and public policy and in putting these into effect. To be sure, a free society ought to have a healthy skepticism about politics—or at least about recourse to the state to solve every problem—and a democratic people ought to be vigilant about the conduct of those they choose to represent them. Moreover, a just government proceeds lawfully, and the interposition of politics into the impartial application of law is rightly decried. Nevertheless, self-government is a great achievement, rare in the annals of human history and fragile in most places where it has been tried, and it is only accomplished through the virtue of those who participate in it. That, at any rate, is what I plan to argue in the essay that follows, though powerful opponents stand in the way.

WHY POLITICS GETS A BAD NAME

Why is politics, or why are politicians, looked down upon? First, there is the accusation and sometimes the fact of corruption. A corrupt politician enriches himself at the public's expense while neglecting or even betraying the public good. Any decent society has laws against bribery, the most obvious form of corruption, but there is a large gray area where politicians act within the law while serving their own interests before the public's. Classical republicanism celebrated the independent yeoman who left his plow, did his public duty, and returned with no reward but honor. In a dynamic commercial society, by contrast, we often expect our politicians to work at politics full-time, in which case they develop their own interests as public employees. Or we worry about the influence of their outside interests on their public work if they work part-time, if they have sufficient independent wealth not to depend upon their government job, or if they make investments on the side. If they need to raise funds to campaign for office or for reelection, are their donors expressing shared objectives, or buying access and influence? If they anticipate leaving public service, voluntarily or by losing an election, might their actions in politics have been designed to build a portfolio for future profit? In short, precisely if "the regulation of these various and interfering interests forms the principal task of modern legislation,"[1] and if the public interest is contested and hard to identify, the line between serving the public and taking care of one's own might be hard to draw and thus the accusation of corruption easy to make.

A second reason democratic politics is widely scorned is the constant need to compromise. In the legislature of a diverse and dynamic society, majorities usually form only through a coalition of interests, and this often requires give-and-take, bargaining and negotiation, even logrolling and vote-trading, as each group settles for less than it wants in order to achieve more than it otherwise would. Nowadays, compromise is rarely praised as a moral achievement but is instead often denounced as a betrayal of principle; politicians who make a willingness to compromise their trademark find themselves excoriated by their own party and then challenged at reelection time. Moreover, opponents of compromise promote those institutions of government that are less oriented to compromise, particularly courts, where the adversarial system yields a clear winner and loser in most cases. Because of the practice of judicial review—whereby courts strike acts of legislation and executive policy they find to violate the Constitution—American law professors have come to celebrate the courts as a forum of principle,[2] however simplistic the principles and however obstinate their enforcement. Those with a preference for principle over compromise tend to move important issues into the courts and out of the hands of political institutions, further reducing the authority of those whose deeds are then treated with additional scorn.

A third reason politics is looked down upon in our society is that its practitioners are thought meddlesome, inefficient, and even ignorant by people with a clear sense of what they want to accomplish in their own area of expertise. Business executives find their plans thwarted and their profitability threatened by politically imposed regulations, not to mention taxes. If established businesses know how to lobby legislatures and even use regulation to entrench their advantage, entrepreneurs and start-up businesses find politically imposed obstacles in the way of innovation and growth. Scientific experts, such as in medicine or environmental protection, complain about the interference of politicians in what they think are matters better left to their professional judgment. We all deplore politics in the office or on the job site if some individuals' jockeying for position or influence or some other personal reward interferes with the task of our organization. Politics in this sense appears inferior to rational expertise or to settled experience in governing the matter in question; it's an unwelcome bully deserving of scorn.

Fourthly, politics is invariably partisan, and that means it promotes bias rather than reason and the advantage of a part over the good of the whole. With only a few exceptions, and even then only in exceptional circumstances, democratic politicians have to identify with a political party, and this necessity compels them to impugn the ideas and the character of their opponents and to exaggerate the value of the same among their friends. Whether or not an objective observer would consider this lying, they accuse each other of dishonesty all the time. Partisans make enemies of fellow citizens, or at least cast suspicion on their opponents, making it hard to act in common even for clearly shared purposes—for example, in foreign affairs. Indeed, partisans sometimes feel they have more in common with similar partisans in other countries than with fellow countrymen of the opposite party. Parties lead politicians to seek partisan advantage in the next election rather than to seek bipartisan agreement in the present. Partisans talk past one another, trying at once to appeal to voters whose own partisanship is unsettled and to rally their loyalists and cement their support. Just as parties seem to absorb the attention and energies of politicians, they repel citizens who are not committed to one party or another, particularly the young and others whose interest in politics is intermittent or unformed. And partisans themselves want parties—that is, other parties—to go away.

Finally, government sustains its assertion of authority with coercive force, and the threat of force probably casts a shadow over every political exchange. On the one side, politics attracts those who are not afraid of exercising power and perhaps even take pleasure in doing so, from the bully to the boss to the tyrant. On the other side, most people do not like being forced to do things, even things they know are for their own good, and this is bound to make government seem irksome and those who strive to master it, dangerous. Because modern politics usually affects large regions with diverse populations, every law and policy is likely to work harm somewhere beyond its intent, compounding the irksomeness of force with the sting of injustice. Except the anarchist, people acknowledge that government is necessary, but it is often seen as a necessary evil; indeed, necessity itself seems to be the opposite of freedom. Not all governments are equally oppressive, but no government that lacks repressive force will survive for very long. And if coercion is a complaint against government at home, it is a chronic problem abroad, where the use of lethal force is sanctioned in warfare, and victory belongs to the ones with the greatest force or the strongest will.

(ANTI-)POLITICAL SCIENCE AND PHILOSOPHY

If these five clusters of opinion are not enough to drain the dignity from politics, consider that major intellectual movements in our time undercut attributing anything distinctive to political action. The dominant approaches in political science—empiricism and rational choice—systematically assume that political ends can be explained by social or economic goals. Since Harold Lasswell defined politics as "who gets what, when, and how,"[3] empiricists have analyzed cause and effect in political life as a matter of costs and benefits. The coin of political economy is not only money, but the structure is the same: Legal constraints count as costs, and the acquisition of power and the reinforcement of values count as benefits. Political life is a competition for goods, just like economic life, with the silent assumption that those who lose in the market can recoup their losses by political success. Do you take pleasure in political action itself, not just in winning? Add that then to the balance sheet as a psychic award.

In "rat choice," the assimilation of political institutions to the economic model is complete, and politics becomes a game governed by a complex web of incentives. Actually, the two approaches run together like concave and convex, the one modeling the logic of political action, the other testing whether political action in fact is logical and trying to explain what is not.

Notoriously, political scientists suppose that it is irrational for the individual citizen to vote, since a single vote almost never decides an election; the closest they come to finding dignity in politics is in the subjective sense of dignity voters feel when they go to the polls or the indignation they feel when excluded.[4] Politicians are supposed to be more rational than voters and so are hypothesized to gain for themselves through public service; for those who don't, the subfield of political psychology is available to explain their folly. As for public opinion, it is measured by scientific polling and its causes probed by scientific analysis of every possible correlate. The fact that opinion is a stage in the acquisition of knowledge and gains its dignity as it approaches knowledge remains invisible to this technique.

If the methods of social science make the dignity of politics invisible, something similar results from a dominant strain in liberal political philosophy. In his influential *Theory of Justice* and even more especially in its sequel, *Political Liberalism*, John Rawls relegates ordinary politics to secondary status. In his original work, politics has a role to play only regarding what he called the second principle of justice, the "difference principle," which permitted economic and social inequalities only to the extent they are necessary to improve the lot of the least advantaged. Judging what was necessary was left to legislatures, presumably because the science of incentives had not sufficiently progressed to allow a rational accounting of what was needed.[5] In this, as in much else, Rawls echoed the jurisprudence of the U.S. Supreme Court, which treats as political only those questions that cannot be settled by rational standards. Actually, Rawls went much further, denying to the state any determination of what constitutes the human good, leaving all such value judgments to individuals; what the state must ensure is that no one is pressured to choose some values over others, justice being the fair distribution of the right to live as one pleases. In recent years, in dicta that deny the power of states to regulate morality, and in cases striking down traditional attempts to do so, the Court appears to have adopted Rawls's individualism. Government—and so politics, the struggle to rule or to govern—concerns only the just, not the good, and that means that the experts on rights, namely the courts, have priority in the state.

One might have supposed that in revising his theory to explain that justice as fairness is "political, not metaphysical," Rawls might have enhanced the status of the political, but in fact, paradoxically, he further constricted the role of actual politics in human life.[6] Critics of *A Theory of Justice* had contended that, despite his intention to construct an account of justice that rested solely on the hypothetical choices individuals would make if they knew nothing about their personal capacities or their personal values, he had actually supposed quite a bit about human nature: that people are radically individual in their views of the good, that they are rational and value choice, that they are generally risk-averse and concerned with self-preservation, and so on. Rawls conceded the point but denied that his suppositions were about what human beings really are—denied making "metaphysical" claims. He asserted rather that his whole theoretical edifice with its hypothetical social contract merely systematized an actual consensus in society about moral intuitions—for example, that everyone is equally entitled to live as he pleases provided he does not harm others, that nobody deserves his talents or is more worthy because of them, that social wealth belongs fundamentally to society at large and should be distributed to members of society according to principles of justice, and so forth. This consensus does not, he thinks, negate genuine differences of opinion—remember, everyone is entitled to his own notion of the good—but life together, political life, requires working out in some detail the overlapping consensus on basic moral intuitions, and that is the political work of "justice as fairness," which is what Rawls calls his liberal theory. Liberalism is "political" in the sense that it applies to particular societies in our time, not to all societies of men in every era; it is contingent upon our shared moral intuitions, which Rawls insists we actually have. In other words, in speaking of "political liberalism," Rawls means that the fundamental political issues in a society are settled matters of consensus, and he develops an idea of "public reason" that defines and limits what kinds of arguments can be made in the public sphere: only such arguments as can be assented to by anyone, regardless of his more particular ideas about what is good (or good for him and his friends and family).[7] It is the liberal, Rawlsian philosopher who determines what counts as a legitimate public reason and thus what political opinions are permissible in a just society. Whether or not in practice Rawls means to censor arguments he considers illegitimate, the concept of "public reason" gives liberals permission to ignore arguments that cross their code. Once again, politics is confined to the less fundamental, or, since Rawls now admits that his theory is not impartially philosophical but political, politics becomes deeply divisive, since what is at issue is who belongs to the consensus that constitutes society and who is shunted outside. The business of politicians is minor, for the most important political decisions are too deep for them to grasp—or to make.

THE POLIS AND POLITICAL FREEDOM

All of the various critiques of politics I have summarized thus far, both those in common opinion and those in academic circles, might be said to depend upon the principal tenets of liberalism and the liberal understanding of human beings as self-interested and self-defining individuals. There is, however, a movement in political theory to restore dignity to political life in the face of the liberal demotion of politics. With variants on both sides of the spectrum—sometimes emphasizing philosophical principles, sometimes historical understanding—the political theorists in question turn our attention back to the Greek polis or the Roman republic and to their citizens' self-understanding, with the thought that something can be learned from the classical origin of politics (the word means literally "the things of the polis") for political life today. Put briefly, and in modern terms, what is learned is the fact of freedom and the value of virtue. Since the most successful Greek cities and the republic at Rome were mixed regimes—partly aristocratic or oligarchic, partly democratic—the lessons operate at several levels, which I will consider in turn.

The dignity of politics is most apparent when political freedom is recovered after authoritarian or totalitarian rule, particularly if that recovery results from popular rebellion.[8] Even the Universal Declaration of Human Rights, generally considered a liberal document, includes the right to vote, and while modern dictators typically hold regular elections—"winning" with ridiculous percentages—there is something undeniably stirring when an oppressed people first participate in a genuinely competitive election to decide who their governors will be. Perhaps it is simply the indignity of having been denied the right to have a say about the conditions under which one lives and the future direction of one's community. Even in long-established democracies like our own, where voters often grow cynical about their efficacy and frustrated at the choices available when they go to the polls, great indignation always accompanies any perceived threat to voting rights. Though the secret ballot was introduced to protect the independence of the individual voter, particularly from those who exercise authority or influence over him in daily social or economic life, voting is not seen by republican theorists as a private act, like the purchase of a product, but as a public exercise. More apparently public is mass action in the streets, the protests that in recent decades have sought to bring down dictators (and sometimes succeeded) or, in established democracies, have drawn attention to specific issues where large numbers of people find representative institutions inadequate to their grievances. Especially in the former case, but sometimes also in the latter, real courage is shown by those who protest in the public square, and that earns respect from fellow citizens and foreign observers, if not always from rulers intent on crushing opposition.

Still, popular movements need spokespersons or representatives, and in practice, they need leaders who articulate their objectives, coordinate their actions, and steadily pursue their aims. Republican theorists are aware of the heroic character of classical politics and struggle to define its meaning in the modern world. Perhaps the clearest endorsement of something like classical heroism appears in the writings of Hannah Arendt, who makes the case for political action as the freest and thus most choice-worthy human activity.[9] Distinguishing physical labor and productive work from action undertaken for its own sake, Arendt follows Aristotle. For Aristotle, many of the finest virtues were habits of excellence in the souls of men, manifesting in the common life of the polis, and political life was defined by the love of honor.[10] (Arendt departs from Aristotle, however, by including the life of the mind wholly within the political world, rather than positing a separate happiness for philosophers moved instead by the love of wisdom.) Arendt writes that political life originates in the human condition of plurality (we live together as many minds in a shared community) and that the energy of the polis developed in the exchange of speeches and deeds among equals and in their competition for distinction. She writes of the American revolutionaries who rediscovered this freedom in their common action against the British monarchy:

> The point is that the Americans knew that public freedom consisted in having a share in public business, and that the activities connected with this business by no means constituted a burden but gave those who discharged them in public a feeling of happiness they could acquire nowhere else.[11]

Key to political liberty in her account is the willingness to initiate something new, not just to act within settled law and institutions. That is why she saw in revolution the genuine source of political freedom and praised the American founders for their embrace of a revolutionary opportunity and their completion of a constitution. Although this thirst for distinction in the display of excellence seems aristocratic, Arendt complains that "the failure [of the Constitution] to incorporate the townships and the town-hall meetings, the original springs of all political activity in the country, amounted to a death sentence for them":

> Paradoxical as it may sound, it was in fact under the impact of the Revolution that the revolutionary spirit in America began to wither away; and it was the Constitution itself, this greatest achievement of the American people, which eventually cheated them of their proudest possession.[12]

The importance of the people in a similarly aristocratic account of political liberty, signaled without complaint, appears in a recent book by Pierre Manent: "The true city comes into being, or rather strives to exist, through the effort of the many to have a share in the city of the few. In this sense politicization is identical with democratization, the city with democracy, more exactly with the movement toward the democratic regime."[13] Political liberty, in other words, emerges in a dynamic that involves both the people and the few; it involves the aspiration both to have a say and to speak well, to consent and to reason.

Both Arendt and Manent, indeed all who comment on the ancient city, are aware of its collapse and perhaps of its inherent instability: The Greek cities turned on one another in war and were unable to meet the challenge of Macedonian conquest, and the Roman republic was so successful at war that it transformed itself from a polis to an empire. When political liberty reemerged in modern Europe among the city-states of Renaissance Italy, it was in a very different set of circumstances: A millennium or more of imperial and monarchical rule had driven Europeans to cultivate private life and feudal orders in the absence of a true public space. Among the consequences was the cultivation of private wealth, not unknown to the ancient world, of course, but often seen as an obstacle to public service. Moreover, the advent of Christianity at the very moment that the Roman republic went into eclipse gave men an alternative city to which to attach their loyalty and their mutual activity. It at once overlaid new virtues upon the classical virtues, oriented men to a kingdom of heaven that made the polis seem futile and misdirected, and established in the church (in Greek, *ecclesia*, meaning "assembly") an alternative institutional framework and a source of law independent of the emperor or king. The modern state eventually arose to address these new circumstances, to protect and promote men in their private interests and to counter the authority of the Church with an independent secular power; as the ancient city gave birth to classical philosophy as its companion and critic, the modern state promoted modern science as its client and instrument. Though states were often made by monarchs, they became subject through revolution to nations, and in these nations, a recognizably revived political liberty could be found, but again in unstable form. Within a century and a half of the French Revolution, the leading states of continental Europe had either taken totalitarian form or were under imminent threat from totalitarians, whose abuse of political freedom had suppressed not only that freedom but the very private life and personal security that modern states had been invented for in the first place. They replaced what remained of independent religion with neo-pagan state spectacle or atheistic ideology, or both.

CONSTITUTIONAL GOVERNMENT AND POLITICAL FREEDOM

Americans and also the British escaped the scourge of totalitarianism in the twentieth century. The shooting war they fought and won against the Nazis and the "Cold War" they sustained against the Soviets were testimony to the endurance of their political liberty and remain monuments in memory to their glory. These victories were not accidents. In the American case in particular, the country was and still remains governed by a political order that is not a nation-state on the European model but a constitutional government, and it remains open to the exercise of political liberty and dependent on the presence of political virtue. Constitutional government is limited government; it has assigned duties and purposes, but each office of government leaves much to be done by others, as well as much to be left to the private initiative of individual citizens acting on their own. Moreover, although constitutional government respects the rule of law, its representative officers are also a source of legislation, and the people themselves give legal authority to the constitution. Law then is not only a constraint imposed upon them, or that they impose upon themselves, but a rule that they make their own and in whose spirit they learn to act. Law lends its majesty to their dignity but derives its majesty from their assent. Let me sketch the outlines of American constitutional government—as it was designed and as it might still be exercised—and comment as I do so on how the constitutional frame gives dignity to American politics. The principal girders in the frame are representation, the separation of powers, federalism, and the guarantee of rights, and I will discuss these in turn.

Representative government is government by the people and for the people, but not exclusively of the people. Although John Adams would write in his early essay "Thoughts on Government" that a representative assembly ought to mirror the composition of society at large, when Alexander Hamilton and James Madison defend the scheme of representation in the new federal Congress under the Constitution, they insist upon the right of the people to choose whomever they please, emphasizing their choice and describing their representative as their agent, not their exemplar.[14] Whatever might be true at the level of the state, in a continental republic, it is impossible that every interest appear in miniature. Madison hopes that election of representatives will "refine and enlarge" the public's views, and he writes that "the aim of every political Constitution is or ought to be to obtain for rulers, men who possess most wisdom to discern, and most virtue to pursue, the common good of the society." Of those "qualities in human nature which justify a certain portion of esteem and confidence," he says, "Republican government presupposes the existence of these qualities in a higher degree than any other form." Representative government makes room for statesmen, men who exercise political virtue in high office, and relies at base upon a "free and gallant" citizenry. The "genius of the people" and "the fundamental principles of the revolution" endorse "the honorable determination, which animates every votary of freedom, to rest all our political experiments on the capacity of mankind for self-government."[15] By this account, there is nobility both in the people's making of political choices and in the offices held in their name.

But Madison also points out, famously, that "enlightened statesmen will not always be at the helm" of government. Republican government is a noble ideal, but American constitutional government adds "auxiliary precautions" to republican virtue, recognizing both that ambitious men might be tempted to abuse power and that even popular majorities can work injustice or ignore the public good.[16] One such precaution is the separation of powers: To ensure the rule of law, those who make the law must allow a separate branch of government to enforce it, and legal judgment in a particular case belongs to a third branch, the judiciary. Madison explains that powers are kept separate, paradoxically, by being shared—that is, the powers are mixed just a little so that each power as a whole remains intact. This description has suggested to some commentators a self-regulating system, explained as a game of interest and ambition, not a particularly dignified affair. But each office or kind of office also has its specific virtue: The House is the people's tribune; the Senate lends stability and wisdom to legislation; the president is the locus of energy and responsibility for the whole; the courts are the seat of judgment and learning. "If men were angels, no government would be necessary. If angels were to govern men, neither external nor internal controls on government would be necessary."[17] That men are not perfect and so obliged to check one another does not establish that there is nothing dignified about exercising the virtues available to them and the virtue of keeping within the limits drawn.

Federalism is another "auxiliary precaution," and it is particularly complex, as national and state governments keep one another in check in part by having different responsibilities and in part by having their responsibilities overlap. Arendt is wrong to say the Constitution fails because it makes no provision for subnational government; the Constitution does not constitute the states, because these are formed by the people directly and independently, and the states secure by this independence their various and vibrant political cultures and distinct communities. Representation in the states is usually a better mirror of society than is national representation, and it makes sense that it should be, since the states have general, residual responsibility for law and government. On the whole, still today, it is state law that prohibits violent crimes and secures the rights of property. And federal interference with the states' police power to protect the community's health, safety, and morals often proves inept and disruptive even in the age of the nationally integrated economy that the Founders promoted. Madison recognized that, because majorities can become tyrannical (perhaps especially in smaller communities), the federal government had a role to play in the protection of rights as well as in the regulation of the economy and national defense. Indeed, what most discredited state power in the early twentieth century was the role some of the states played in enforcing racial injustice, and the federal government's success in dismantling segregation helped gain it admiration and authority on the issue of civil rights. Still, that victory came from the bottom as much as from the top, from the courage and creativity of the Civil Rights Movement, which not only marched on Washington but organized and protested within the states. And the changing politics in the states—where African Americans serve in much higher numbers than in federal elective office—helps lock the gains of fifty years ago in place. It has been noticed that the states can serve as "laboratories" for reform in law and public policy, sometimes modeling future federal legislation, sometimes competing against one another for population and investment.[18] The Constitution gives the people through the states ultimate authority over its own amendment and gives them, by means of the electoral college, ultimate say over the election of the country's highest officer. American democracy, in other words, is participatory rather than plebiscitary because of the many opportunities for action provided by state politics and because federal politics for the most part percolates up from the states. The dignity of our politics is peculiarly dependent on continued dignity of the states.

    The protection of individual rights plays an essential role in American politics. According to no less a source than the Declaration of Independence, this is the end or purpose of government itself. The guarantee of religious liberty and prohibition on religious tests for office mean that the United States demands no common creed of its citizens, only consent to its Constitution and to the basic political principles it entails. Political rights have often been seen as instrumental to private rights as a result, but I think this mischaracterizes our republicanism, which instead relies upon a continuum of rights. At least until the recent reconceptualization of rights as a means of self-expression, most rights in one way or another entailed self-government, from the governance of one's own estate to the right to speak and write about the governance of the community's and the country's affairs. "Self-government" is not quite a synonym for "virtue," but it is pretty close.[19] Because the settling of specific rights in particular disputes is the business of the courts, they have often seen themselves as in a special way the guardians of rights. In specific cases, they were certainly meant to be, and because Americans incorporated the common-law tradition, particular decisions can count as precedents and have general effect. At the same time, when the Supreme Court has presumed to pronounce abstractly on rights, they have often done harm: in extending the rights of slave-holders in *Dred Scott* and helping to precipitate the Civil War, in defining civil rights so narrowly as to allow the entrenchment of segregation in *Plessy v. Ferguson*, in creating a right to abortion in *Roe v. Wade* and to sexual autonomy in *Lawrence v. Texas*, and perhaps more. Even *Brown v. Board of Education*, seen by many as the Court's finest achievement, mostly just undid the harm of *Plessy*, and seen from the perspective of sixty years, the actual racial integration of schools, which proceeded under judicial administration, is less successful than the integration of the military and the marketplace, which resulted respectively from executive and legislative action. In securing the rights of due process, especially ensuring the integrity of criminal trials, the courts are within their authority, and there are certainly times when they have vindicated the clear commands of the Constitution against political drift or partisan hostility. But every assumption of judicial power in the definition of fundamental law diminishes political liberty, for it removes critical issues from public debate and deliberation and allows political institutions to shirk their own duties.[20] The majesty of law and the dignity of politics are not inherently at odds, but each can encroach upon the other. The Constitution is to be admired, not condemned, for leaving liberty and nobility ultimately to depend on self-restraint.

ANSWERING THE OBJECTIONS TO POLITICS

Constitutional government, then, vindicates the dignity of politics without exaggerating the sovereignty of politics in the manner of the modern state. It leaves room for great virtue in high office—think, for example, of the presidency of Abraham Lincoln—without unrealistically relying upon virtue and without unduly glorifying ambitious men. It ensures popular consent without denying the need for political prudence and legal justice. It allows for growth and change while preserving respect for the wisdom and achievement of the past. At least it does all this if it is rightly understood, and in that way, it might be said to summon right understanding. It does not suppose that politics is the highest good, and in that way, it perhaps reminds us that human beings are not the highest beings.[21]

How can the objections raised at the outset against the dignity of contemporary politics be answered? To the charge of corruption, it might be admitted that men are presumed to be self-interested and recalled that a man's prudence in the administration of his own affairs is probably evidence of his capacity for prudence in the affairs of the commonwealth. Beyond that, the glorification of wealth in our society today—not just the appreciation of wealth as a means to genuine goods, but the social attitude that a person's acquisitive success is a proxy for his human worth—must be a temptation to contemporary politicians, who think less of themselves and of their ability to move among the wealthy if they feel the pinch of necessity in their own lives not as a mark of virtue but as a badge of shame. As for compromise, though dishonorable when it involves capitulation on a matter of moral duty, it has its own moral authority. Compromise requires listening to, understanding, and respecting the interests and opinions of one's opponents, admitting the limits of one's own interests, and accepting one's own fallibility. And it entails a promise (signaled in the term itself, of course) to adhere to what is agreed upon. It is the art of peacemakers, and there is a time for making peace as much as a time for competition.

Politicians can probably never avoid exasperating experts, but even when they listen to them, as in matters of their expertise they surely should, it remains their duty to judge competing goods and weigh them against one another. Precisely because human goods are incommensurable, there is no expert who can replace political institutions in performing this task. How to balance protection of the environment with economic health and strength? personal privacy and autonomy with social morality and public virtue? the pursuit of human excellence with compassion for human neediness? All these are chronic issues that can never be fully settled, if only because resources are always scarce and change is constant. To some extent, we assign the care of different ends and interests to different institutions of government, but it remains the task of politics to settle for the present the disposition of the whole.

Partisanship is inevitable if men have political liberty, and it is the genius of modern republicanism to accept the alternation of parties in power through the means of competitive elections—in contrast to the republicanism of the ancients, where officeholders routinely were scrutinized and often punished at the end of their terms in office, giving them an incentive not to relinquish power if also an added motive not to misbehave. Charles Evans Hughes, when governor of New York, nicely described the duty of politicians in relation to parties:

> In my judgment, participation in the work of one of the great parties offers an opportunity for service to the community, greater than that afforded by political activity outside them.... What party a man shall join, or whether he shall join any party, is a question for his own conscience, and if he is upright and honourable in his conduct, and seeks justice in his decisions, he will be of public service. But the paradox is that the influence of the non-partisan who abhors party, must in the main be exercised through party.... Belief in party, identification with one of the great parties, an intense desire to have it true to its best traditions and to enhance its public usefulness is not inconsistent with independence of character. Free expression of sentiment within the party, and forceful expression of conviction, whether or not it coincides with the wishes of the party managers, is essential to keep the party vigorous and wholesome.... When, therefore, the temporary attitude of party threatens the interests of the community, when an ill-chosen policy invites general disaster, when party success means the debasement of the standards of honor and decency, the party man should recognize the superior obligation of his citizenship.[22]

This seems to me to get the matter precisely right, insofar as it is possible to make a universal maxim out of a judgment that is inevitably prudential. As for the coerciveness of politics, this ought to be admitted, not denied by sophistry—even the venerable sophistry that in obeying a law he or his representative has made, a man obeys only himself and is thus uncoerced. Because human nature is unruly, there is rarely respect without an element of fear, if only the fear of losing one's good reputation. Politics earns its dignity if the fact of coercion makes citizens courageous in the face of fear and reminds rulers, in spite of interest and ambition, to be just.

I have written about the dignity of politics without much regard to the political positions of the parties in question, as though the critiques of politics do equal damage to citizens and politicians on both sides. This is probably not the case: Those who glorify economic gain likely have the most trouble identifying political corruption (and those who denounce economic profit probably see corruption everywhere), while Rawls's exclusion of religious faith from "public reason," though in principle applicable to religious citizens and politicians of both parties, in practice is typically used against religious conservatives. Still, as enemy soldiers respect one another's courage even when they despise one another's cause, so it seems we can applaud the establishment of political freedom and admire the exercise of political virtue even when they give advantage to our political opponents. Seeing freedom as an occasion for virtue, not merely a formal process, reminds us that the relation of means and ends in politics is complex, again because political ends are incommensurable. Political freedom is a genuine good without necessarily being the highest or the only political good.

NOTES

1. Alexander Hamilton, James Madison, and John Jay, *The Federalist*, ed. Jacob E. Cooke (Middletown, CT: Wesleyan University Press, 1961 [1788]), no. 10, p. 59.
2. The phrase is from Ronald Dworkin, "The Forum of Principle," *New York University Law Review* 56 (1981), 469–518.
3. Harold Lasswell, *Politics: Who Gets What, When, How* (New York: McGraw Hill, 1936).
4. The classic texts are Angus Campbell, Philip E. Converse, Warren E. Miller, and Donald E. Stokes, *The American Voter* (Chicago, IL: University of Chicago Press, 1960) and Gabriel A. Almond and Sidney Verba, *The Civic Culture: Political Attitudes and Democracy in Five Nations* (Princeton, NJ: Princeton University Press, 1963). On indignation, see Nick Bromell, "Democratic Indignation: Black American Thought and the Politics of Dignity," *Political Theory* 41 (April 2013): 285–311.
5. See John Rawls, *A Theory of Justice* (Cambridge, MA: Harvard University Press, 1971).
6. See John Rawls, *Political Liberalism*, expanded edition (New York: Columbia University Press, 2005).
7. See ibid., lecture VI. See also the critique by Robert P. George, "Public Reason and Political Conflict: Abortion and Homosexuality," in *In Defense of Natural Law* (Oxford, England: Clarendon Press, 1999), ch. 11.
8. See, for example, the discussion in Seyla Benhabib, *Dignity in Adversity: Human Rights in Turbulent Times* (Cambridge, England: Polity, 2011).
9. See Hannah Arendt, *The Human Condition* (Chicago, IL: University of Chicago Press, 1958).
10. See Aristotle, *Nicomachean Ethics*, esp. books I and II; *Politics*, esp. books III and VII.
11. Hannah Arendt, *On Revolution* (New York: Viking Press, 1965), 119.
12. Ibid., 239. As I note below, Arendt seems to have been misled by the silence of the federal Constitution about local townships and associations, which nevertheless long remained vital, at least if we trust the observations of Alexis de Tocqueville, *Democracy in America*, vol. 1, part 1, ch. 5; vol. 1, part 2, ch. 4; vol. 2, part 2, ch. 4–7.
13. Pierre Manent, *Metamorphoses of the City: On the Western Dynamic* (Cambridge, MA: Harvard University Press, 2013), 98. The discussion in the following paragraph draws upon Manent's important book.
14. Compare John Adams, "Thoughts on Government," pp. 401–409 in Charles S. Hyneman and Donald S. Lutz, eds., *American Political Writing During the Founding Era: 1760–1805*, vol. 1 (Indianapolis, IN: Liberty Fund, 1983) with *The Federalist*, no. 52, and Alexander Hamilton's statement in the New York ratifying convention that "the people should choose whom they please to govern them," *Elliot's Debates on the Federal Constitution*, vol. 2, p. 257.

15. *The Federalist*, no. 10, p. 62; no. 57, p. 384; no. 55, p. 378; no. 46, p. 322; no. 39, p. 250.
16. Ibid., no. 10, p. 60; no. 51, p. 349.
17. Ibid., no. 51, p. 349.
18. The analogy was introduced by Justice Louis Brandeis in his dissent in *New State Ice Co. v. Liebmann*, 285 U.S. 262 (1932), at 311. See Michael S. Greve, *The Upside-Down Constitution* (Cambridge, MA: Harvard University Press, 2012).
19. See Harvey C. Mansfield, "Responsibility Versus Self-Expression," pp. 96–111 in Robert A. Licht, ed., *Old Rights and New* (Washington, DC: American Enterprise Institute, 1993), and more generally, Mansfield, *America's Constitutional Soul* (Baltimore, MD: Johns Hopkins University Press, 1993).
20. See the dissent by Justice Felix Frankfurter in *West Virginia State Board of Education v. Barnette*, 319 U.S. 624 (1943), at 646, and the classic article he cites, James B. Thayer, "The Origin and Scope of the American Doctrine of Constitutional Law," *Harvard Law Review* 7 (1893): 129.
21. See Aristotle, *Nicomachean Ethics*, book VI, 1141a20.
22. Charles Evans Hughes, *Conditions of Progress in Democratic Government* (New Haven, CT: Yale University Press, 1910), 71–72, 74, 75–76.

8

The Vital Role of Religious Institutions

Michael O. Emerson

Religious congregations in the United States are pervasive, currently well over 340,000 in number.[1] To put that number in context, religious congregations are more common than the locations of Subway, McDonald's, Burger King, Wendy's, Starbucks, Pizza Hut, KFC, Taco Bell, Domino's Pizza, Dunkin' Donuts, Quiznos, and Dairy Queen ... combined ... and multiplied by three. And these congregations represent millions of Americans. In fact, most Americans regularly participate in or visit a congregation in any given year.[2]

Why are congregations—churches, temples, mosques, synagogues, and the like—so numerous, and why do they involve so many people in the United States? What is the meaning of these congregations—and their congregants—for society? To answer these questions, we must first ask, why religion? Is it useful for society? What functions does it serve?

WHY RELIGION?

For as long as there have been humans, there has been religion. People, as my colleague Christian Smith put it, are "moral, believing animals."[3] That is, all people live by a moral code and believe in something. They must, or they would be unable to live. This is part of the human condition, different from other animals. We have relatively few instincts, and thus we must live—as communities, as individuals—by a moral code, by what we believe is the right, the good, the decent.

Take the simple example of eating. We must eat, or we die. Yet even in this most basic of human activities, we cannot escape developing morals and beliefs around it. What should we eat—not only what tastes good (and this is of course shaped by how we are raised and our culture), but how much of what types of food? What should we *not* eat? Is it acceptable to eat dog? As we know, in some cultures it is acceptable, while in others it is considered not only disgusting but an egregious act of uncaring. How often should we eat—whenever we are hungry, or at set times during the day? When we eat, what should we use—our hands, or chopsticks, or forks, spoons, and knives? Should we eat standing up, sitting down on chairs, or sitting down on the floor? Can we talk to others with food in our mouths?

I could go on, but the point is that humans must have rights and wrongs, do's and don'ts, what is acceptable and what is abhorrent, in order to survive and live together. And as humans, we go further. We are "moral, believing animals" because we have a natural inclination to seek meaning, order, belonging, and security. Without instincts to guide our way, we must understand our world. We must create paths of what to do and not do, for as finite beings, we cannot do everything. The search for meaning—from why we eat what we eat to the deepest of questions such as what is our ultimate purpose and what happens when we die—is an essential, unavoidable human activity.

For billions of people across the earth, vital meaning is found in religious traditions and organizations. It is there that they find answers to questions they ask. It is within their religious communities that they gain purpose, focus, and direction. Religion scholar Peter Berger wrote that religion is so powerful across the globe because it, better than any other system, provides what humans seek: meaning, order, belonging, and security. It does so by creating what he calls a "sacred canopy" over a human community.[4] For believers, religion does not provide direction, purpose, and rights and wrongs simply because it is "how we do it" in the United States, or in our family, or in current times. These reasons are ultimately too limited to sustain human community, action, and virtue.

Rather, religion is so powerful precisely because it is so all-encompassing, because its reasoning rests on transcendence—the spirit world. Religion, to use Peter Berger's imagery, fights against the terror of meaninglessness, chaos, and aloneness by placing a strong, caring, transcendent covering of meaning, order, and belonging over human communities. It is this all-encompassing nature to which some people react negatively. They feel it impinge upon them, limiting their choices and ultimately their freedom. They want out from underneath the sacred canopy, to choose a different path. What they often find instead is exposure to confusion, chaos, and uncertainty.

For the past several decades, social-science research has documented with thousands of studies the benefits of religion to people and communities. Philosopher and avowed atheist Bruce Sheiman summarized much of this work in his provocative book, *An Atheist Defends Religion: Why Humanity Is Better Off with Religion than without It*. In his book, he argues that "religion provides a combination of psychological, emotional, moral, communal, existential, and even physical-health benefits that no other institution can replicate."[5] Echoing Immanuel Kant's dictum, "Science is organized knowledge. Wisdom is organized life," he argues that there is a difference between truth (facts, knowledge, the observed world) and Truth (wisdom, values, meaning, an existential framework that overflows with purpose). The latter, he argues, is necessary for the proper functioning of people and societies, and religion is, in his view, the single most powerful institution to do this.

Sheiman organizes religion's benefits into three main components: caring for humanity (which we will explore later), a force for progress,[6] and health and happiness. Let us focus here just on the health and happiness of religious participants. Sheiman notes that three-quarters of U.S. medical schools now offer courses in spirituality and medicine. Why? Because research has found the following benefits from increased participation in formalized religion—especially attendance at religious services: less depression, less drug abuse, fewer suicide attempts, more life satisfaction, better marriages, less divorce, higher levels of perceived well-being, higher self-esteem, lower blood pressure, less time spent in the hospital, faster recovery rates, slower mental decline from Alzheimer's, lower criminality levels, longer lives, greater physical health, and less suffering when one is unemployed, ill, or adjusting to the death of a loved one.

These benefits accrue because religion and being in a religious community provide meaning and purpose, altruism and generosity, consolation and coping, social connections, optimism and hope, gratitude and forgiveness, relaxation and mediation, commitment, and healthy lifestyle choices. Given that we are fundamentally social beings, we do substantially better when we are part of a caring, committed community of like-minded believers. This is why as scholars of religion, we find over and over that the single most powerful predictor of all these health and happiness benefits is frequency of religious-service attendance. It is a proxy, a shorthand measure for social connection with others and with the transcendent.

But seemingly, not all societies or humans are religious. Modern day Scandinavian societies, for example, are overwhelmingly secular—almost no one attends religious services, and high percentages of people are either atheist (believe there is no God) or agnostic (don't know and generally don't care if there is a God). Still, the people of those nations report high levels of happiness, good health, and long lives. How do we understand such findings?

The people of these nations are still moral and believing, still meaning-seeking, still in need of order and belonging, but their small (not one of these nations even has a population the size of the Chicago metro area), well-to-do, homogenous, social-welfare states currently provide most of what humans seek. Their long-existing, stable societies largely provide the canopy of meaning and direction. They are tucked away from much direct conflict with other nations, with a culture designed for sustained interaction with family and friends. Religion and religious institutions in these societies seem to be largely unneeded yet remain there for high holy days, weddings, funerals, baptisms, and confirmations.

But lost in this description is the fact that in these societies, the state is the religion; state and church are intimately tied together. There is a state church, and the government provides the sacred canopy. It funds religious organizations, licenses the ministers, and incorporates religious ideals such as caring for all in the community (in this case, through government programs). It gives meaning and order and belonging. What it cannot do, of course, is define why humans ultimately exist or provide a definitive response to what happens when we die. Thus, the apparent secular nature of Scandinavian societies may be context- and time-dependent. Should these societies grow substantially more diverse, should the government be unable to support all of its citizens at current levels, should substantial tragedies—such as war, disease, or massive climate change—impact these far-northern nations, the government-provided canopy may rip, and its people will seek meaning, order, and belonging elsewhere.

Contrasted with modern-day Scandinavian societies, the United States has always had separation of church and state, it is vast in land and people, it is substantially diverse, and it celebrates its rugged individualism. As noted, the United States is highly religious among Western nations, and religious institutions play a significant role there in providing what humans seek and in shaping virtuous people, so essential for the functioning of the United States.

RELIGIOUS CONGREGATIONS ARE ESSENTIAL FOR U.S. LIFE

In the United States, religious congregations have always played an essential role for Americans. By "religious congregation," I mean any group of people who gather regularly for religious purposes (such as worship) and have an official name, a formal structure that conveys a purpose and identity, an openness to all ages, and no restraints on how long people may remain in the group. Congregations are typically associated with a place where the congregating occurs, but this place—a mosque, temple, church building, synagogue, or any other place of worship—can change as the congregation's size or resources change. R. Stephen Warner convincingly argued that congregations are the center of religious life in the United States and that even religions that are not traditionally congregationally based, such as Buddhism, become so as they adapt to U.S. life.[7]

In a fifteen-nation study, the United States scored highest in religious membership (55 percent) and with the exception of Northern Ireland, had membership rates twenty or more percentage points higher than every other nation in the study.[8] To varying degrees, more than 150 million Americans are involved in religious congregations.

Congregations, then, are where Americans most often go to seek the meaning of life, to worship, to find direction, and to receive social support. Major life events happen within these groups. Religious congregations are where very many newborns are officially recognized and welcomed into the human community, where Americans most often get married, and where people most likely gather to say goodbye to deceased loved ones and friends.

But the role of congregations goes far beyond these essential functions. Allow me to illustrate with an example.

At the request of China's central government, I recently gave a talk to their religion commission about the relationship between religious congregations and social services in the Houston metropolitan area. In this region of six million people, our surveys found that 3.6 million attend religious services at least monthly. The area's several thousand congregations—ranging from only ten participants to the nation's largest, Lakewood Church, with nearly fifty thousand attending on any given weekend—produce approximately 2.2 million volunteers for the region and tens of millions of volunteer hours per year.

What are these volunteers doing? I found that the type of work engaged in by a volunteer was shaped in part by the religious tradition within which that volunteer's congregation was located. Combined, the work of the volunteers involved nearly every conceivable aspect of society. Volunteers provided child care so parents could take a break; served at the Houston food bank; worked on park-beautification projects; created care packages for the military and gift baskets for women's shelters; served as volunteers at these shelters; offered (literal) drive-through prayer services for needs and requests; gathered shoes, blankets, and blood donors to meet community needs; supported the homeless; started and operated adoption services; engaged in immigration and refugee advocacy; and provided financial assistance, legal assistance, counseling services, disaster recovery, and support for families, foster families, those with HIV/AIDS, pregnant women, seniors, orphans, and those in halfway houses and prisons. They implemented antipoverty campaigns, housed and staffed boy and girl scouting troops, and provided holistic community development, housing development, financial-literacy training, art training, singing lessons, language instruction, and health fairs in schools, hospitals, and homes. They delivered over a million meals (per year) to shut-ins, helped locals prepare for disaster, offered interfaith and interethnic training, and even served as a significant component of volunteers for the annual Houston Marathon.

The different faith traditions provided services not only through their individual congregations but also through their denominations. These included, to name a few, the Islamic Society of Greater Houston, Lutheran Social Services,

Catholic Charities, Jewish Family Service, the Jewish Federation of Greater Houston, and (joining them all together) Interfaith Ministries.

The Chinese contingent, upon hearing and viewing my presentation, were stunned. How is all of this possible through volunteer organizations, they wanted to know. Who coordinates all of this? How is it funded? Was Houston somehow unique in the degree to which its religious congregations engaged in social services? They were even more surprised when I answered, without hesitation, "No, not unique in the least."

And then came their most important question: What would Houston be like without the work of the congregations and their denominations? That, I answered, is a frightening thought. If all the organizations founded and operated by religious congregations closed their doors, if the flood of volunteers dried up and the services they offer disappeared, Houston would cease to function. It is that simple. Community life and well-being would not be possible in the Houston region without its congregations and its local religious associations. A radical restructuring would have to occur, massive rises in taxes and fees would have to be implemented in an attempt to pay people to do the work of the volunteers, and new organizations would have to be created overnight. It would be, to understate the case, a difficult task.

Professor Ram Cnaan of the University of Pennsylvania fully agrees. He conducted both a census of Philadelphia congregations and a full national study of congregations. In his 2006 study of Philadelphia, he and his colleagues concluded that congregations are an essential component of the city's civil society. Without them, the quality of life for residents would deteriorate immeasurably. The authors found that congregations there go about their work quietly and serve a heroic role in improving the lives of all Philadelphians. Ultimately, they reported, "religious congregations and other faith communities shoulder a considerable portion of the burden of care for the needy people in America."[9]

In his national study, Cnaan found similar results. Clergy and congregations are Americans' number-one refuge when they have serious problems, not the government or human- and health-service professionals. Congregations serve as one of the most critical safety nets for the nation's poor, with three quarters of them operating some mechanism for assisting people in economic need. In fact, Cnaan and his colleagues found that congregations provide service in more than two hundred areas, from summer day camps for children and scholarships for students, to visitation of the elderly and sick, to credit unions and health clinics.

In the United States, more volunteering occurs in and through religious congregations than anywhere else.[10] Most importantly, the more frequently someone attends religious services, the more often that person volunteers.[11] The same is true for monetary donations. Church members are more likely to give than are nonmembers, and the more frequently people attend religious services, the more broadly and the more generously they give. Along the same vein, those who frequently attend religious services are more civically engaged and in turn more politically active.[12]

These findings point to the important work of Nancy Ammerman, who argues, based on her extensive national study of congregations in 2005, that it is through religious congregations that American civic life is strengthened and that democracy flourishes. Congregations and faith traditions teach, operate within, and reinforce the democratic system: "Even those convinced that God is on their side are . . . shaped by deep convictions that acceptable democratic civic participation requires them to win their struggle through persuasion rather than violence."[13] She goes on to say,

> Making commitments to a local congregation and learning to be religious in the particular way of that congregation's tradition, far from being antidemocratic, may provide exactly the sorts of experiences, skills, and commitments that enhance the abilities of women and men, native and immigrant, small-town resident and big-city cosmopolitan to engage their fellow citizens, working together to build up our store of social capital.[14]

We can define social capital as the features of social organization that foster cooperation and mutual benefit among people. These might include friendship networks, traditions, and trust. Social capital is the stem from which blooms the flower of democracy. According to religion scholars Donald Miller and Corwin Smidt, religion contributes more to U.S. social capital than does any other institution.[15]

Ammerman concludes much the same. Congregational life, as structured in the United States, requires "constant voluntary investment if any local community of faith is to thrive."[16] The benefits of this work are not wasted—or limited to just the members of individual congregations. Such activity provides models and resources for larger life together. We learn lessons, Ammerman notes, for how to work together, how to speak with confidence and humility, and how to care for the world. Congregations are so essential because for their participants, "worship is where their eyes are opened, religious education is where they get their focus, caring communities of faith are where people practice the arts of compassionate response."[17] In short, the American democratic life, rooted in volunteerism and participation, benefits continually and powerfully from the functioning of healthy, vibrant, active religious congregations.

Consider one of the most characteristic features of the United States. It is, we know, an immigrant nation. Currently about one-fifth of all people on earth living in a nation other than the one in which they were born live in the United States. American society operates effectively only insofar as immigrants adapt to and contribute to U.S. life. Here, too, religious congregations play an essential role.

In our book, *Religion Matters*,[18] my colleagues and I outline the immense benefits of religion and religious congregations for immigrants to the United States. Often, we note, religion is more important for immigrants in their new nation than it was in their old. It helps them adapt to an unsettling, new environment. They benefit from a transcendent framework in understanding their experience and gain a new sense of purpose. In congregations, they connect socially, get help navigating a new system, take language classes, give and receive financial assistance, find support for family needs, and much more.

In a process that initially seems counterintuitive, immigrants attending ethnic congregations learn to become American. It is here that they learn the American practices of volunteerism, leadership within organizations, the democratic process, and other cultural norms. It is here that they learn English, discover job and child-care connections, access information on becoming a citizen, and learn to navigate the healthcare system. As Will Herberg pointed out in his classic 1955 work, while immigrants may be expected to eventually abandon their nationality and language, they are not expected to abandon their faith.[19] Indeed, attending religious services is a way for immigrants to become American and adapt to American society.

Congregational life is not perfect—far from it. People argue over issues as broad as theology and as small as the color of the new carpet. In her fine work on congregational conflict, Penny Edgell Becker finds four main types of congregations, each viewing the purpose of a congregation differently. She terms these "houses of worship," "family," "community," and "leader" congregations. Most conflict, she says, occurs "within frame," meaning within agreed-upon understandings of what congregational life should be. Occasionally, conflict occurs *between* frames. Some congregants desire, for example, a house of worship (which emphasizes providing religious goods and services to individuals, and religious reproduction), and others desire a family congregation (which emphasizes close, family-like relationships and building community). Resolution strategies needed and used vary considerably for within-frame and between-frame conflicts.[20]

But the conflicts themselves both teach and are the fruition of democracy. People learn how to negotiate, how to give and take, how to win, how to lose, how to compromise. Whether they do it well or struggle, they learn. Ironically then, congregational conflict contributes to a dynamic democracy, enacted in small ways across America's hundreds of thousands of congregations.

CONCLUSION

We have seen the often unrecognized but extensive role religious institutions play in American life. They are, to put it directly, essential. Government does well, then, to maintain the separation of church and state, allowing congregations and other religious organizations in all their diversity to flourish. Government must continually walk the difficult line of allowing for maximum freedom of its citizens to gather for religious purposes while not allowing any particular religion or organization to act above the law. U.S. history is largely positive in these respects, and these efforts must be seen as necessary for the continued healthy functioning of the nation.

After the family, it is religious organizations that most contribute to the formation of upright citizens, schooled in the importance of virtue, cooperation, and democracy. It is religious organizations that buttress and support families. It is in congregations that faith grounds Americans in the transcendent dignity of the human person made in the image and likeness of his Creator, in the value of rights and obligations, and in the connection of all humans as God's community. In the final analysis, America thrives because its religious congregations thrive.

NOTES

1. See Clifford Grammich, Kirk Hadaway, Richard Houseal, Dale E. Jones, Alexei Krindatch, Richie Stanley, and Richard H. Taylor, *2010 U.S. Religion Census: Religious Congregations and Membership Study* (Association of Statisticians of American Religious Bodies, 2012).
2. See Michael O. Emerson, "Analysis of the 2012 Portraits of American Life Study," working paper (Houston, TX: Kinder Institute for Urban Research at Rice University, 2012).
3. See Christian Smith, *Moral, Believing Animals: Human Personhood and Culture* (New York: Oxford University Press, 2003).
4. See Peter L. Berger, *The Sacred Canopy: Elements of a Sociological Theory of Religion* (Garden City, NY: Doubleday, 1967).
5. Bruce Sheiman, *An Atheist Defends Religion: Why Humanity Is Better Off with Religion than without It* (New York: Penguin, 2009), vii.
6. For a complete list of religious resources that lead to social change, see Christian Smith, *Disruptive Religion: The Force of Faith in Social Movement Activism* (New Brunswick, NJ: Rutgers University Press, 1996).
7. See R. Stephen Warner, "The Place of the Congregation in the Contemporary American Religious Configuration," pp. 54–99 in James P. Wind and James W. Lewis,

eds., *American Congregations, Volume 2: New Perspectives in the Study of Congregations* (Chicago, IL: University of Chicago Press, 1994).
8. See James E. Curtis, Edward G. Grabb, and Douglas E. Baer, "Voluntary Association Membership in Fifteen Countries: A Comparative Analysis," *American Sociological Review* 57 (April 1992): 139–152.
9. Ram A. Cnann, with Stephanie C. Boddie, Charlene C. McGrew, and Jennifer Kang, *The Other Philadelphia Story: How Local Congregations Support Quality of Life in Urban America* (Philadelphia, PA: University of Pennsylvania Press, 2006), xvi.
10. See Nancy Tatom Ammerman, *Pillars of Faith: American Congregations and Their Partners* (Berkeley, CA: University of California Press, 2005); Robert Wuthnow, *Learning to Care: Elementary Kindness in an Age of Indifference* (New York: Oxford University Press, 1995).
11. See David E. Campbell and Steven J. Yonish, "Religion and Volunteering in America," pp. 87–106 in Corwin Smidt, ed., *Religion as Social Capital: Producing the Common Good* (Waco, TX: Baylor University Press, 2003).
12. See Roger J. Nemeth and Donald A. Luidens, "The Religious Basis of Charitable Giving in America," pp. 107–120 in Corwin Smidt, ed., *Religion as Social Capital: Producing the Common Good* (Waco, TX: Baylor University Press, 2003).
13. Ammerman, *Pillars of Faith*, 262.
14. Ibid., 267.
15. See Donald E. Miller, "Religion, Privatization, and Public Life: The Nature of Civic Engagement in a Changing Religious Environment," presented at Conference on Religion, Social Capital, and Democratic Life, Grand Rapids, MI (October 16–17, 1998); Corwin Smidt, John Green, James Guth, and Lyman Kellstedt, "Religious Involvement, Social Capital, and Political Engagement: A Comparison of the United States and Canada," pp. 153–170 in Corwin E. Smidt, ed., *Religion as Social Capital: Producing the Common Good* (Waco, TX: Baylor University Press, 2003).
16. Ammerman, *Pillars of Faith*, 276.
17. Ibid.
18. Michael O. Emerson, Susanne C. Monahan, and William A. Mirola, *Religion Matters: What Sociology Teaches Us about Religion in Our World* (Boston, MA: Allyn & Bacon, 2011), ch. 11.
19. See Will Herberg, *Protestant, Catholic, Jew: An Essay in American Religious Sociology* (Chicago, IL: University of Chicago Press, 1955).
20. See Penny Edgell Becker, *Congregations in Conflict: Cultural Models of Local Religious Life* (New York: Cambridge University Press, 1999).

9

The University

Candace Vogler

"The advancement of knowledge through research, the transmission of knowledge through teaching, the preservation of knowledge in scholarly collections, and the diffusion of knowledge through publishing are the four legs of the university table, no one of which can stand for very long unless all are strong."[1]

Although established by crown and church in the Medieval Ages—and since then, by particular states—the university stood above the local interests of its host community and was granted distinct freedoms not commonly enjoyed by the wider society. It was expected to serve universal interests of truth seeking, of knowledge gathering, of learning and critical reason. The university was partial only to such global concerns. It stood for important aspects of human life, aspects that were universal in character.[2]

John Henry Newman gave his inaugural lectures as rector of the new Catholic University of Ireland in 1852[3] and inadvertently set in motion a train of twentieth-century Anglophone work on the nature of the university.[4] Newman was concerned with a crisis that he took to have its roots in the increasing emphasis on professional research—research dictated by the needs of Victorian industrial development and heavily skewed toward the sciences—and in a model of education oriented to the production of appropriately credentialed provincial lawyers, doctors, and schoolteachers. He argued that these trends damaged teaching, stunted learning, and ultimately worked against knowledge itself.

Most of those taking up Newman's topic in the twentieth and twenty-first centuries share his concern over the relations between the university and the larger economic and political world in and through which institutions of higher learning operate.[5] It has become characteristic of the contemporary university[6] that faculty and administrators find themselves moved to reflect on the place of the university in the larger society. This is partly because of the unprecedented growth of the university over the course of the twentieth century: the increasingly broad demand for university education and the sheer number of universities formed in order to meet that demand.[7]

It has become commonplace in most of the world that young people hoping to find ways of making a living that do not grind them into the dust need to earn at least a baccalaureate (bachelor's) degree. This is not just because secondary-school (high-school) education is rarely enough to equip young people with what they need in order to succeed. It is also because the kind of labor required in many sectors of the economy has changed dramatically. People in the developed and developing world look to universities to prepare young people for the challenges of contemporary economic life. Meanwhile, the work produced by both research and applied-professional faculty in universities fuels economic growth. Some scholars see the economic role of the contemporary university as in tension with its larger ideals.[8] There are threats to both the educational and the research missions of the university when the market has undue influence over the curricular initiatives, pedagogic approaches, or research agendas of the faculty. Nevertheless, for better or worse, there is no way of understanding the life of the contemporary university without a healthy appreciation of its economic aspects.

THE UNIVERSITY IN THE ECONOMY

Basic research in the arts and sciences—research undertaken with no particular application in view—serves the interests of expanding, organizing, and disseminating knowledge in specialized fields. It is certainly the case that this work increases both the scope and the depth of our understanding. But at the same time, it questions our bases, provides new ways of conceiving our objects of inquiry, focuses and refocuses curiosity, and invites creative and imaginative ways of extending inquiry—all the while holding itself accountable to the high academic standards and critical scrutiny of the many and varied disciplines. *Applied* research— sometimes undertaken by faculty members of the arts and sciences, but more often by professional faculty—is directly concerned with practical matters. Sometimes, basic research interacts with professional (applied) research in complex ways. For example, basic research into plant genetics informs work by nutritionists, agricultural specialists, and policy-oriented social scientists in the service of developing sustainable methods of increasing the world's food supply. Commenting on measures to stop the advance of famine, Jaroslav Pelikan remarks on the interaction:

> While some of the most decisive and abstract basic research was the result of work done in the laboratories of industry and government, these laboratories remain accountable to their chief executives, and ultimately to shareholders or legislators and taxpayers, who have a right to demand justification for any such basic research in relation to

the primary mission of the institution. It is an oversimplification but not a distortion to point out that in the faculty of arts and sciences of the university basic research *is* a primary mission of the institution.[9]

In short, in order for the university to fulfill its core commitment to knowledge, it cannot be held hostage to the exigencies of pressing practical concerns that have only a tangential relationship to the organization, advancement, and development of human understanding.

For all that, it is virtually inconceivable that contemporary industry could thrive without advances directly tied to new knowledge that came to fruition in universities; that the financial sector could operate in the absence of instruments and research nurtured through basic research in university social-science departments; that governments could do without university research projects—in the arts and sciences and the professional fields—tied to specific governmental goals or initiatives; that medicine could advance without basic and professional university research; or even that cultural institutions could flourish without the historians, scholars, and critics whose principal source of support is the universities. For that matter, in many parts of the world nowadays, it is doubtful that high-performance sport could flourish in all of its variety without university athletics.[10] And this is not even the first place where one looks to understand the importance of the university to the economy.

The *first* place to look in asking about the economic significance of the university is to university students and alumni—those who are pursuing or have already completed degrees in specialized fields. We look to the university to preserve, extend, and develop organized knowledge; to foster critical engagement with this knowledge and its sources; and to provide the labor force needed for an increasingly complex global economy. Sociologists Harald Schomburg and Ulrich Teichler put the point this way:

> Higher education has to prepare students to become highly skilled specialists and to be versatile in many other domains, to increase their body of knowledge and to learn to transfer academic knowledge into practical problem solving, to be trained to cope with established job requirements and to question the established rules and tools, to foster the cognitive competences and to provide opportunities of developing socio-communicative competences and to develop work attitudes and values that are not in the domain of cognitive training.[11]

Schomburg and Teichler reached this conclusion after a tremendously ambitious study following the fates of alumni who earned their undergraduate and graduate degrees in eleven European countries and the United Kingdom over the decade following major reforms in higher education. There is nothing especially European about their conclusions. Notice the tensions in their list of things that students need in order to fare well in the larger world:

- highly specialized professional training and the ability to be flexible and versatile—to extend, modify, adapt, or leave behind something of what they have acquired through professional training,
- obedience to requirements of various positions and the ability to question those very requirements, and
- academic strength and social and personal development that floats free of strictly academic achievement.

Schomburg and Teichler do not focus on formation or character or wisdom, but their list is struggling to say that a body of knowledge and a suitable set of skills is not enough for students to flourish. We want these to exist in the larger context of the students' integrated intellectual and social development—we want students to grow not just by acquiring skills and information but by developing something of wisdom. The history of work in technical fields—in the sciences, in mathematics, in medicine, in computational work generally—is enough to show that the exact *content* of what students learn, and the skills they acquire in working with this information, are likely to become obsolete very quickly. What does *not* outlive its utility is the larger social, intellectual, and practical orientation to inquiry that students cultivate, when all goes well. And this is the place where something of wisdom enters into a liberal-arts education.

What is it about the university that allows it to inform and to staff the work both of public and private institutions at virtually every level of economic activity? And why is it that the increasingly focused collaboration between universities and economic institutions has been a source of criticism and concern among many prominent theorists of higher education?[12]

The answer to both questions can be found in the traditional mission of the university.

THE MISSION OF UNIVERSITIES

For the most part, university mission statements in the Anglophone academy say the same things. These institutions exist in order to advance society through research, creative activity, scholarship, the discovery or development of new knowledge, and education. The description of the larger society served by a center of higher education sometimes reflects the character of the institution. Consider, for example, a system of state-funded campuses, or a private institution with a specific religious affiliation or historic aim, or a private institution that locates its public function in an international frame. Whether the institution announces its intention to serve the citizens and economy of a given state or province, a people sharing a given religious tradition, or the nation or world at large, the announced purpose of a university centers on contributing to the long-term advancement of society. To this end, universities big and small are committed to full and free inquiry; critical discussion; high standards of research, scholarship, and teaching; and some sort of public outreach.

Given the aims of universities, it is easy to see why we need them and why it is important that they retain a measure of independence from the public and private entities that fund them. It is hard to conceive of a modern university that will not depend on corporate sponsorship or government funding for research in the natural and social sciences—or one that can support vibrant programs in the arts or humanities without strong private and public support. But if universities are to provide both the kind of knowledge base and the kind of education that the mission statements describe, they need a measure of autonomy. The very character of the core task of the university—open-ended inquiry—tells against the urge to try to harness university research to the practical interests and demands of even those groups who help to fund the work. Stefan Collini brings this out beautifully:

> Intellectual enquiry is in itself ungovernable: there is no predicting where thought and analysis may lead when allowed to play freely over almost any topic, as the history of science abundantly illustrates. It is sometimes said that in universities knowledge is pursued "for its own sake," but that may mis-describe the variety of purposes for which different kinds of understanding may be sought. A better way to characterize the intellectual life of universities may be to say that the drive towards understanding can never accept an arbitrary stopping-point, and critique may always in principle reveal that any currently accepted stopping-point *is* ultimately arbitrary. Human understanding, when not chained to a particular instrumental task, is restless, always pushing onwards, though not in a single or fixed or entirely knowable direction, and there is no one moment along that journey where we can say in general or in the abstract that the degree of understanding being sought has passed from the useful to the useless.[13]

Collini's sketch of the character of open-ended inquiry gives some sense of how the university can begin to address the *prima facie* puzzling desiderata for higher education that frame Schomburg and Teichler's study.[14] Teaching students to answer to both the standards governing work in their field and field-specific modes of presentation for work is *how* university education prepares them to become specialists. At its best, an undergraduate education that includes thoughtfully composed general educational requirements in the humanities begins to prepare students to be not only specialized and disciplined, but versatile. Liberal-arts education requires a strong, general background in humanities and the sciences. In a time where many universities are trying to be increasingly devoted to professionalization and hyperspecialization, it is important to fight to preserve liberal-arts education.

Significant work in mathematics and natural science or formal social science gives students opportunities to work with empirical data. They can develop a healthy appreciation for the standards governing respectable empirical inquiry, for the kinds of conclusions that can be warranted, and for the ways empirical work provides a basis for those conclusions. In the larger context of a liberal-arts education, however, students also need to develop ways of understanding the *limits* of what can be known about the natural and social world on the basis of the data and models generated and deployed in empirical research. Good scientists and social scientists are as alert to the limits of scientific understanding as they are to the strengths of empirical work. Even if we share the popular conviction that science, adequately developed, can tell us what we want to know about how things are in the human world and the terrestrial world more generally, no amount of information about how things are is enough to show how things ought to be, or how we ought to go about improving life in the world that we share. We look to universities both to give young adults an understanding of how things are and to help them develop insight into larger questions about how, when, and why we might intervene in the world for the sake of humankind.

The humanities and humanistic social sciences provide the kind of literacy demanded by many desirable careers: not just skills working with different kinds of documents but general experience with serious attention to written material; not just an ability to cope with primary sources, scholarly articles, and books of literature, say, or history, but an active orientation to the content of these. One learns the point at which a reader loses interest or understanding, the conclusion of an argument outruns its premises, or an analogy ceases making contact with what it was meant to illuminate. This learning, in turn, forms part of the basis of what Schomburg and Teichler had in mind in urging that a university education should provide students with opportunities to develop "socio-communicative competences and . . . work attitudes and values that are not in the domain of cognitive training."

Beyond this, strong education in the humanities provides students with opportunities to grapple with central questions in human life at exactly the point in their lives when these questions begin to become vivid and personal for them. How do the structures of basic social and political institutions influence the lives of citizens? How do moral norms, rules of etiquette, and basic standards of civility and decency shape human activity and experience? What sorts of things impede people's efforts to lead meaningful lives? What sorts of things help people to flourish? How do love, romance, and family contribute to good lives? How is ethical conduct both possible and problematic for human beings? How do people go about pursuing good and avoiding evil? What sort of knowledge is presupposed about human beings and human lives when we meet these questions in literature, in philosophy, and in humanistic social science? These kinds of questions endure in human history. They endure cross-culturally. They inform work—explicitly or implicitly—in every humanistic discipline. And they are precisely the kinds of questions that begin to emerge in the lives of undergraduates at the point they find themselves away from home and thrust into a world with new people, new activities, and new opportunities. The chief educational challenges for humanistic academics center on helping students to work with the content of humanities coursework anchored by such questions.

Strong general education in the sciences and humanities comes to fruition when students begin to work accurately, critically, and creatively with what they are learning in classrooms and laboratories. What they get from university coursework is not just packets of knowledge and a set of disciplinary skills for working with words and formulas. What they get, if all goes well, is a general intellectual and practical orientation to serious inquiry—to flexible, creative scholarly work that is, for all its imaginative charms and freedoms, disciplined and governed by standards of thought and criticism and alive to the challenge of at once learning how things are or have been, and looking for ways to make things better.

THE ROLE OF CAMPUSES

How do the campuses of universities contribute to the work of universities? The answer to this question is straightforward in the physical and biological sciences and allied professional fields. Research (and teaching) in these fields requires well-equipped laboratories. Medical schools fare best when attached to teaching hospitals. And so on.

Beyond this, as is the case in any other area of open inquiry, the sciences progress through creative conversations among colleagues, and while these *can* happen at conferences or through electronic media, plain physical proximity—sharing a department, having offices along the same hall, for instance—can help enormously. For example, the Gravity Probe B experiment—one of the most important experiments aimed at testing predictions based in Einstein's theory of general relativity—received its initial thrust in conversations between Leonard Schiff (then chair of Stanford's physics department) and his colleagues William Little and William Fairbank. The experiment ran from 1963–2011, a NASA experiment under the leadership and management of Stanford faculty. Although it is increasingly true that, in many fields of inquiry, research and collaboration involve significant use of internet resources and many university courses operate in part through course websites, the life of university campuses—in classrooms, in laboratories, on quads, and in residence halls and libraries—provides the infrastructure for intellectual community.

It is not *impossible* for faculty to teach students they never see in classrooms, laboratories, or lecture halls—students the faculty will never bump into at campus eateries, in the halls of their departments, on the quads, or at campus athletic events. Learning is not impossible for students who commute to a campus a few hours a week or work online at a distance. But it is very difficult to model or to cultivate an active, practical, and intellectual orientation to inquiry without old-fashioned conversation and discussion.

This is not to say that hopes for near-universal access to higher education pinned to university-sponsored online instruction, research opportunities, and course offerings are in vain.[15] But the kind of educational opportunities afforded by online resources are fundamentally different from the sort provided by even a routine commuting relationship with the university campus. A faculty member giving an online lecture—even a live lecture delivered electronically in real time—can't have even the limited eye contact she can have with students in a lecture hall. She might be able to answer questions that arrive as text messages, but she can't ask students to turn to their neighbors and take a moment to think together about how to approach a problem. She can't sense the restlessness in a room when students are having trouble following her lecture. She can't tell if some students have fallen asleep. She can comment on written work and go back and forth with her students over email about their writing, but she can't follow up later in her office.

And her students will be deprived of one of their most important educational resources—each other. The whole of the embodied aspect of cultivating an orientation to disciplined open inquiry—tone of voice, facial expression, the simple camaraderie that forms when everyone faces the same challenging assignment, experiences the same weather on the way to class, hears the same noises drifting in from outside, and waits in the hall together for the students in the earlier class to file out—*none* of these things can help to frame and guide the establishment of intellectual community in an online course. Online courses may be excellent vehicles for a lot of content—for packets of knowledge. But it is the *orientation to content* that the students need most, together with the community that provides the living support for cultivating that orientation, as they don't just encounter and acquire new information but feel their way around the content in community with others. The way that such an orientation is nurtured and developed is through thinking together in conversation, feeling the mood of a room, being alive to both the material under discussion and the whole range of responses that the other people around have to its content. This is as true for faculty collaborating on a research project as it is for students taking an introductory course.

CONCLUDING REMARKS

Contemporary universities face tremendous challenges. The demand for higher education has never been greater; a national economy, or an entire sector of transnational or international activity, can rise or fall with the quality of its educated labor force. Rapid changes in technology and shifting political circumstances mean that there is no single, easily specified set of concrete skills or kinds of information that people need in order to make their way in the larger world. Arts and sciences faculty can no longer presume that their students share a common educational background. Distinctions between pure and applied university research blur more often than not, and rising costs and cultural pressures combine to make it increasingly difficult for most universities to achieve their missions. In the heady rush to find ways of promoting research and expanding access to higher education while lowering the costs of both, many institutions have made compromises that leave research at the mercy of market forces, preventing open inquiry and failing to provide curricular leadership and oversight that could serve to ensure the health of these institutions in the long run.[16]

Human beings are rational and social animals. The university answers to both of these central aspects of human nature to the extent that it promotes high intellectual achievement in relatively autonomous academic communities devoted to open inquiry. In this way, it has a distinctive role to play in promoting human good in a thriving society. This role is nowhere near enough to ensure a healthy and flourishing human society, but it is a piece of the life of such a society that we cannot do without.

NOTES

1. Jaroslav Pelikan, *The Idea of the University: A Reexamination* (New Haven, CT: Yale University Press, 1992), 16–17.
2. See Ronald Barnett, "Recapturing the Universal in the University," *Educational Philosophy and Theory* 37 (December 2005): 785–797, pp. 785–786.

3. Newman was dissatisfied with the lectures, and their publication history bears the marks of his dissatisfaction. He revised and added to the material. The final edition, prepared under his direction, was published in 1873 as *The Idea of a University: Defined and Illustrated* (London, England: Basil Montagu Pickering).
4. Pelikan gives a thoughtful survey of books written in homage to, or in dialogue with, Cardinal Newman in Pelikan, *Idea of the University: A Reexamination*, 1–10.
5. For example, José Ortega y Gasset (*Mission of the University* [London, England: Kegan Paul, 1946]) and Robert Maynard Hutchins (*Education for Freedom* [Baton Rouge, LA: Louisiana State University Press, 1943] and *The Higher Learning in America* [New Haven, CT: Yale University Press, 1936]) echo Newman in stressing the educational mission of the university. Both were especially concerned with seeking some remedy in university education for the threat of fascism. Karl Jaspers (*The Idea of the University* [London, England: Peter Owen, 1963 (1946)]) urged that a properly constituted university should function as a social conscience, again, partly in response to the specter of fascism. Clark Kerr (*The Uses of the University* [Cambridge, MA: Harvard University Press, 1963 and four additional expanded editions through 2001]) provided a prescient account of the troubled development of the university from an institution modeled as a community to one modeled as a kind of industrial complex geared toward producing useful knowledge and young professionals (see also Stanley Aronowitz, *The Knowledge Factory: Dismantling the Corporate University and Creating True Higher Learning* [Boston, MA: Beacon Press, 2000]), to one radically decentralized and largely in the service (and at the mercy) of disparate market forces. Throughout, he is concerned to reclaim some of the place for the university that formed the backbone of Newman's account.
6. By "university" I mean a self-governing, public or private, not-for-profit, accredited academic institution granting baccalaureate (bachelor's), master's, and doctoral degrees in specialized fields of the arts and sciences and conferring postgraduate professional degrees in at least one of the learned professions (law, medicine, or divinity) or in at least two other professional fields: engineering, architecture, journalism, education, etc.
7. For example, in the United States, there were 977 universities in 1900, a number that had risen to 3,535 by 1990. Only 382 doctoral degrees were awarded in 1900, compared with 38,238 in 1990. In 1900, 27,410 baccalaureate (bachelor's) degrees were awarded, and in 1990, 1,049,657. See Thomas D. Snyder, ed., *120 Years of American Education: A Statistical Portrait* (Washington, DC: National Center for Education Statistics, 1993), 75 (ch. 3, table 23). For general and studiously comparative work on growth in the university systems in North America and Europe, see Martin Trow, "Reflections on the Transition from Elite to Mass to Universal Access: Forms and Phases of Higher Education in Modern Societies Since WWII," in Philip Altbach, ed., *International Handbook of Higher Education* (Dordrecht, Netherlands: Kluwer Academic, 2005).
8. Former Harvard President Derek Bok explores these concerns in his *Universities in the Marketplace: The Commercialization of Higher Education* (Princeton, NJ: Princeton University Press, 2003).

9. Pelikan, *Idea of the University: A Reexamination*, 17–18.
10. This is especially true in so-called nonrevenue sports (like track and field and most water athletics) along with most women's sports, although it applies as well to any men's sport where university student athletes provide the talent pool for professional organizations. In North America, Europe, Australia, and some Asian countries, for example, the members of national teams competing in the Olympics tend to be drawn primarily from university athletic programs—90 percent of the membership of the U.S. Olympic team in 2012 was made up of student athletes. See D. Knapp, *Performance of Student-athletes at Olympic Games* (Sydney, Australia: Australian Sports Commission, 2012) for a discussion of student athletes in the United States, France, Australia, and the United Kingdom. Although university faculty rarely look to university sports programs in thinking about the place of the university in society more generally, university athletics programs were the first region of the university to pursue direct commercial ventures, a point emphasized and explored in Bok, *Universities in the Marketplace,* 50–71, 137–154.
11. Harald Schomburg and Ulrich Teichler, *Higher Education and Graduate Employment in Europe: Results from Graduate Surveys from Twelve Countries* (Dordrecht, Netherlands: Springer, 2006), 6.
12. For a powerful statement of concern, see Aronowitz, *The Knowledge Factory* (Boston, MA: Beacon Press, 2001).
13. Stefan Collini, *What Are Universities For?* (London, England: Penguin, 2012), 63.
14. See Schomburg and Teichler, *Higher Education and Graduate Employment in Europe.*
15. For a serious look at the impact of these new technologies on universities in Europe and the United States, see Martin Trow, "From Mass Higher Education to Universal Access: The American Advantage," Center for Studies in Higher Education, Research and Occasional Paper Series 1.00 (2000).
16. In the United States, the celebrated modular course model, which has taken the place of a serious, shared general-education curriculum, is largely to blame for this. When students can satisfy their general-education requirements by taking a grab bag of courses in different fields of the arts and sciences, utter incoherence in the course of study at its very base is virtually inevitable.

10

Institutions of Research Vital to a Thriving Society

Sanjeev R. Kulkarni and Donald W. Landry

Dramatic advances in electronics, computing, and communication ushered in the current technological age, though history may well judge this moment to be only its barest threshold. Ongoing developments in biotechnology are yielding similar revolutionary impact. These and other advances have propelled us beyond the Industrial Age within a single lifetime.

Nonetheless, age-old scourges prevail—poverty and disease, crime and ignorance. Clearly, many of our problems as a society are more spiritual in nature than material or technological, deriving from less tangible contributors such as alienation, family breakdown, and political deadlock. Substantial progress might be made on our material problems through more effective use of existing technology. But a thriving society needs sources of hope and renewal, and on the material side, these emanate from our institutions of research.

Research in science and engineering leads to new materials, new processes, and new industries—and prospects for innovations that provide feasible solutions to our most pressing problems. But these innovations are not launched in isolation. They operate in the context of society and in the service of humanity. Research in the social sciences and humanities provides a greater understanding of the societal, economic, and political systems within which innovations are developed and deployed. Research in all these disciplines leads to the development of new technologies, new occupations, the creation of wealth, improvements in the standard of living and the quality of life, greater health and longevity, and increased opportunity for the pursuit of happiness. Moreover, for those with an interest in the pursuit of knowledge, institutions of research provide a structure for learning, a venue for fulfilling employment in research and in teaching, and an opportunity to contribute to society—all foundations for a good life.

Broadly speaking, research and development (R&D) refers to activities in the pursuit of knowledge and understanding and/or the creation of new ideas, products, or processes. R&D is often broken down into subcategories, though the boundaries between these is sometimes ambiguous:

- basic research: research activities aimed at increasing knowledge or understanding without being directed toward specific applications,
- applied research: research activities aimed at specific applications to fulfill a particular identified need, and
- development: activities aimed at developing prototypes of new products or processes in preparation for commercialization.

Basic research, applied research, and development are all important in creating and developing innovations that impact society, but the focus here is on basic research. While some argue for a "demand side" view of research (the premise that all research should be need-driven and hence in some sense, applied), a broad consensus endorses the proposition that basic research serves a critical role for a thriving society. Basic research creates a repository of knowledge and understanding that may be drawn upon as needed, serving as a foundation for innovations less likely to arise through a narrow and applied focus. Taking the importance of basic research as a given, we focus herein on the integrity of the basic-research enterprise and the institutions that comprise it.

INSTITUTIONS OF RESEARCH

The institutions of basic research are, in the main, the universities. Even as teaching is highly valued, the prestige and ranking of a university depend overwhelmingly on the impact and productivity of the research of its faculty. Academic institutions spend approximately $60 billion per year on science and engineering R&D, accounting for more than half the nation's total basic research funding and more than a third of all U.S. research funding (basic plus applied).[1] The institutions of research also include a variety of organizations not engaged in undergraduate education, such as the Scripps Research Institute, the Salk Institute for Biological Studies, the Institute for Advanced Study, and a number of governmental laboratories, such as the Intramural Program of the National Institutes of Health (NIH) and a variety of Department of Defense (DoD) and Department of Energy (DoE) laboratories. Research also is conducted in industrial labs to varying degrees, but these labs tend to focus more on either applied research or development.

"Institutions of research" also can be taken to include the institutions that *fund* research. The federal government provides approximately 60 percent of academic spending on science and engineering R&D, virtually all from six agencies:

the NIH, the National Science Foundation (NSF), the DoD, the National Aeronautics and Space Administration (NASA), the DoE, and the Department of Agriculture. Academic institutions themselves are the next major source of our R&D funding, contributing about one-fifth of the total, with substantial contributions from philanthropy.[2] The remaining fifth of academic spending on R&D derives more or less equally from state government, industry support, and other sources. This last category includes foundation support that ranges from the behemoth Howard Hughes Medical Institute to smaller, focused enterprises such as the American Cancer Society, the Juvenile Diabetes Research Foundation, and the Cystic Fibrosis Foundation.

The various sources of funding organize the processes of grant application, peer review, and funds allocation. Other key stages in the basic research enterprise include the execution of the research, the dissemination of results, and the use of these results. This system operates in the ambient social, political, and economic environment, which creates a sort of feedback system for basic research. The output of this system—namely research results and the way these results are used—can help shape policy that in turn drives the availability and allocation of future funding. The importance of research to a thriving society renders the integrity of the research system a paramount concern.

INTEGRITY OF THE RESEARCH ENTERPRISE

When integrity is mentioned in relation to research, it is usually in the context of an individual researcher or research project/group and typically refers to adherence to certain ethical principles and standards in the conduct of the research. Various types of research misconduct such as plagiarism, fabrication, falsification, sabotage, and usurpation—founded in the seven deadly sins[3]—have their infamous examples scattered throughout the history of science. A case of misconduct in research from more than a century ago is that of the Piltdown Man (1912). Bone fragments from an orangutan skull and a human skull were deliberately misrepresented as having been collected together from a pit in Piltdown, England, and belonging to a previously unknown human ancestor. More recent examples involving questions of scientific integrity include the cases of Thereza Imanishi-Kari (1989–1996), Jan Hendrik Schön (2001–2002), Eric Poehlman (2005–2006), and Marc Hauser (2007–2012).

There is some controversy regarding the frequency of research misconduct, and there is some ambiguity as to what actually constitutes misconduct. On one extreme are the clear-cut, outright violations, which seem to be relatively uncommon, but there are also ambiguous, and more frequent, cases of exaggeration and self-promotion. Some famous cases of egregious but innocent errors include "polywater" (what appeared to be a startling discovery in the 1960s of a new form of water, but that actually represented poorly cleaned containers) and "cold fusion" (events in 1989 that led to a false hope for inexpensive energy production through nuclear reactions at room temperature). In any case, the impact of failures of integrity by individual researchers on the body of knowledge should be minimal for several reasons. First, these cases seem to be fairly infrequent. Second, they typically involve a narrow scope of inquiry and thus are very localized in effect. Third, if the research system is structured appropriately, then the impact of these problems should be self-correcting. If the result is of significant interest, then independent studies will be conducted—and these either will support or refute the original claims.

Much more pernicious problems arise when assaults on the integrity of the research system are systemic and/or if they occur at higher levels of the research system. Here "integrity" is meant broadly, referring to the overall soundness of the enterprise and the results arising therefrom, including all steps from the appropriation and allocation of resources through the dissemination and use of research results. This is not referring to actions by individuals (whether innocent, venal, or pernicious) but rather pressures from the culture to think in a particular way. The impact of this systemic bias is not erroneous conclusions in a particular study, but distorted research in many studies, across entire organizations, or across large swaths of the research enterprise. Pervasive and persistent, these pressures can exert broad and long-lasting effects through hiring, promotion, and tenure; funding and publication; and response to and reception of the research, including the bestowing of honors and awards. Such pressures arise through a lack of diversity of thought, and once present with sufficient strength, the self-organizing feedback elements of the system can serve to further strengthen the resulting bias. This in turn can distort policy and diminish the capacity of a society to thrive.

SYSTEMIC BIAS

Academic freedom in institutions of research supports the integrity of the research enterprise. The tenure system is meant to enhance academic freedom by eliminating the fear of dismissal of a researcher without just cause. But while tenure may protect a faculty member's position, the researcher and her work can still be marginalized through decisions made at the level of her department, her university, or the research community at large. There is the possibility of selection bias with regard to who gets hired, who receives tenure, funding, or promotion; which research gets published; and which has support—or lack thereof—from colleagues in one's research community. For example, faculty members in almost any department of obstetrics and gynecology whose work does not support abortion on demand, or faculty members in various departments whose work does not support the theory of global warming, will likely not advance far in their fields. In fact, even the work performed by graduate students and postdoctoral researchers is subject to these pressures, since a department's faculty typically play a strong role in shaping the projects of students.

Regardless of which position one takes on a particular issue, the institutionalization of bias is an unfortunate state of affairs antithetical to the best interest of research. Needless to say, the goal of research is to seek truth, not advocate for a position. When seeking truth, opposing views are beneficial, as contrary opinions can challenge false or sloppy work or facile conclusions. On the other hand, if one's interest is to advocate for a position, bias is useful. The more widespread the bias, the greater the forces in the system that can preserve and strengthen it. A monolithic academy produces distortions in research and impairs self-correction in a meaningful timeframe.

The crucial distinction here is between bias in the research *system* versus bias in any particular research *study* or in the studies of a particular researcher. Various types of research and experimenter bias have been studied extensively, and of course, care should be taken to avoid inadvertent bias to the extent possible through the proper design of protocols, practices, and analyses. Since drawing inferences from limited data requires favoring some hypotheses over others, a certain kind of salutary bias is inevitable. But in the process of conducting a study, the data, in principle, should be able to lead a researcher to abandon an initial hypothesis in favor of one more consistent with the data. Even if a favored but incorrect hypothesis is retained for the moment, eventually it will yield to the weight of additional data. Valid scientific theories must be falsifiable, and researchers must have an openness to the falsification of a favored hypothesis—a subordination of personal agenda to the truth as we are best given to see it. Of course, a certain humility is required to be able to do this.

In pursuit of truth, the rate of progress on a given research problem depends on a number of factors, including the degree of bias among the researchers. When independent researchers study the same problem and bring different perspectives, progress generally will be faster. Independent studies can more quickly falsify an incorrect hypothesis, whereas studies tainted with the same bias thwart the process of hypothesis refinement.

This issue with bias in the system is not confined to just the process of conducting research nor to any particular institution involved in the research enterprise. Bias can be, and seems to be, present in academia, industry, and government. Bias in industry tends to exhibit itself most strongly through the self-interest of the particular industry and manifests itself through research support that bolsters the corporate interest. Bias in academia, perhaps amplified on study sections of granting agencies, can be more far-reaching. Bias knows no partisan boundaries; it can exist on the left, right, and center, and can be present in any stage of the system from allocation of funds through the use of research results. The reception that scientific results receive from the research community can have significant impact on the careers of individual investigators and ongoing funding of specific projects or entire research areas.

The dominant position of federal funding in the hierarchy of support for academic research, as well as the role of government in shaping the political and economic environment within which basic research is conducted, places research firmly in the grip of politics. To the extent that research reflects the important needs and considered judgments of the populace, the political process would be an efficient mechanism for the allocation of resources aimed at research. However, interest groups, through lobbying and pressure tactics, can leverage their limited resources with the federal largesse to the detriment of the body politic. For example, in the medical/biological fields, consider the funding preference for juvenile diabetes (type 1) over adult-onset diabetes (type 2), despite the tenfold greater incidence of type 2 diabetes. Another example is the preference for federal funding of breast cancer research over that of other, more prevalent cancers. In fiscal year 2012, the NIH provided $800 million in support of breast cancer research and $233 million (only 29 percent as much) for lung cancer research. However, the American Cancer Society's estimates for the current year are 40,000 deaths due to breast cancer and 159,260 deaths from lung cancer.[4]

Direction of funding allocations to specific fields are not the only way that government policy distorts the conduct of research. Another concerns the preference for applied research over basic research (or translational over basic research). Governments prefer rapid, practical results with smaller risk to capital and lesser opportunity cost. Basic research need not have any immediately discernible use, and hence, its application is more speculative and the time course to an application more protracted. On the other hand, basic research yields a repository of knowledge that can have profound impact many years after its completion and in ways never originally contemplated. The chosen balance between basic and applied research, then, reflects a bias in time horizon and risk tolerance.

A variation on this theme is to bias the funding opportunities for basic research toward short term, practical ends. Thus, there is a trend to require that proposals discuss the broader impact and significance of the proposed work, with funding decisions based in part on this description. If the aim is to support basic research, then the value of forcing investigators to concoct statements on the impact and significance of their proposed work is questionable.

Two other trends over the last few decades have been the move toward funding groups of investigators (often with a preference for multidisciplinary collaborations and researchers from different institutions) versus funding projects by individual researchers, and the requirement to discuss a project's impact on "K–12 education." These pressures seem to be driven by the funding agencies, although the underlying origin of these trends is unclear. Researchers respond accordingly, forming (multidisciplinary and/or multi-university) groups of investigators, sometimes contrived, or discussing the impact on K–12 education, to the extent possible. If funding decisions are based on these criteria, then they are distortive. If not, then they are distracting. That is not to say that these criteria are without merit. On the contrary, K–12 education is vitally important and multidisciplinary and multi-university collaboration can be extremely productive. But if the goal is to fund basic research, the process should not be distorted with a bias toward other considerations.

THE POWER OF PREVAILING MINDSET AND POLITICS

The power of politics, beyond biasing the selection of research topics, can also affect the dissemination of research. In a prior age, a typical example of politics would be local and limited. Prominent members of a field might resist a paradigm shift and for a time, groundbreaking research might be difficult to publish or slow to become accepted. A particularly dramatic historical example is that of the Copernican revolution. In 1543, Copernicus published his heliocentric model of the solar system, turning upside down the prevailing Ptolemaic worldview of the earth as the center of the universe. Despite the simpler model and a better explanation of observable data, it took nearly 200 years and the work of many scientists, including Galileo and Newton, before this view became widely accepted. Another famous historical example, this time from the mid-1800s, involves the pioneering work of Ignaz Semmelweis on the value of hand-washing and antiseptic procedures in medicine. Despite compelling results, his ideas were largely rejected and sometimes derided by his contemporaries during his lifetime. It took several decades and the work of Louis Pasteur, Joseph Lister, and others before the work of Semmelweis became widely accepted. The term "Semmelweis reflex" or "Semmelweis effect" is sometimes used to refer to a reflexive rejection of new knowledge that runs counter to prevailing beliefs. In the examples of Copernicus and Semmelweis, ideas that were once heresy or ridiculed became self-evident in time. One is reminded of various quotations about the stages of truth (ridicule, violent opposition, and finally self-evident acceptance). A modern example in the biological sciences might be the rejection of Stanley Prusiner's first grant proposals and his early publications on prions, only to have these be the basis of his Nobel Prize in 1997. In the present age, a pervasive political perspective can serve as a self-organizing principle that allows disparate individuals distributed across funders—such as members of private corporate funding boards, members of foundations, philanthropists, members of editorial boards, and reviewers—to advance a particular theory and exclude competing perspectives.

Climate change, and global warming in particular, is a topic of great current interest that involves a broad range of the issues discussed above and intertwines science, politics, policy, and public opinion. There is near universal agreement that CO_2 levels have increased significantly since the late nineteenth century or so. Discussions regarding increases in surface temperature depend on the time frame under consideration, and there are differing estimates of the amount of increase. There is strong, though not universal, consensus among scientists on the anthropogenic theory of climate change. There is less agreement on projections going forward and the likely consequences of global warming, and there is little agreement on what if anything should be done about it. Among the general public, there is probably a wider range of views on all of these issues. Regardless of the position one takes on them, the pressure from politics and the press is not constructive from a scientific standpoint, though it undoubtedly plays a role in furthering an agenda. In fact, such pressure is worrisome and detrimental to science; the 2009 "Climategate" controversy[5] did not help to move research forward. Consensus is most meaningful if achieved in the absence of pressure, other than the weight of scientific evidence. "Truth by consensus" is a dangerous approach to science under any circumstances—but especially when consensus is coerced.

This raises some epistemological and practical questions. When is the evidence for a position on a research issue sufficient to warrant making decisions on hiring, promotion, and tenure based on whether or not an individual agrees with this position? Is broad agreement on a particular issue evidence of actual bias or settled truth? If a researcher today proposed a geocentric model of the universe, we should not be surprised if there is "bias" against such a position. In fact, we would expect it. Nor, at this point, would we expect a paper espousing geocentrism to prompt a thorough review of all details; few would take issue at a quick rejection of such a paper. But this may not have been the case four centuries ago. On the other hand, presumably there are contemporary issues that are at a stage where the claims of Copernicus were in the late sixteenth century. That is, on some current issues, the truth isn't clear, and yet there seems to be positional pressure. For clarity on these issues, perhaps the data should speak more loudly and the politics less so, at least as far as science is concerned. Progress in research hinges on its integrity and, in the current age, pervasive bias in our institutions of research is one of the greatest threats to the integrity of science and to the role of research in promoting a thriving society.

NOTES

1. See National Science Board, "Research and Development: National Trends and International Comparisons" (ch. 4), *Science and Engineering Indicators 2014*, table 4-3, p. 4-14, nsf.gov/statistics/seind14/content/chapter-4/chapter-4.pdf.
2. See National Science Foundation, *Higher Education Research and Development Survey: Fiscal Year 2012*, table 1, "Higher Education R&D Expenditures, by Source of Funds and R&D Field: FYs 1953–2012 (Dollars in Millions)," ncsesdata.nsf.gov/herd/2012/html/HERD2012_DST_01.html.
3. The traditional "deadly sins" or "capital vices" are wrath, greed, sloth, pride, lust, envy, and gluttony.
4. See American Cancer Society website, cancer.org/cancer/breastcancer/detailedguide/breast-cancer-key-statistics and cancer.org/cancer/lungcancer-non-smallcell/detailed-guide/non-small-cell-lung-cancer-key-statistics (accessed August 8, 2014).
5. By way of explanation, see Andrew C. Revkim, "Hacked E-Mail Is New Fodder for Climate Dispute," *New York Times* (November 20, 2009), www.nytimes.com/2009/11/21/science/earth/21climate.html?_r=0.

11

Economic Sustainability

Michael D. Bordo and Harold James

Today, in the aftermath of what was the most severe financial crisis since the Great Depression, there is a great deal of uncertainty about the proper framework for economic policymaking, and about the appropriate relationship between fiscal-, monetary-, and financial-policy tools available to government. The purpose of this chapter is to outline a framework for coherent thinking about the economy, its present problems, and its future directions.

Most discussions about the economy today are either narrowly focused on specific aspects or conducted at the level of general policy and economic theory. As a result, what is often missing is a "middle ground" perspective that can help us think about the economy in a way that is practical and not excessively theoretical but also not overly focused on day-to-day issues and debates. We aim here for such a discussion.

THE ECONOMIC CHALLENGE

The aftermath of the financial crisis, now often called the Great Recession, has raised many questions about policy responses to the crisis but also about larger and fundamental issues concerning the role of the economy in a well-developed and healthy society. In particular, it has produced a debate in many countries about fiscal policy, the sustainability of deficits and debt, and the use of inflationary monetary policy as a way of reducing dangerously high levels of both government and private-sector indebtedness.

As in the case of monetary- or trade-policy reform, action will only come when there is a widespread and deep recognition that something is really broken. We have now reached that point: a crisis. To use the original medical sense of the term, this is the moment when the disease is either cured or it moves on to a termination fatal for the patient.

LEARNING FROM CRISES

Learning is partly about analyzing what went wrong and partly about finding solutions. Collectively, we have done well on the first part but poorly on the second. There is actually much conventional agreement about the causes of the post–2007 financial crisis. Most explanations of the problem rely on some combination of the following five sources of instability.

First, precipitants of the crisis included peculiarities of the U.S. real-estate market, government incentives for increased house ownership, and imprudent lending by financial institutions.

Second, wrong incentives within financial institutions led to the assumption of excessive risk. Internally, bankers had enormous potential to benefit from risky moves but were insulated from the costs of failure. Compensation packages may also have contributed to excessive risk-taking. For institutions as a whole, this was not seen as a problem, because the whole institution was protected by the logic of "too big to fail." The public sector then had to absorb the contingent liabilities built up in the financial sector.

Third, global imbalances, with long-term current account surpluses in some countries (such as China and other rapidly growing Asian economies and Gulf oil producers) allowed the long-term financing of deficits in others (the United Kingdom, Australia, Spain, Ireland, and above all, the United States). This so-called savings glut led to cheap money.

Fourth, excessively loose monetary policies by many of the world's central banks, especially the United States Federal Reserve, significantly increased the amount of cheap money circulating in the world's economies, thereby fueling a number of bubbles, such as the United States' housing bubble.

Finally, once the crisis erupted, the fiscal consequences of major banking problems led to problems of debt unsustainability. Unsustainable public debt in turn has the capacity to destabilize the banking sector.

None of these issues really have been solved. Real estate and other asset bubbles are beginning to appear again. That all these problems are still with us is an amazing feature of the world today—and a terrible indictment of current ability to learn.

Though there is some discussion of financial-sector reform, with a gradual consensus building around sliding[1] or incremental capital-adequacy rules, many systemically important banks became bigger rather than smaller as a result of the crisis.

Global imbalances[2] were immediately reduced in the course of the initial crisis, with the United States adjusting its deficit relatively rapidly, but they are emerging again.

The world's major industrial economies are maintaining very low interest rates. Before 2007, such policy was seen as at worst a mistake, but now it is interpreted as a malign strategy. There is a widespread suspicion that the United States is deliberately following a strategy of currency depreciation (or "currency wars" in the phrase of Brazil's finance minister, Guido Mantega). The answers suggested as an appropriate response rely on the application of some variant of capital controls, yet there is a great deal of evidence that capital controls have been destructive and counterproductive in the past. Their widespread adoption now would put at risk the continued development of an integrated international economy, in which capital can flow to productive uses.

Measured inequality, which was rising in the growth period before the financial crisis, has increased at an even faster rate since the outbreak of the crisis. And it looks as if the anticrisis measures that are so often lauded as having prevented a Great Depression have actually intensified the pressures resulting from globalization that contribute to the new inequality. Nonconventional monetary policies fueled an asset boom, with share prices soaring and property prices in global centers such as New York, London, Paris, Rio, and Shanghai squeezing out domestic purchasers. The wealthy did very well. Meanwhile, the middle classes were squeezed by nominal interest rates that were near zero—and thus in real terms, allowing for inflation, actually negative. Working-class incomes were hit by the rising competition for jobs as well as by global competition.

We do not know how to handle the fiscal issues posed by the financial crisis. Doubts about the sustainability of government debt produce sudden surges of interest rates, as risk premiums rise dramatically with perceptions of the likelihood of default. Such rises do not take place in a linear way but occur with great suddenness.

For countries on the brink, a perverse logic follows. Government debt service had in general become easier because of the low-interest-rate environment. But hints of new fiscal imprudence or of the abandonment of plans for long-term debt consolidation and reduction would drive up borrowing costs dramatically. In those circumstances, the additional costs of debt service easily outweigh the effect that might result from some measure of fiscal relaxation.

Fiscal uncertainty in consequence is affecting all major industrial countries and producing political paralysis.

So while we understand quite well what may have produced the financial crisis, we are pretty helpless when attempting to actually draw useable lessons.

From a longer historical perspective, the paralysis may not be surprising. It took a good deal of time to learn what we all now take to be the lessons of the interwar Great Depression. It was only thirty years later, in the 1960s, that fiscal Keynesianism was widely accepted. It was also only in the 1960s that Milton Friedman clearly formulated the monetary lessons of the Great Depression.

In trade policy, a much quicker lesson was drawn. In the Great Depression, a spiral of trade-protection measures was used to combat monetary deflation. What political process produced the reaction? The trade quotas and tariff restrictions came about as a result of logrolling[3] in the legislature as well as a general demand for political action. A political-science analysis of the process, by Elmer E. Schattschneider, was influential in transferring responsibility for trade measures from the U.S. Congress to the president.[4]

The modern equivalent to that learning about trade policy would be to think about mechanisms for the long-term improvement of fiscal policymaking. In particular, it would be helpful to devise a mechanism to identify potential risks to fiscal stability (such as those implied by an overextended banking and financial system). Moreover, there is a need to limit legislative pressure (logrolling) for additional spending on projects that are a local priority but whose importance ought to be measured up against overall needs and means.

The constructive (and relatively quick) response to the Great Depression in trade policy did not pay off immediately. But in the long run, it produced a much better policy environment. This is the moment to make an analogous move to improve the political process that produces fiscal policy. That exercise requires thinking about the appropriate aims of fiscal policy.

SOME FUNDAMENTALS

The proper and efficient working of an economy allows for the basic conditions necessary for the existence, interaction, and well-being of human beings: clean water, adequate food, housing, and means of communication. It is also the basis for more creative forms of expression and for innovations that allow a realization of more opportunities for people. People are not isolated islands but thrive only in society. Economic activity is a necessary part of this normal functioning.

Positive institutional and economic development occurs as a result of innovations that are socially beneficial but also produce benefits to the innovators. In a society that discourages entrepreneurship, all individuals find their room for action and for self-improvement limited and reduced.

Markets exist as a forum for the articulation of collective choices. They transmit indications about individual wishes, inclinations, and expectations about the future. But through the aggregation of individual choices, markets also produce signals that *guide* the actions and decisions of individuals (what to buy, what to produce, what to invest in for future production) through the price mechanism.

Distortions to the market, such as a manipulation of prices by an authority or powerful players in the market, generate wrong signals, so that too much or too little of a product is consumed, bought, produced, or planned for future production. Replacing a market by a central notion of what people could or should be expected to want not only produces efficiency losses. It can only be achieved at the expense of fundamental aspects of human liberty and human initiative. Seeking to replace the market thus carries a high cost by lowering the scope for realizing human potential.

Choices are articulated within a context; a network of institutions structures the lives and interactions of individuals: the family, local civic communities, religious communities, associations, and enterprises. These all have their own dynamics and make important contributions, but their interactions are regulated by an overall legal framework. It is desirable that they should have as much space as possible—within the bounds of the law—to resolve conflicts and to build the consensus that makes society viable.

Governments can solve some collective-action problems that arise from specific market failures, when some particular conduct produces costs or disadvantages for others. They provide collective goods—in particular, internal and external security and basic infrastructure. The institutions that make free exchange possible—the definition and enforcement of property rights, the arbitration of disputes, and the rule of law in general—depend on government. Governments thus have a fundamental and indispensable role to play in ensuring the proper, competitive, and free functioning of markets.

This role demands as a prerequisite sustainability, and that depends on perceptions of the legitimacy and fairness of the social order as well as sound fiscal policy. There is a legitimate demand that fiscal policy offer a safety net when other—better—mechanisms that should produce social cohesion and solidarity (such as greater levels of entrepreneurship and raised skill levels) for some reason are not effective. Indeed failure to provide a safety net can produce bad and destabilizing consequences as well as dramatic market failures. Sound fiscal policy is also necessary. One of the contributing causes of the financial crisis lay in the perception that widespread access to credit and borrowing could offer a compensation for poor wage growth and falling real incomes. The credit boom—one that was ultimately unsustainable—was thus a compensation for inadequate productivity growth, both for people (above all in the United States) and indeed for whole countries (above all in Mediterranean Europe), as well as a nontransparent mechanism to advance social-policy aims. It was a nongovernment way to effect a large social transfer.[5]

Sustainability is also threatened by rapid changes of policy or by policy inconsistency. Some commentators identify a fundamental "economic policy problem."

Democratic societies find credible commitment to a long-term policy almost impossible, even if there is a broad consensus that such a long-term orientation would be desirable. Political scientists show that there are no really adequate mechanisms to reward current majorities for future economic performance that comes at a current cost and where the payoffs lie several electoral terms in the future. Some even suggest that one of the reasons that fiscal reform and consolidation may work better in the United Kingdom than in the United States is that a five-year electoral cycle gives a longer horizon than a four-year one that is punctuated by midterm elections. The difficulties lie in part in the fact that present pain and future gain have often been misused as political slogans (perhaps most dramatically in Stalinist and Soviet claims about the benefits of forced industrialization), and there is therefore a great deal of public cynicism about them. But in part, there is only a poor and limited understanding about the relationship between present policy and future economic outcomes. A great deal of argument consequently occurs about notions of a "free lunch," made most often in the case of monetary policy where low interest rates are supposed to deliver greater growth, employment, and prosperity levels.

Considerations about long-term sustainability and justice thus require an approach that takes into account fundamental considerations about the proper scope of government.

THE SCOPE OF GOVERNMENT

Dealing with market failures might appear to be a particularly urgent function of government in situations where many of the preconditions that might lead to the development of efficient markets are absent. As more sophisticated private-sector institutions develop and society becomes more complex, the necessary scope for government might be expected to be reduced. In Ancient Rome, for instance, ensuring the supply of grain to the city was a major task of government; now we think that markets can supply food needs rather effectively and efficiently. Most twentieth-century governments organized telecommunications services; now we like competitive provision by private suppliers. In practice, however, governments have become more and more active and also more and more complex.

Government action is constantly expanded, because there is a sense that existing control provisions are inadequate and should consequently be extended. When government starts to be active in a particular field of endeavor, that action requires new legal provisions. The creation of such a framework by itself often means that it is more difficult for the private sector to be active in the same area, and it establishes an assumption that government has a proper role here. Such calculations contribute to the ratchet effect[6] that characterizes a great deal of modern government activity.

One particular example has been frequently highlighted in recent discussions. Distortions of the housing market played a prominent part in the financial crisis. An increased share of mortgage lending came from government-sponsored enterprises, notably Fannie Mae and Freddie Mac. (That share fell slightly in the Great Recession but has since increased again.) The Community Reinvestment Act required private lenders to expand their lending to borrowers below the median income levels in the areas in which they were active. There were also more general distortions that followed from the particular fiscal treatment of favored activities, in particular, house purchase through mortgage tax relief. Tax calculations prompted a higher level of engagement in housing than would otherwise have been undertaken. The result of the extension of government subsidies and regulations produced a complex and large-scale system of distorted incentives that affected and altered market behavior.

One of the features of complex tax deductions is that they create an increasing demand both for complexity and for access to special treatment. This is a powerful argument against the often-made attempt to use tax policy to promote particular kinds of activity. A simplified tax system would reduce the extent of lobbying to produce new distortions.

Furthermore, public programs establish powerful and politically influential coalitions and lobby groups. The operation of legislative assemblies in framing budgetary laws often generates the inclusion of additional spending authority that initially seems of minimal overall cost to the society at large but of great benefit to individual legislators and their constituents. The building up of such authorizations of expenditure in the end may, however, become very costly when all are aggregated together. There is an analogy between the buildup of fiscal claims and the way congressional discussion of trade policy in the interwar years led to the addition of a multitude of small measures of protection that in the aggregate became costly and destructive.[7]

Sometimes government may spend rather aimlessly, simply in the hope of achieving an aggregate stimulus that may promise a political payoff. It is hard to see how this kind of spending is constructive. In the words of a leaked 2006 UK cabinet memorandum, "We've spent all this money, but what have we got for it?"[8]

Finally, many programs are established with an initially modest cost but later expand, perhaps as the result of the availability of new technology (for instance, in medical provision) or because of the expansion of recipient categories because of demographic change (as most notably, in Social Security provision). Both developments mean the opening up of large funding gaps. The impact and the significance of such a process go well beyond merely fiscal considerations. The expansion, for instance, of Supplemental Security Income payments for mental disability has led to parents of children with mental disabilities looking for pharmaceutical solutions that may be harmful or redundant as a way of increasing income.[9]

There is in general a tendency inherent in the operation of many legislatures to accept a buildup of expenditure that cannot be financed in the longer term and thus imposes high costs and limits on the actions and choices of subsequent generations. While it is clear that there are highly exceptional circumstances in which unanticipated economic or financial shocks may demand a temporary increase in the extent of government activity in order to stabilize both economic activity and economic expectations—and that such an increase may be expected to raise government debt—the long-term stabilization of expectations also requires that such increases in expenditure need to be funded. These are circumstances in which appropriate government action may contribute to the building of confidence and trust. Confidence and trust are important factors in generating successful economic outcomes; their absence leads to suboptimal equilibria. In the long term, government debt that increases at a faster rate than the overall growth of the economy will eventually become unsustainable and will erode confidence and sap trust.

Different societies will choose different levels of government activity. It is possible to identify some societies (mostly lower-income countries) in which the small size of government leaves basic tasks unprovided; there is inadequate security, enforcement of law, and/or infrastructure. People are required to provide privately for their own security and are constantly mistrustful of others. The absence of an effective state makes it impossible, then, for anything that we might identify as society to exist.

It is also possible to identify societies where the size of government has become so large as to crowd out the room for individual action and initiative. In Sweden in the 1970s and 1980s, the average marginal tax rate was close to 90 percent, and the share of government in GDP was close to 60 percent. This was unsustainable. A government that is too big may well undermine society just as surely as a government that is too small. But whatever the size of government society chooses, its activities should be transparent to minimize distortions.

The creation of new tasks for government in response to a buildup of political lobbying often means that some of the most basic tasks of government are left undone. For instance, complex welfare systems exist alongside inadequate or antiquated infrastructure. Some economists have tried to identify a maximum sustainable level of government activity as 30 percent of GDP, but such precision is quite hard to justify on the basis of general principles.[10] For some societies, higher rates may be sustained for long periods of time if they are adequately funded; other societies would find even a 30-percent level corrosive. The historic concerns of American society in limiting government activism may mean that a preference for a lower level fits most easily with U.S. political traditions.

Markets have been distorted more frequently by overoptimistic claims about the effectiveness of government than by inadequate expectations. Such claims build up anticipation of positive outcomes, and when they prove too ambitious, the failure is blamed on the partiality or the inadequate extent of government action. There is in consequence an even more vocal call for government action. The state's overextension, then, tends constantly to excite larger demands for state altering of the market process. The distrust of government that is produced by overambitious or overextensive demands for state action would also harm markets by leading to a neglect of investment in those collective goods needed to support market activity. To avoid the damaging effects of excessive expectations for government action, a clear delimitation of the appropriate area for and extent of state activity is required.

THE SCOPE OF MONETARY POLICY

Money plays a special role in economic life, as it is a store of value and a unit of account. It developed as a result of both private and public law, of private contracts and of the requirement to pay taxes in a particular unit. Money could be issued by the state because of a government's ability to define the unit of account in which taxes should be paid. In the *Nicomachean Ethics*, Aristotle explained that money owes its name to its property of not existing by nature but as a product of convention or law.[11] Greek coins usually carried depictions of gods and goddesses, but the Romans changed the practice and put their (presumed divine) emperors on their coins. In the New Testament, Christ famously answers a question about obedience to civil authorities by examining a coin and telling the Pharisees, "Render unto Caesar what is Caesar's."[12] Alternately, it is possible to conceive of money arising out of conventional agreements about the exchange of goods, between parties who are not necessarily in the same political unit. Aristotle in *Politics* set out a theory of money as arising out of exchange, a theory that seems at odds with the account in the *Nicomachean Ethics*.[13] Aristotle is thus cited by both traditions. Both traditions also make the important points that markets are distorted by a fluctuating unit of account and that political orders lose their legitimacy as monetary values oscillate.

Markets have been distorted by inappropriate price signals following from mistaken monetary policy. A rising general level of prices (inflation) increases incentives to consume and spend now while penalizing longer-term investments in the future. Inflations of the kind that occurred in the 1970s distort market signals and have particularly destructive effects in financial markets, because they destroy the ability to make long-term calculations. A highly inflationary environment such as occurred in Germany in the 1920s or more recently in Zimbabwe encourages living for the moment, without a thought of future activity and future generations; this ultimately kills economic activity. Unanticipated inflation redistributes income and wealth from creditors to debtors. The belief that it is possible to use politics to affect the monetary process and hence also the distribution of resources increases the stakes in political conflicts and generally produces political instability.

But even apparently noninflationary monetary growth can produce the same sort of effect. In the aftermath of the crisis, the adoption of nonconventional monetary strategies has created a problem of legitimacy. Quantitative easing (QE) has not as yet substantially affected consumer price levels or headline inflation, but it has generated substantial increases in asset prices. The result has been an increase in measured wealth inequality and a challenge to the ideals and principles of justice.

There is a symmetry between the operation of inflations and deflations. If imperfectly anticipated, inflations are a tax on creditors and a subsidy to debtors. Unanticipated *de*flations subsidize creditors and tax debtors. Both have redistributive consequences, and both increase to an unsustainable point the pressures on the political process (groups try to use the levers of policy to achieve their own specific and partial advantages at the cost of other groups).

A falling general level of prices (deflation) increases debt burdens and acts as a constraint on business activity; this explains the malaise of many economies in the 1930s. Deflation pushes businesses and individuals into bankruptcy, makes credit inaccessible, and blocks the realization of new and innovative possibilities. The effects of deflation are especially severe if the deflation is unanticipated and if wages and prices are inflexible. Unanticipated deflations have major redistributive consequences, in which debtors are highly burdened and creditors claim more assets. Rigid prices and wages produce an underutilization of resources. In a highly deflationary environment, few potential entrepreneurs are willing or able to do anything; they wait for a better future. With the resulting underactivity, however, the possibilities of a better future are also diminished. In the Great Depression of the 1930s, monetary-policy mismanagement (leading to deflation) produced bank panics and financial-sector instability. There is a powerful tradition among prominent economic analysts that suggests that for the United States and some other countries, the bank problems were the consequence of gold-standard-induced price deflation.[14]

Severe deflations also lead to a politicization of economic decision-making and to greater political instability—as do severe inflations. Here there is a symmetry in effect between monetary disorders, though in the twentieth century, inflationary problems generally proved to be more common than deflationary ones.[15]

A long-term framework for economic and social sustainability—and for the transmission of chances and opportunities from one generation to the next—thus depends on a basic commitment to monetary stability. An independent central bank bound by rules to limit discretionary power provides a credible nominal anchor, stabilizes expectations, and also may serve as a lender of last resort.

THE SCOPE OF THE FINANCIAL SECTOR

In the course of the recent financial crisis, fiscal and monetary policies have both been caught up in the need to undertake urgent action to stabilize the financial sector. Central-bank balance sheets have expanded, and there has been an explosion of public debt.

Before 2008, there was a general consensus that central banks were primarily concerned with price stability and monetary policy. However, the financial crisis has brought an involvement of central banks in financial-sector stability issues and in issues of credit allocation and credit policy. These are fundamentally fiscal issues, and the involvement of central banks in distributive policy gives rise to a demand for greater political control of central banks. In addition, governments intervened directly in order to recapitalize financial institutions threatened by failure. The aftermath of the threat of failure of giant financial institutions has thus given a powerful shock to the economy that undermines sustainable expectations about both fiscal and monetary policies.

Financial-sector instability can pose a serious threat to normal economic activity, and the demand for action to tackle the problem is legitimate and urgent. Markets involve a constant trading of claims. Some (like equity) are contingent on economic performance and share in the chances and risks of profit and loss from productive activity. Other claims (like credit or bonds) are not associated with exposure to profit or loss and depend only on the solvency (ability to pay the debt) or insolvency of the borrower. An excessive growth of debt claims (which can alternately be described as a credit bubble or a debt bubble) raises the chances of large-scale (rather than individual) insolvency. The risk of such a danger of related financial collapse makes financial crises dangerous and complicates normal productive activity. A buildup of high amounts of debt can create a pyramid of vulnerability, in which the effects of one particular default have wide-reaching and inherently unpredictable consequences.[16]

Some market distortions have followed not directly from the actions of government but from the way in which businesses have structured themselves. Flaws in corporate governance may be a consequence of wrong overall incentive structures, though they may also reflect particular developments in the business community. Too often individuals within enterprises and in management have been encouraged to promote their own advantages at the expense of the institutions within which they are operating. The result is that some businesses have focused too much on short-term profitability (often as expressed in the share price) rather than longer-term sustainability and innovation.

Distortions may often result from incentives springing out of public policy. Some businesses have become large and complex less as a response to market conditions than as a result of calculations that a big business will be seen as so indispensable to the general welfare that it needs to be rescued by government in the case of self-generated failures or unanticipated shocks. This has been a problem of the financial industry, but it is not confined to financial services. Conspicuous examples of other large bailouts are those of General Motors and Chrysler. The result is that the balance of risk and reward that applies to small business units does not seem to apply to larger and more powerful units, which can in consequence play for short-term gains while ignoring the possibility of long-term failure. After all, the reasoning goes, public authorities would intervene to help in the case of disaster, because of a belief that these businesses are so central to the economy that they ought not be allowed to fail. Financial institutions took inappropriate levels of risk, then, because they saw that they would benefit from any gains while being able to spread losses to government and the taxpayer. The potential extent of damage that a financial-sector collapse would cause thus made for a greater willingness to take risks that would make collapse more likely. The idea of "too big to fail" poses a fundamental threat to a sustainable balance of economic policy and to fiscal and monetary stability.

INTERACTIONS

For the purpose of policy design, fiscal-, monetary-, and financial-sector policy are best viewed as having separate objectives—long-term sustainability of public accounts, monetary stability, and financial-sector stability—and separate means of achieving those objectives: a responsible fiscal authority, a correctly operating central bank, and a framework for financial activity that limits the danger of financial shocks.

But in practice, there are many potential and potentially dangerous interactions among the elements of policy: the buildup of public debt increases the appeal of inflation as a way of reducing that debt; inflation distorts the tax system through bracket creep, as progressive tax systems are not adjusted for inflation; price instability can destabilize the financial sector; and loose monetary policy can generate asset booms. In the past, notably in the post–World War II period, higher levels of government debt have produced a dangerous sentiment that inflation is the most politically convenient way of reducing public and private debt. That temptation will be acute again in the wake of the financial crisis. Bursting asset bubbles and financial-sector distress have been associated with increased demands for state rescues and interventions. Sound rules to maintain fiscal balance, monetary stability, and incentive-compatible financial oversight should minimize these spillovers.

CONSEQUENCES

The following consequences may be derived from these fundamental observations:

1. There is a need for sustainable long-term fiscal guidelines or rules that hold the size of government stable and limited, exclude a long-term increase in government debt, and limit government deficits over the course of a business cycle. Such guidelines do not exclude the possibility of short-term responses to unanticipated events (such as severe recessions and natural disasters), but require that emergency responses cannot be made into a permanent mechanism.
2. It is desirable to make an explicit, visible, and transparent link between public consumption of goods such as social services and the tax revenues needed to pay for such goods.
3. In some circumstances, government may need to borrow in order to undertake long-term public-investment projects, and such investments need to be carefully priced and funded so that the general level of return is proportionate to the investment undertaken. Governments may also need to borrow to finance wars by tax smoothing, i.e., borrowing during the war (when taxation of labor income would reduce work effort at the time of greatest need) and retiring the debt after the war by raising taxes.
4. There is a need to avoid particular distortions of the tax system that act as encouragement to hold individual, corporate, and public debt rather than equity participations. The special tax treatment of corporate debt, household mortgage debt, or municipal debt encourages the unsustainable growth of debt. Tax simplification could aim at treating profits, dividends, and interest in an equal way.
5. There is a need to think of institutional arrangements that might better provide for long-term sustainability and provide a general (rather than a partial or class-based) vision of the country's interests. Councils of nonpolitical experts might have a greater role in assessing the extent of future

public liabilities (which are often masked in normal budgetary procedures) in defining what truly constitute public goods, and in ascertaining long-term equity with regard to future as well as present generations.
6. There is a need to address the question of how the Federal Reserve can be insulated from partisan pressures. This requires an institutional commitment to a credible means of ensuring monetary stability. This is best achieved by central banks, whose independence is ensured by strong, legal provisions and whose goals include a clear and overarching commitment to overall price stability, manifested in a sustainable price level or inflation target over the medium term. A credible mechanism for ensuring that the long-term inflation (price level) target is met would mean that short-term responses to temporary shocks would not produce market expectations that undermine the effectiveness of the short-term response. In an earlier era, and at a lower level of financial development, tying the value of the currency to a commodity such as gold was capable of achieving these goals in advanced countries. But the monetary stability provided by a rule-based approach in the age of fiat money (money that derives its value from authority rather than from any intrinsic value) is considered by many economists and monetary theorists to be superior to that of the nineteenth-century gold standard.[17] Today the greater complexity of modern economies and financial markets generates a need for mechanisms in a fiat-money regime that can be confidently expected to produce similar stable outcomes. Hence the need to ensure a viable governance structure.
7. In the sphere of monetary policy, expectations are anchored by a credible and explicit inflation target, which in general is not set by the central bank itself but by the political authority. The desired rate of inflation is a political objective or choice; it is up to the central bank how to achieve it.
8. The "too big to fail" issue can be tackled with legal measures to ensure the operation of effective competition and the removal of barriers to entry, as well as with a regulatory requirement to contemplate how individual parts of the enterprise can become independent in the event of an overall corporate failure. The problem of the excessive growth of particular financial institutions is not appropriately dealt with by arbitrary legislation that limits size, which could simply generate a replication of the phenomenon among a larger number of cloned enterprises.

NOTES

1. "Sliding" involves higher capital ratios for firms with large capitalization than for smaller firms.

2. Here we mean current account deficits in some countries (notably the United States, the United Kingdom, Ireland, and Spain) and large surpluses in others (notably China but also many Asian states, Gulf states, and Germany).
3. Logrolling is the process through which one congressman gets a particular tariff for his area (say, on rope-making equipment, in which his area specializes). No one else will support that by itself, because it makes rope more expensive, but if the representative from the next area gets a tariff on fishing rods and the next one on bicycle pumps and so on, there will be general support. The same process obviously applies to particular appropriations.
4. See Elmer E. Schattschneider, *Politics, Pressures and the Tariff: A Study of Free Private Enterprise in Pressure Politics, as Shown in the 1929–1930 Revision of the Tariff* (New York: Prentice-Hall, 1935).
5. See on this Raghuram G. Rajan, *Fault Lines: How Hidden Fractures Still Threaten the World Economy* (Princeton, NJ: Princeton University Press, 2010).
6. By ratchet effect, we mean the metaphor that once government has intruded upon a sector, the ratchet has been moved to the next notch and can't easily be turned back.
7. See Douglas A. Irwin, *Peddling Protectionism: Smoot-Hawley and the Great Depression* (Princeton, NJ: Princeton University Press, 2011).
8. See Robert Winnett, James Kirkup, and Holly Watt, "Labour Spending: Gordon Brown and Ed Balls Ignored Warnings and Wasted Billions," *Telegraph* (June 10, 2011). Accessed at www.telegraph.co.uk.
9. See David H. Autor and Mark G. Duggan, "The Growth in the Social Security Disability Rolls: A Fiscal Crisis Unfolding," *Journal of Economic Perspectives* 20 (Summer 2006): 71–96.
10. See Vito Tanzi and Ludger Schuknecht, *Public Spending in the 20th Century: A Global Perspective* (Cambridge, England: Cambridge University Press, 2000).
11. See book 5, ch. 5: "Money has become by convention a sort of representative of demand; and this is why it has the name 'money' (*nomisma*)—because it exists not by nature but by law (*nomos*) and it is in our power to change it and make it useless."
12. Matthew 22: 21.
13. See Curzio Giannini, *The Age of Central Banks* (Cheltenham, England: Edward Elgar, 2011); Carl Menger, *Grundsätze Der Volkswirthschaftslehre* (Wien, Austria: W. Braumüller, 1871).
14. See Milton Friedman and Anna Jacobsen Schwartz, *A Monetary History of the United States, 1867–1960* (Princeton, NJ: Princeton University Press, 1963); Michael D. Bordo, Ehsan U. Choudhri, and Anna J. Schwartz, "Could Stable Money Have Averted the Great Contraction?" *Economic Inquiry* 33 (July 1995): 484–505; Ben Bernanke and Harold James, "The Gold Standard, Deflation, and Financial Crisis in the Great Depression: An International Comparison," pp. 33–68 in R. Glenn Hubbard, ed., *Financial Markets and Financial Crises* (Chicago, IL: University of Chicago Press for the National Bureau of Economic Research, 1991).
15. However, we need to distinguish between good (productivity driven) and bad deflation (collapsing aggregate demand). The Great Depression of the 1930s was an example of a bad deflation; the low deflation and significant growth in the United States in the

1870s and 1880s is an example of good deflation. See Michael Bordo and Andrew Filardo, "Deflation and Monetary Policy in a Historical Perspective: Remembering the Past or Being Condemned to Repeat It?" *Economic Policy* 20 (October 2005): 799–844. In addition, expected deflation equal to the real interest rate produces the "optimum quantity of money" and the most efficient allocation of resources in a money economy. See Chapter 1 in Milton Friedman, *The Optimum Quantity of Money and Other Essays* (Chicago, IL: Aldine, 1969).

16. See Carmen M. Reinhart and Kenneth S. Rogoff, *This Time Is Different: Eight Centuries of Financial Folly* (Princeton, NJ: Princeton University Press, 2009).

17. For instance, see Bennett McCallum, "Monetary Standards and the U.S. Constitution," Shadow Open Market Committee (March 28, 2011), economics21.org/files/pdfs/in-depth-research/mccallum-spring-11.pdf; Luca Benati, "Long Run Evidence on Money Growth and Inflation," European Central Bank, Working Paper Series 1027 (March 2009).

12

Republican Prudence: The Founders' Foreign-Policy School and Its Enduring Legacy

Paul O. Carrese and Michael Doran

Should the president of the United States order military action against states such as Syria to enforce a century of international law prohibiting the use of chemical weapons in war—despite the war-weariness of the American public and its Congress? This is only one of the thorny foreign-policy questions that the United States, and the principles for which it stands, faces in our day. Is a military strike the best way, or any way, to prevent Iran from acquiring nuclear-tipped missiles? How can the United States prevent North Korea from engaging in nuclear blackmail? As American troops withdraw from Afghanistan, will the country fall into the hands of the Taliban again, or of al-Qaeda? Are drone attacks a wise way to destroy or degrade the capacities of terror networks? Should the United States ally itself with dictators who serve its material interests or who represent a lesser evil in thwarting a more dangerous foe?

None of these international problems, or others we could list, admit of simple answers. Some are interconnected. Their difficulty is increased by the fact that the world has changed radically since the end of the Cold War. Alliances that the United States established after World War II are no longer particularly well-suited to the most serious problems that we face, or even to sustaining the international order we built together. Yet significantly altering those alliances or building new ones hardly seems possible. China and Russia are resurgent as great powers (the former after several centuries of relative weakness), but they are neither liberal nor republican. Moreover, America as a constitutional republic was founded in war but has been devoted to peaceful aims of protecting and enjoying natural rights, which largely has meant rejecting war or militarism (at least until recently). Today's bewildering complexity has revived an American instinct to turn away from international affairs as of secondary importance or as an arena from which we should hold ourselves aloof, in the exceptionalist belief that we embody higher standards of justice and progress.

In short, we are living through an awkward period. The liberal democracies won the Cold War, but this brought no reprieve from America's global interests and burdens. We know that something new and different is afoot, but we are not sure what it will be, and we lack a national consensus on how to shape it. Whom should we consult for commonsense guidance?

THE INADEQUACY OF OFF-THE-SHELF ANSWERS

Unfortunately, the established schools of thought regarding foreign policy are as outmoded as our alliances, and in many ways are themselves Cold War relics. On university campuses, two foreign-policy schools dominate: realism and liberal internationalism. Realists tell us to pursue the national interest by first considering calculations of relative power among states, with limited if any concern for moral values. Liberal internationalism, by contrast, emphasizes the importance of moral principles and international law and thus of working through global institutions, the United Nations especially. As different as the two schools are, they both hold one attitude in common: foreign policy as largely the domain of experts, based on universal principles that experts understand even if they disagree about what those principles are. Each school, in its own way, therefore regards the influence of domestic politics on foreign policy as an unwelcome intrusion. Neither is concerned with distinctively American principles when considering U.S. foreign-policy options and behaviors. The realist concern with power and interests speaks to a people from anywhere, since all states supposedly think alike about international affairs (despite plentiful evidence that they don't). The liberal internationalist emphasis on ideals and international law speaks to a people from nowhere, since all thinking should rise above the specific places, interests, and histories of any given people (despite plentiful evidence that it doesn't, and sound theoretical doubt that it ever could do so in human affairs).

This universal or theoretical attitude alone ensures that such schools will have only limited influence on flesh-and-blood American leaders, for whom it is axiomatic that a successful foreign policy must pass the test of the ballot box, or consent of the governed, as guided by fundamental and enduring American principles. Precisely because American principles aspire to a kind of universal status—invoking basic rights of individuals and states that at a minimum are accessible to all reasonable peoples everywhere—a proper attention to these principles need not forsake justice for an exclusive focus on national interest.

Off campus, two additional schools of thought are worthy of note. The first of these is neoconservatism, which has only a small following in the professoriate but which is deeply influential in the Republican Party. At the heart of the neoconservative perspective is a belief in American exceptionalism—the conviction that the United States has a uniquely beneficial role to play in the world. Among the benefits that it offers is the spread of liberal democracy, the best form of government. George W. Bush's decision to make democracy promotion a mainstay of Middle Eastern strategy owed much to the influence of neoconservatism, which is currently in retreat. In the past decade, the United States has supported the removal of four Arab dictators: Saddam Hussein (Iraq), Hosni Mubarak (Egypt), Zine El Abidine Ben Ali (Tunisia), and Muammar Qadhafi (Libya). The ensuing turmoil has left the American people wary of deep engagement in Middle Eastern politics. Combined with the long war in Afghanistan to build some form of constitutional government after deposing the Taliban in November 2001, it also has left many American leaders and citizens reticent about nation-building or democracy promotion as a prominent element of U.S. foreign policy.

The decline of neoconservatism has certainly benefited the realists, but it also has opened up a space for what might be called neo-isolationism, which at this stage is more a mood than a fully articulated school of thought. In the 2012 presidential election, Representative Ron Paul expressed this mood more explicitly than any other candidate, but it is by no means confined to the libertarians or, for that matter, to the political right. His son, Rand Paul, now serves in the U.S. Senate and has given new energy to such ideas. His voice is joined by some on the political left who believe America largely has been a force for ill in world affairs in the past century. Together, they seem to be converging on an inversion of an old Cold War doctrine: American *self*-containment as the best path for America (and everyone else). Only time will tell how influential this impulse toward disengagement will prove to be. But the fact that the two Pauls enjoy particularly strong support among young people suggests that it may be a significant voice in foreign affairs for years to come, no less so, perhaps, than the post–World War I isolationist pulse, which lasted over two decades.

While each of these schools has its attractions, all have obvious defects. Realism enjoins us to pursue our interests in a pragmatic fashion. While this sounds commonsensical, the school offers few clear principles about how to define interests, particularly for a rule-setting, order-guarding great power with expansive and diverse interests like the United States. "Self-preservation," for example, doesn't clarify whether to focus on short-term calculations at the expense of long-term prevention as the best means. Moreover, in a liberal democracy, realism's rejection of values-based policy will inevitably meet with strong opposition. Indeed, America has thought of itself as exceptional since its founding in the eighteenth century, and not only for separating itself from the great-power wars of Europe. Alexander Hamilton voiced the first arguments for an American navy that could be a world power, precisely in order to liberate the Americas from European powers and thus "vindicate the honor of the human race," in *The Federalist*, no. 11 (1787)—three decades before the Monroe Doctrine was announced.

For its part, liberal internationalism also has a political tin ear. It cannot explain persuasively why the will of the United Nations—packed as it is with unrepresentative autocrats—is superior to the will of the American people. Liberal internationalists will never convince Americans that the workings of the collective-security machinery of the United Nations will protect them better than unilateral action by their own elected Congress and president directing their own military. Moreover, both free peoples and their academic elites ought to have sober doubts about replacing public deliberation, in self-governing and sovereign states, with new norms of international law and "global governance" fashioned by supranational elites. The European Union has discovered that it cannot ignore longstanding criticisms about the "democracy deficit" inherent in its attempt to replace national political institutions and sovereignty with policy organs in Brussels that rarely seek or consider the consent of the governed. Even if such a model could work, it entails a loss of freedom and political responsibility by citizens to shape their common destiny. Only political institutions rooted in national identity permit the civic engagement required for a thriving society. This principle will not inevitably lead America into either isolationism or conflict with other sovereign peoples, as history itself proves. Three centuries of foreign policy have demonstrated that it is possible to balance the demands of a self-governing sovereignty with a commitment to peace based on the law of nations.

Unlike realism and liberal internationalism, neoconservatism does appeal to the democratic nature of the American people, but its emphasis on democracy promotion, the assumptions of which are highly questionable from a social-science perspective, looks like a recipe for endless foreign adventures. It also doesn't address the republican tradition in America that warns of the excesses and temptations of militarism. We wonder if the sound elements of this school, those which reflect longstanding principles and practices of American policy, will reappear under a new name or new guise as the weaknesses of alternative views reveal themselves under the pressures of our complex, globalized era.

Isolationism—or, to avoid offense, an inclination to disengagement and a focus on "America first"—is certainly on the rise. However, this is an era of globalization. The dark side of our world includes weapons of mass destruction, global terrorist networks, and cyberattacks that could disrupt our economy and threaten millions of lives. Those threats alone guarantee that America will have to remain deeply engaged in global affairs, given the commonsense principle that threats are best opposed or deterred by steady mitigation and a respected reputation, rather than waiting for attacks to arrive on our shores. Moreover, whether one's views incline toward retrenchment or assertive internationalism, we are, as already mentioned in passing, still the primary guarantor of the global order as defined by peaceful commerce, mutual recognition of states under international law, and prevention of great-power war and use of weapons of mass destruction. We cannot withdraw from our leading role in sustaining this free, dynamic, and predominantly peaceful global order without endangering the prosperity and peace it brings. Many realists, and the isolationists or restraintists, apparently think this global order can sustain itself and will survive an American retreat from leadership. They either trust in the magical efficacy of the balance of power (despite the somber history of those balances) or they suppose that illiberal great powers will somehow be eager to support liberal ideals (and the mutually beneficial multiple-sum security arrangements that serve our interests and principles as well as the larger aim of global peace and prosperity). Liberal internationalists have not figured out how to give American leadership the latitude it needs to enforce international law and norms rather than being bound by legalisms and ineffective institutions (including a U.N. Security Council stymied by Russia and China). The neoconservatives join these other schools in overlooking the distinctively American tradition of balancing interests with justice—and of balancing exceptionalism with obedience to international standards.

OUR PARTICULAR DANGER: THE ALLURE OF DISENTANGLEMENT

This brief survey of the major schools suggests that, as we attempt to answer the thorniest foreign-policy questions, we will not find any readymade solutions. We seem to be on our own, forging a new path in a dangerous new age. Fortunately, we have before us the example of our forebears, who also faced unprecedented challenges. We not only have the advice of the Founders but Abraham Lincoln's example of consulting that advice.

Though Lincoln's problems were more domestic than foreign, he showed how the Founders, who guided the colonies out of the British Empire and into a brave new experiment, could counsel his own time. Lincoln understood that America was the first polity in history to be deliberately founded upon ideas and that our subsequent rise to prosperity and global prominence hardly justified amnesia about our original aims. Lincoln's greatness lay in a strategy of rededication to the principles of the Founders. This included a commitment to prudence rather than rigid doctrines in navigating the ship of state toward high ideals, and a commitment to balancing military power and the higher ends it should serve. We can do the same.

One lesson for the twenty-first century to be gained from reconsidering the Founding is that today's temptation toward isolation or disengagement is nothing new. Our continent-sized republic has been blessed with natural resources and waves of immigration, making it uniquely self-sufficient and safe in comparison with all other great powers. The protection provided by geography convinced some Founding Fathers that it was possible to separate the United States from the rest of the world. The leading Founder, George Washington, was aware of this temptation and resolutely sought to guide the new republic to avoid either militarism or isolationism. This is especially true of his Farewell Address of 1796,[1] the first great statement of American foreign-policy principles.

Many pundits and academics persistently misinterpret Washington as warning against "entangling alliances" in the Address. He did no such thing. Those words are Jefferson's—from his First Inaugural Address of 1801—and they express a characteristically Jeffersonian idealism: If only we could avoid all political engagement with the great powers of the old world, and avoid a standing army and navy, we could peacefully develop in isolation while still enjoying the benefits of international commerce. By contrast, Washington warned against "permanent alliances" that would subordinate our fledgling republic to any great power; he recommended "temporary alliances" and a permanent military capability to weather the storms of international affairs. He did defend his policy of "neutrality" regarding the European wars provoked by the French Revolution but indicated that the "predominant motive" for restraint toward Europe was to "gain time" for our young nation, and new Constitution, to "mature" toward a position of "strength." Thus the Farewell hoped that America, if it followed these prudent and balanced policies, would become "a great nation." By sticking to a principled prudence, our republic could develop the "strength and consistency which is necessary to give it, humanly speaking, the command of its own fortunes."

The wisdom of Washington's more balanced view, as opposed to Jefferson's idealistic isolationism, became apparent soon enough—indeed, during Jefferson's two terms as president. In what is among the clearest of history's judgments on nonintervention or disengagement as a valid strategy, it was Jefferson who sent the young U.S. Navy and Marines to North Africa to suppress the Barbary pirates. Indeed, to eliminate a threat to American commerce, he deployed a blue-water navy that he once had resisted creating. His deal with Napoleon to purchase the Louisiana Territory, which doubled the size of the republic, was a similar retreat from idealistic principles that he hoped would forestall potential American militarism and international engagement. To raise the capital to pay Napoleon and manage the whole transaction, Jefferson turned, in part, to the national bank—the creation of which he had opposed as both a violation of strict constitutional interpretation and as inviting the easy financing of wars and a militaristic political culture.

Jefferson's followers fared no better than he in their attempts to toe the disentanglement line. We might use the fresh memory of our bicentennial commemorations of the War of 1812 to reflect on why America entered that war, and

Republican Prudence: The Founders' Foreign-Policy School and Its Enduring Legacy

what we immediately learned from it. The first severe price America had paid for holding to isolationism—by cutting its minimal army and navy still further—was the lack of respect the Royal Navy showed for American commerce on the high seas. British harassment and impressment provoked an outraged America to declare war on the British superpower and to provocatively set fire to the town of York (today Toronto), which resulted in the disaster of the British invasion and burning of our nation's capital city on August 24, 1814. It was the profound shock of this foreign policy threat that led Jefferson, and other Jeffersonians such as Madison, to change their minds about the constitutionality of a national bank—and the need to recharter it. Its absence had proven that it was (as Hamilton and Washington originally had argued) indispensable for financing an adequate national defense that could deter threats by signaling our capacities. (Alas, the argument, sound as it was, did not persuade Andrew Jackson.)

In our contemporary foreign-policy debate, we frequently hear restatements of Jeffersonian idealism. Its unassailable origins and its purity of principle give it an air of unique authority and timelessness, especially after American power has encountered setbacks or frustrations abroad. Those who have recourse to it, however, almost invariably forget the early tests that unadulterated Jeffersonianism failed to pass. For example, those who argue against a more forward-leaning American posture in the world frequently quote John Quincy Adams, as Jefferson's most important foreign-policy heir. They especially like the description by Adams of America's attitude toward the struggles for freedom of other peoples. From a July 4th address in 1821, it is a perfect distillation of the Jeffersonian ideal of nonentanglement:

> She has, in the lapse of nearly half a century, without a single exception, respected the independence of other nations while asserting and maintaining her own. She has abstained from interference in the concerns of others, even when conflict has been for principles to which she clings, as to the last vital drop that visits the heart. . . . Wherever the standard of freedom and Independence has been or shall be unfurled, there will her heart, her benedictions and her prayers be. But she goes not abroad, in search of monsters to destroy. She is the well-wisher to the freedom and independence of all. She is the champion and vindicator only of her own.[2]

Those who invoke this passage rarely remind us that Adams, as well, had as much difficulty as Jefferson in living up to these ideals. Two years later, he was emphasizing his Washingtonian, Federalist roots, for it was none other than Secretary of State John Quincy Adams who formulated what became known as the

Monroe Doctrine—effectively proclaiming America the great-power hegemon of the Western hemisphere. The context is revealing, since this declaration was, in part, another response to the War of 1812 and the sacking of Washington. It was, in short, a response to vulnerability. The successful British invasion, and America's general incapacity to deter a war given the international awareness of our passivity and lack of military and financial capability, taught the Americans a simple lesson of the sort credited, a century later, to Leon Trotsky: "You might not be interested in war, but war is interested in you." Protecting the American experiment in republican government and promotion of international peace required a forward-leaning foreign policy, backed by a credible military capability.

As historian John Lewis Gaddis has recently argued, the American response to the 2001 attacks on New York and Washington followed a similar pattern to the shocks of 1814 in Washington and 1941 in Pearl Harbor. Rather than retreating from the world beyond its shores, the United States became more deeply engaged in it. After the wars in Iraq and Afghanistan, the pendulum is obviously swinging back toward American disengagement and the idea of self-containment of the globe's foremost power. Still, if history is any guide, many contrary forces eventually will weaken this isolationist impulse. To be assertive and vigilant about international affairs is simply a predominant trait in our national character, although we occasionally grow weary of and frustrated by its burdens. This was the strategy developed by Franklin Delano Roosevelt and other national leaders in the 1940s, a strategy sustained by presidents and Congresses of both parties for nearly seventy years—including forty-five years of the Cold War—and then for over a decade beyond. Even after our current period of expending blood and treasure abroad with mixed success, we must remember that assertive vigilance is also our most prudent trait. Our best leaders have followed the example of the Founders who, in word and deed, sought to find a balance between forward engagement and restraint.

FOUR PRINCIPLES FOR AMERICAN FOREIGN AND SECURITY POLICY

Of all our foundational documents, Washington's Farewell Address provides the clearest commonsense guidance about the principles needed for our time. It is evergreen, not least because Washington was contending with heated arguments between versions of realism, idealism, and isolationism among his own advisers—to include Hamilton and Jefferson as well as Madison. He sought moderation—a prudence to apply principles, in murky circumstances, in a way that would balance America's highest ideals with our practical interests. Washington's successors have been most successful when they deliberately sought this larger balance between ideals and interests, and between the ends and means of American power.

With these ideas in mind, one can glean from the Farewell Address and its legacy in American foreign policy four broad principles for a distinctively American strategy.

In what follows, we cite President Dwight D. Eisenhower's Farewell Address from January 1961 as an example of the enduring echoes and relevance of America's first strategy, and of Washington's conception of statesmanship. While many other national leaders and instances could be cited across our three centuries, we note that Eisenhower's foreign-policy decisions have been widely praised across partisan and intellectual boundaries in recent years. His parting words thus provide a fairly recent basis for rediscovering a national consensus on first principles. Indeed, because Eisenhower himself sought such consensus in a very difficult time—of open and global superpower conflict, potentially involving catastrophic weapons—it is remarkable to note that he consciously modeled his Farewell Address on Washington's. We should follow Ike's example in discerning the deeper relevance of these founding principles despite intervening changes in technology, society, and international affairs.

1. The Primacy of Natural Rights and Religious Ideals

"Of all the dispositions and habits which lead to political prosperity," Washington stated, "religion and morality are indispensable supports." A republic, in his view, should neither ignore the mutual influence between governmental and private morality nor adopt religious zealotry in its policies. The Declaration of Independence called upon "the Laws of Nature and of Nature's God" as well as "the protection of divine Providence" as sources of our highest ideals. Two decades later, Washington applied these principles to foreign affairs, arguing that religion enjoined America to behave with "good faith and justice towards all nations" and to "cultivate peace and harmony with all." Thus America should "give to mankind the magnanimous and too novel example of a people always guided by an exalted justice and benevolence." Successors such as Lincoln, Franklin Roosevelt, and Eisenhower similarly invoked these religious and metaphysical principles to guide the practical, pressing issues of war and power that they confronted in their times.

Washington, of course, was no pacifist. Like the other Founders, he defended the Revolutionary War with legal and philosophical principles that are applicable to today's problems. The Declaration of Independence, for instance, carefully justifies rebellion on the basis of natural rights and the legitimacy of constitutional government. At the same time, it specifies unacceptable forms of warfare. This principle, too, has formed a lasting legacy in American policy, upheld in word and deed by most presidents and Congresses. Americans have at times fallen short of these standards of protecting human dignity and the rights of the person even in war, but our enduring consensus is that the standards themselves must hold our actions to account.

Washington and his greatest successors were no strangers to public affirmations of religion, because they knew that high ideals are hard to achieve and therefore require extraordinary support. From the time of Washington's leadership in the Revolutionary War, the military always has provided chaplains and conducted religious services—not only to console and comfort troops and sailors but also to remind them of the higher ends that force and war must serve. Moreover, to this day, our presidents and other national leaders invoke divine guidance about decency, perseverance, and honorable conduct in war and crisis.

Adherence to republicanism, natural justice, and transcendent truths about humankind made Washington confident that America would be "at no distant period, a great nation." Such discipline brought about the founding of America and was adhered to by Washington's successors as we rose to become a world power, then a superpower, across three centuries. On what grounds should we ignore it now?

2. The Maintaining of Civilian Authority and Military Readiness

In his Farewell Address, Washington speaks disparagingly of "overgrown military establishments." They are, he says, "inauspicious to liberty" in general but "particularly hostile to republican liberty." One of the most famous echoes of this warning in living memory is in Eisenhower's Farewell, regarding the "unwarranted influence" possibly arising from the new "military industrial complex."[3] We often forget that, in a true echo of Washington, Eisenhower first defended such a permanent military capability and then warned of its possible excesses.

Throughout Washington's career, he noted the dangers of both militarism and weakness. A professional military, he believed, was necessary to protect liberty. At the same time, he was mindful of the question posed by the collapse of the ancient Roman Republic: Who will guard the guardians? Rome devolved into dictatorship when the military became too prominent and took it upon itself to rule. Washington therefore insisted on civilian authority in deciding how to achieve the distinctively moderate aims of American foreign policy.

In Washington's day, fear centered on these "military establishments," but today we might think more in terms of striking a balance between civilian authority and our entire "national security establishment." In an age of cyberwarfare and global terrorism, it is inevitable that much of the important work of national defense will take place in secret, and secrecy and liberal-democratic government are potentially antithetical. The recent revelations by Edward Snowden regarding internet surveillance programs of the National Security Agency illustrate the difficulty of maintaining civilian oversight of intelligence organizations. While few would suggest that the United States is teetering on the brink of tyranny, it would be equally fanciful to suggest that the rule of law and liberal-democratic institutions simply will take care of themselves.

Maintaining a healthy balance between the citizenry and the military requires constant vigilance—and education. Citizens must be educated not only to respect the virtues of public service but also to understand the challenges that confront those professionally responsible for defense and national security. While a professional class of foreign-policy experts is necessary to the health of the republic, we also need an active citizenry capable of guarding the guardians. We might ask ourselves, therefore, whether our current educational system, and our broader political culture, is living up to its national duty. If not, how should it be reformed? Washington and Eisenhower, among many other great national leaders, supported as strong a military capability as was needed to preserve liberty as circumstances changed, without endangering it. Eisenhower thus affirmed "the imperative need" for the new military-industrial complex, given new global threats, while insisting upon maintaining it in balance with other national principles and priorities. Like Washington, he also insisted this balance could arise only through vigilance and debate among citizens and leaders alike.

3. Wariness of Faction but Adherence to Constitutional Roles

One method of amassing power unjustly, Washington warned, was "to misrepresent the opinions and aims" of others. "You cannot shield yourselves too much against the jealousies and heart-burnings which spring from these misrepresentations; they tend to render alien to each other those who ought to be bound together by fraternal affection." Moderation in our rhetoric and debates, as well as in our policy aims, is a difficult but necessary discipline. Eisenhower reminded us of this when warning that "mere partisanship" among political leaders must not obstruct proper pursuit of "the business of the nation."

Indeed, Washington has conveyed to the best of his successors the principle that the president should represent all the American citizenry, not any one "faction." The presidency embodied the common principles and highest ideals of the entire nation. Especially with respect to war and foreign affairs, he therefore counseled moderation as striking a sober balance between rival ideas or courses of action. He exemplified respect for diverse viewpoints and a confidence that allowed consultation of a wide range of intelligent advisers leading to decisive policy choices. He selected a Cabinet that formed the original "team of rivals"[4]—including both Hamilton and Jefferson—while also seeking the advice of other leaders similarly accomplished in both domestic and international affairs, such as John Adams, James Madison, and John Jay. For this Cabinet, general moderation did not mean mushy compromise or merely splitting the difference but finding the higher middle ground in addressing difficult problems.

Guided by these principles, Washington set the model of a strong, moderate, and faithfully constitutional president, justifying decisions with principles and working patiently with an increasingly divided Congress. He sought to ameliorate the factionalism gripping America—and gripping his own Cabinet and advisers, given the French Revolution and its aftershocks in America—by calling his countrymen to the enduring interests and higher ends that united them. For Washington, this culture of constitutionalism was indispensable for a sound foreign policy. A complex structure for formulating policy was the best way to balance liberty and security. His example of wide consultations, prudence, and flexibility is difficult to emulate today, since we now embrace populism, partisanship, and permanent campaigning—not to mention, among most intellectuals, a blind adherence to off-the-shelf foreign-policy doctrines. Nevertheless, American officeholders could do worse than to strive to meet the standard of the first administration, which launched a new federal republic and safely navigated the great-power conflict then engulfing Europe, all while faithfully adhering to constitutional ideals. It is no accident that Eisenhower invoked these same principles of philosophical balance and constitutional complexity in an era marked by new challenges of nuclear missiles, computers, and truly global conflicts; he believed that technology and circumstances might change, but the basic challenges of statesmanship and policy endured.

In common with all the leading Founders, Washington sought to safeguard liberty and security by dividing responsibility for defense between two branches of government—thus applying the principle of checks and balances as well as division of labor to foreign policy. The president would lead in articulating particular policies, given the advantages of executive branch secrecy, speed, and unity, but he would do so while consulting Congress (especially the Senate) and striving for a high-minded national consensus on the best means to achieve American interests. Vetting policies through both the executive and legislative branches is almost always tedious and sometimes feels as if it is producing the lowest common denominator. More often than not, however, it actually generates the highest possible consensus on means and aims. Eisenhower opened his Farewell by affirming this principle of seeking "essential agreement" between the presidency and Congress and of cooperation on "vital issues" of national and international policy, as the basis for a sound American strategy.

4. Statesmanship as Balancing Interest and Justice

The approach to formulating foreign policy that Washington favored required the president to balance speed and secrecy against consultation and transparency. Moreover, he argued that an American policy must balance our distinctive domestic political ideals with the realistic international interests held by any state. We might sum up this complex approach in one word: statesmanship. It is the word Eisenhower used in a seemingly quite different era to summarize his own first principles and approach to strategy, stating that "it is the task of statesmanship" to "balance, and to integrate" the various enduring principles, new developments and challenges, and multiple viewpoints and factors of our complex politics and the complicated world he faced.

The concrete benefits of this traditional ideal of statesmanlike judgment also were noted by no less than the great philosopher of liberal democracy, Alexis de Tocqueville, who credited Washington with preventing disaster as the French Revolution and Europe's great-power struggles roiled American politics. In *Democracy in America*,[5] he wrote, from the vantage point of the 1830s, that "nothing less than the inflexible character of Washington" could check popular opinion and "prevent war from being declared on England" in the 1790s. Although "the majority pronounced against his policy; now the entire people approves it," and if not for Washington's prudence, "it is certain that the nation would have done then precisely what it condemns today." Tocqueville was gracious enough, as a foreign visitor, not to mention that in between Washington's statesmanship and his later observations stood the disastrous War of 1812—which apparently had taught Americans to think more highly of Washington's prudent approach.

Washington's advocacy of practical judgment and moderation over doctrines or "isms" would be Machiavellian if the aims were immoral or amoral, or if the ends were thought to justify any means. The pattern throughout his career, however, was to avoid either amoral expedience or an impractical moralism. Both as general and as president, he employed hard-nosed intelligence and covert operations while stopping short of ruthlessness.

Like Lincoln, Churchill, and other great statesmen after him, Washington is a model for successfully yoking day-to-day policies to larger moral ends. He managed to strike a balance between interest and justice, through prudent recourse to just war principles. The just war tradition, first developed in medieval Christianity and then adapted by more secular Enlightenment thinkers, articulated principles about the ends and means of war to ensure that states held legitimate and largely defensive aims and sought to limit the carnage and passions of war. This high level of statesmanship is difficult to achieve. It is the product of education, native intelligence, character, and above all, experience. But if Washington could manage it when the fledgling nation was still surrounded by stronger powers, it is certainly not impossible for us in the present day, when the country is more powerful than ever. This is the achievement of Franklin Roosevelt, and also of Truman, Eisenhower, and subsequent leaders of Cold War America—to balance engagement and restraint, and to adapt American ends and means to face new global threats, while shouldering the unique responsibilities that come with America's status as a global superpower that propels the world's economy, innovations, and spirit of liberty.

REPUBLICAN PRUDENCE FOR A GLOBALIZED WORLD

The Farewell Address ends by declaring that America should seek both independence and justice in foreign affairs. Tocqueville discerned that this was the basic charter of American foreign and defense policy, and he saw a national principle of enlightened self-interest in Washington's declaration that a truly independent, capable America would be able to "choose peace or war, as our interest, guided by justice, shall counsel." Washington argues that a secure, independent nation should surrender neither to crude pursuit of interest nor to abstract justice but rather must balance and find moderation among these rival propensities. Since Washington placed statesmanship and prudence at the center of his own strategy, he would understand that, in the present day, America as a global superpower would need to build a network of alliances extensive enough to deter global threats and secure the blessings of liberty while not undermining our liberty and our national independence. His counsel hardly precludes the judgment that a thriving republican society in a globalized world must be simultaneously an independent society and a globally engaged society, so as to serve both our ideals and our interests.

These Washingtonian counsels do not fit neatly into any of the established schools of foreign policy today. On the basis of that fact, one might argue that his thinking is inappropriate to the twenty-first century. On the other hand, it might be wiser to conclude that nothing is more characteristically American than Washington's blend of realism, idealism, and constitutionalism. Perhaps it is more fitting to argue that today's foreign-policy schools simply fail to fully comprehend the essential nature of the United States. Perhaps we should revise such theories accordingly and rediscover our original American school.

In many ways, our challenges are indeed new, but the highest consensus of the founders is still the unified aim of both political parties—to benefit mankind and ourselves by respecting, as Washington stated, "the obligation[s] which justice and humanity impose on every nation." This advice eludes snappy slogans and is difficult to follow in practice, because it cannot possibly provide us with a clear roadmap for every situation—but then no sort of advice can do that properly or reliably. Nonetheless, it does allow us to find due north—the fundamental balance of interest and justice—better than any alternative. Indeed, it indicates some of the failings of the existing maps while also alerting us to some of the worst hazards along the way.

Moreover, the Founders' school of foreign policy encourages us to maintain a flexible but *principled* disposition. Washington hoped his moderate, balanced principles would "prevent our nation from running the course which has hitherto marked the destiny of nations." This presupposed civic vigilance by citizens and leaders alike. The Farewell Address thus calls his "friends" and "fellow-citizens" to take up the hard work of learning about and debating difficult issues while avoiding passion and partisan rancor to the degree humanly possible. In foreign policy, as in all aspects of political life, neither the experts nor the public have a monopoly on insight. Both are capable of error. A successful, long-term American strategy toward any given problem, or any given era of international realities, will command the respect of a large part of the public and a significant percentage of the experts. Such strategies must be a product of cocreation and must be rooted in our deepest principles and values.

NOTES

1. Available at avalon.law.yale.edu/18th_century/washing.asp.
2. John Quincy Adams, "Speech to the U.S. House of Representatives on Foreign Policy," July 4, 1821, available at millercenter.org/president/speeches/detail/3484.
3. Available at eisenhower.archives.gov/research/online_documents/farewell_address.html. This site also contains letters and other documents revealing the administration's mindfulness of Washington's Farewell.
4. By this we mean long before Lincoln. See Doris Kearns Goodwin, *Team of Rivals: The Political Genius of Abraham Lincoln* (New York: Simon & Schuster, 2005).
5. Available at gutenberg.org/files/815/815-h/815-h.htm. Our quotations are from the translation by Harvey Mansfield and Delba Winthrop (Chicago, IL: University of Chicago Press, 2000), vol. 1, part 2, ch. 5.

13

Missing Persons, Fugitive Families, and Big Brother: The Government in Relation to the Family and the Person

Gerard V. Bradley

America's government and laws have never had more effect upon the flourishing of persons and families, and more influence upon Americans' understanding of personal and familial well-being, than they do today. Yet the same government and law profess to know almost nothing about what it means for a person to be good, or what a family is.

The confluence of these two trends is very unfortunate. Public authorities in the United States possess an ever-growing portfolio of capabilities to affect how our lives go, just when they have lost track of what to do with it. It is as if the American people put their most precious valuables in a "blind trust"—literally: not one in which the trustee acts for the good of his beneficiaries though without explicit instruction from them. It is that the trustee is unseeing, unguided, stumbling about his task.

This is especially unfortunate because, in truth, the state and its laws are for persons—for their genuine flourishing in community, including foremost the community established by marriage, which we call the family. The Roman lawyer Justinian saw the matter clearly many centuries ago: "Knowledge of law amounts to little if it overlooks the persons for whose sake law is made."[1] That is to say, knowledge of law (and government) amounts to little without the prerequisite knowledge of persons' true interests and genuine flourishing. Our founders and generations of their successors would have wholly agreed.

A *functioning* society—one which defends its shores and pays its bills—is possible in today's distressed circumstances, at least for a time. But a *flourishing* one is unavailable so long as government manages our lives as much as it presently does, without the guidance of a sound moral compass. Indefinite functioning is doubtful; at least, the experiment with government as blind trustee is still so new that we cannot identify any long-term success stories.

In fact, we have reason to suspect that within decades, some Western democracies will decompose, either through balkanization (as more or less homogeneous regional populations throw off the meddling of soulless state bureaucrats), de facto colonization by less-neutered regional superpowers (Russia, China), or by creeping Islamization (especially in the natally challenged countries of Europe). The United States is exceptional. It is considerably less exposed to these dangers than are the other Atlantic and Anglophile democracies. But America is not immune to the manifold disintegrative effects of blind trusteeship, which include a certain political lassitude, susceptibility to peaceful but spirited populist uprisings, and a widespread unwillingness of citizens to make the sacrifices required by the common good.

This lamentable situation is not self-correcting. The growth of law's raw impact on persons and families and upon our understanding of their flourishing is inseparable from the explosive growth of government itself over the last few decades. That growth shows no signs of abating or of being arrested. On the contrary, under the headings of (to cite a few examples) protecting national security, fighting crime, assuring equal access to healthcare, keeping up the GNP, and providing national standards for educating a globally competitive workforce, our *national* government is engaged with who we are to an extent that the Framers could never have comprehended and which was unthinkable to us just three decades ago. Besides, many home-grown, culture-determining decisions—such as those about abortion and church-state separation—come from unelected Justices of the Supreme Court.

The social goals just mentioned are good things. After all, it is not good for anyone if her country is attacked or she lacks the basic necessities of life. But even safe, prosperous societies can be like deserts for anyone seeking to live in accord with, say, the Ten Commandments. The key thing is for public authorities to seek prosperity and safety (and other collective ends) while remaining mindful of the truth about persons and families and scrupulous to promote the overriding goal of civil society: helping people lead truly worthwhile lives. This scrupulosity does not promote efficiency and might even reduce security. But it pays a profound dividend.

Expansion of national power not only upends traditional notions of federalism, with their emphasis upon responsive state and local governments; it also suffers a mortgage from overseas. The emergent national behemoth is itself partly shaped by global forces, including international law and United Nations realpolitik, foreign-policy entanglements (political, military, humanitarian), and the transnational character of information flow and so much economic activity. The relevant norms of national governance are therefore often exogenous. They frequently have nothing whatsoever to do with helping America's people to flourish.

As government and law have grown, its apologetics have strangely shrunk. Public authorities generally profess "neutrality" about what is good for people and brand themselves an equal-opportunity facilitator of persons' quests to establish their own "identities." There is a simple reason why this image of government-as-public-utility is—despite its inadequacy—an entrenched ideology: it works. It works well for those in charge, who spare themselves the obligation of defending a substantive vision of human flourishing, and especially of defending any such vision as true. It works well for the rest of us, too, because it tells us that we are free to invent ourselves according to our dreams. What is not to like about that?

It is a curious sort of agnosticism. Government actors justify their actions with a tripartite set of claims, the combined effect of which is to outsource the job. Someone else actually supplies the justification—either real people do (according to the claim that there is a widespread consensus), all reasonable people do (an ideal consensus), or each one of us does for ourselves. Let me explain, so that we have a precise diagnosis in hand before we turn to the possibility of helpful reforms.

The first of these three claims has already been adumbrated. It is that the imperatives of some vast social objective (security, global economic competitiveness, public health) trump reservations rooted in concerns about the kind of people we are becoming. Here the supplier is, basically, "we, the people," who agree that these purposes are indeed worthwhile. The catch is that we are then expected to follow quietly through the dark underworld of means. We are invited to lay down moral qualms about killing and torture, "to save American lives." Education is reduced to vocational preparation in order to "keep up with the Koreans" in math and science. Religious liberty is subordinated to an alleged public-health crisis about contraceptives. The debate about immigration policies marginalizes (but does not quite suppress) the essential question about how so many newcomers can be brought to understand and commit themselves to our political community and its distinctive way of life. The debate is instead dominated by, on the one hand, a jejune rendition of what it means to extend help to the poor and on the other hand, workforce and GNP considerations.

The common mainspring is to displace talk of what is truly good for people by emphasizing what *must* be done to achieve certain goals or to obtain some amenities. This amounts to having an agenda, not to promoting a critically defensible account of the common good. This displacement reduces daily political and administrative decisions to means-ends calculations. It saves no room for a reflective account of who we are and aspire to be.

Another strand of justification has to do with the "objective" truths of science (including medicine and psychology) and of reportable experience, as trumps over the more "subjective" normative claims of religion or morality. This constructed epistemological chasm obscures genuine value by demoting it in the mind of any socially responsible person. It is not here exactly that "we, the people" are suppliers.

It is more exactly that no reasonable person—an idealized "we, the people"—could deny the justification.

We can see more clearly this government apologia by considering its roots. These are both more and less venerable than one might suppose. The prevailing epistemological primacy of technique and experiment is not the Founders' legacy to us. On the contrary, the Founders believed in science, but they believed more fervently in the truth ("objective," if you like) of Scripture and the moral norms expressed in the Decalogue, as well as in the centrality of the virtues to any worthwhile life. I say "more fervently" not to compare temperatures of belief. I mean that the founders believed that morality, religion, and family were more essential to the republic's survival than were science, or even prosperity. The Founders and generations of Americans after them believed that our experiment in liberty could only succeed if the people were virtuous.

Relegating the truth about human flourishing to the private realm of opinion is not Lincolnesque. Nor is it the simple product of twentieth-century progressivism. It is not, however, a hangover from the 1960s, and was most certainly not inaugurated with Barack Obama. This epistemological revolution has an exact birthday: June 14, 1943. For on that day, our Supreme Court decided *West Virginia v. Barnette*, the second Jehovah's Witnesses' flag-salute case.

Barnette famously held, "If there is any fixed star in our constitutional constellation, it is that no official, high or petty, can prescribe what shall be orthodox in politics, nationalism, religion or other matters of opinion."[2] Note well which realms escaped the ban upon officially prescribed "orthodoxy"—science and law. Harvard philosopher Michael Sandel proclaimed that with *Barnette*, the liberal "procedural republic had arrived."[3]

Barnette is a recognizable form of liberal political theory, according to Sandel, because it affirms the priority of fair procedures over substantive ends, a priority rooted in the fact of disagreement about religious and moral ends among citizens.[4] Yves Simon perspicuously diagnosed this same "liberalism" (his word) in a 1943 scholarly article. Simon wrote that this ideological construct was coming to the fore in some Western societies. By its lights, the mind is vouchsafed no freedom from the requirements of "logical and experimental truth" and so none in regard to science (the synthesis of logic and experience). "As regards the so-called transcendental sphere," "the individual should be granted an unlimited freedom of assertion and denial." Simon asserted that these "liberties cannot be safeguarded unless society adopts an attitude of complete indifference toward transcendental objects, and professes some kind of agnosticism."[5]

Barnette was liberalism *in utero*, and then stillborn. Americans throughout the 1950s surely valued science and respected law. But they continued to adhere to the great constitutional tradition, which treated our government as one nation "under God" and which was responsible for inculcating the real human virtues upon which our polity depended for its exceptional existence. The government of a free people was, however, peculiarly hamstrung. It could not directly bring about the virtuous citizenry it needed. Only the constitutionally separate churches, a morality beyond amendment by any principality or power, and the independent realm of family life could do that. An essential part of leading an upright life was, in any event, persons' free choices and commitments to genuinely worthwhile forms of living. So a Grand Bargain was struck.

The Grand Bargain in American political history has been a strategic partnership between government and civil-society institutions, such as the family, community associations, neighborhoods and—most important—churches and other organized religious communities. The law would help people to be good by helping these institutions to cultivate good people. The law would do its job by (among other things) affirming the truths that there is a provident Creator God, that religion is good, that morality is objective and can be found in the Bible, and that marriage between man and woman constitutes the family—and by vigorously promoting religious liberty. Perhaps most important, the law would promote the moral and cultural authority of the churches; indeed, the government would regularly affirm its own dependence upon a Supreme Being.

This bargain came undone during the 1960s. Simon and Sandel are nonetheless right: though inert at first, a new way of mapping the world came to be in 1943. From that point forward, it grew slowly in strength and acquired influential acolytes. One can see its profile clearly in most elite opinions during the 1950s. In legal analyses, constitutional opinions, and in some (but far from all) political thought and practice, the unencumbered self struggled then to be born into a realm of subjectivity. This birth was over against what those resisting the liberal vision held as the truth about chastity, the nature of marriage, and when persons begin (in debates about abortion, divorce, censorship, illegitimacy, pornography, prostitution). Elites dismissed such formulations as either rank superstition or sclerotic religious dogma.

This momentous development is not exactly the priority of the objective over the subjective. In an important sense, that priority, so stated, is sound. The big thing is rather identifying "objective" knowledge with reliably obtained data about the natural world (from the size of distant stars to the power of invisible atoms) and with generalizations about human behavior (the stuff of social sciences, including economics). The rest of "knowledge" simply isn't. It is feeling, speculation, religious dogma, mere opinion—all possessing (at most) the truth-value of poetical expression. Its truth is "subjective."

An English law lord (named Law) gave thematic expression to this development in a recent case; he denied relief to a Christian relationship counselor who could not endorse the same-sex acts of his potential clients. Her refusal was a prima facie case of sexual-orientation discrimination. She sought an exception rooted in ambient legal norms of religious liberty. Lord Law declared that any exemption on religious grounds would be "unprincipled." He reasoned that it would "give effect to the force of subjective opinion" (read: religion) and thus could not "advance the general good on objective grounds."[6]

We come now to the third of three basic justifications for activist government. It is not "neutrality" about value. That is yesterday's mantra. It is instead the genuine value of neutrality. This would justify government exertions by appeal to the overriding importance of each person's self-definition, identity, empowerment, and autonomy. The Supreme Court in *Roe v. Wade* famously confessed its inability to "resolve the difficult question of when life begins." This reticence about metaphysical truth remains an important part of the "pro-choice" position. But it has been undercut by the law's recognition of precisely when people come to be—namely, at fertilization—in contexts *other* than abortion (such as in laws against feticide, whereby anyone [other than an abortionist] who kills an unborn child is guilty of murder just the same as if the victim were ten or one hundred years old. Think of the Scott Peterson murder case.).

The "pro-choice" case is now supported chiefly by the value of choice. And so in 1992, the Supreme Court justified its affirmation of *Roe*: "At the heart of liberty is the right to define one's own concept of existence, of meaning, of the universe, and the mystery of human life." According to this "Mystery Passage," the sun around which law and government revolve is self-invention through unfettered choice—the establishment of one's own identity.

Pick up almost any opinion page or journal article or court opinion that considers the flourishing of persons and families, and you will soon encounter this extraordinary valuation of self-definition. The 2013 Supreme Court decision in favor of same-sex marriage depended upon it. Justice Kennedy (writing for the majority) said that the state "confers" the "dignity" of marriage upon individuals' choices. This "dignity" consists in the "pride in oneself individually and pride in one's partnership with one other person." Two people, he wrote, "define themselves by their commitment to each other." The law recognizes their marriage in order "to affirm their commitment."[7] Marriage is not anymore a specific sort of "partnership" or "commitment"—communion is the better word—which the state is bound to protect and maintain so people can choose it and live up to the moral demands of it. It is rather the mutually agreeable arrangement of the two persons whose "partnership" it is.

This 2013 conclusion extends the reasoning of the Court's family-law jurisprudence back to the 1970s. The anthem of this movement from family as a stable form of life with its own nature and collateral incidents to the variable construction of so many individual lifestyle maestros is the *Michael H.* case, decided in 1989.

There, Justice William Brennan wrote that ours is not an "assimilative, homogeneous" society but a "pluralistic" and "facilitative" one: "Even if we can agree that 'family' and 'parenthood' are part of the good life, it is absurd to assume that we can agree on the content of those terms and destructive to pretend that we do."[8]

The meaning and value of the "family" are thus transparent for the meaning and value which individual persons attribute to them by their choices. The meaning and value of these choices are transparent for the value of them as *their choices*. So the meaning and value of "family" and even of a person's well-being globally reduce to the value of certain choices being really *mine*, authentically Me, truly constitutive of my "identity." Value is the Mystery Passage, all the way down.

The justificatory work done by the Mystery Passage in today's political culture is enormous. It works partly by appeal to consensus: Everyone could agree that, notwithstanding their many value disagreements, deciding for oneself is desirable. It works partly by the sheen of "neutrality"; public authority is not siding with anyone's moral or religious view. And partly it works as a straight-up truth: We are invited to conclude that defining oneself is, simply and really, intrinsically valuable. This last part is, in my judgment, fast becoming paramount. It constitutes an emerging "orthodoxy," which public authority assiduously promotes, especially by and through the law's influence upon culture.

Even religion can be sucked into this reduction. In elite opinion, in most academic legal commentary, in much law, and to a significant extent in the minds of many ordinary people, religious acts have the same dignity and value as do other acts by which persons express and actualize their deepest selves, desires, or self-defining thoughts and emotions. The supreme and perhaps only universal value here is authenticity and thus "identity." As John Finnis aptly writes, religion's "status and immunities are as instances . . . of the only really basic human good, the only intrinsically worthwhile end at stake, setting for oneself one's stance in the world."[9]

The immediate effect of turning religious belief back upon itself—valuing it *as* someone's belief—is to undermine the possibility of taking religion as a zone of truth, as not only one's belief but also a true account of the way things really are (there *is* a God, final judgment, and an afterlife of different sorts). Once religion is transposed into a peculiar form of self-empowerment, it is prone to collapse into psychological categories. As the cultural critic Philip Rieff said in 2005, "I think that the orthodox are in the miserable situation of being orthodox for therapeutic reasons." As Richard John Neuhaus summarized Rieff's words: "People who try to practice orthodox Christianity and Judaism today, he says, inevitably remain trapped in the vocabulary of therapy and self-fulfillment."[10]

One recent synthesis of this epochal liberalism is contained in a judicial opinion by the New Mexico Supreme Court in 2013.[11] This court ruled in favor of a lesbian couple who asserted that, under the state law outlawing discrimination on grounds of sexual orientation in all "public accommodations," a wedding photographer was bound to shoot video at their commitment ceremony. A concurring opinion by Justice Bosson almost congratulated the photographers—the Huguenins—for the integrity of their Christian-founded belief that such ceremonies were immoral and that they could not promote or assist in the celebration by taking pictures of it and then arranging those pictures professionally in an album. Justice Bosson wrote that the Huguenins are "free to think, to say, to believe, as they wish; they may pray to the God of their choice and follow these commandments in *their personal lives*" (my emphasis). They must nonetheless pay what he called the "price of citizenship." In the world of "the marketplace, of commerce, of public accommodation," they must "compromise." They "must channel their conduct, not their beliefs, so as to leave space for other Americans who believe something different." They must adhere to the "glue which holds us together as a nation, the tolerance that lubricates the varied moving parts of us as a people."

Although the Huguenins are not obliged to express words of positive approval, they are now legally required to behave in every respect as if that were exactly their judgment—or get out of the commercial photography business. What Justice Bosson described as a good citizen's "compromise" is instead a relativizing acid, corroding everyone's attempts to hold onto one's commitments as true, as corresponding to an objective transcendent order of value.

The Huguenins wished to avoid participation in same-sex "weddings," not because their disapproval was part of the "Me" which each had created but because they were convinced that what they believe is *true*. The law would have them act as if they are mistaken. The state is frankly telling them that their views may in some sense be "true"—*for them*. But their views are surely not really true. Their views are also rather hurtful to some other people. The Huguenins stand in some peril of being branded "hateful."

Many people, perhaps including the Huguenins, can withstand heavy doses of negative messaging, social recriminations, and legal harassment. Many others cannot, and everyone has their limits. Over time and across various sectors of life, this corrosive privatization of morality and religion will conspire to persuade most of us that it is, really, just about Me.

One way in which law fosters persons' conversion to the morality of self-definition *über alles* is by allying itself with science. Consider the example of state laws (in California and New Jersey) that forbid mental-health professionals to treat minors—even with the enthusiastic support of their parents—for unwanted same-sex attraction. No such professional may engage in what are often called "reparative therapies," upon pain of forfeiting his or her license. The norm at the base of these laws is quite straightforward: there is nothing wrong with same-sex attraction. Scientific interventions to correct same-sex attraction thus amount to psychological mutilation.

Another way in which Mystery Passage–type autonomy can be foisted upon people is by defining deviance around it. British sociologist Nikolas Rose has written most perceptively about how science changes conceptions of human dignity. He describes the entourage of the new imperial Self: "Once the guidance of selves was no longer dependent upon the authority of religion or traditional morality," it was allocated to experts of 'subjectivity.'" The older experts dealt with existential questions about the meaning of suffering and death. The new clerisy, according to Rose, transposed them into "technical questions of the most effective ways of managing malfunction and improving 'quality of life.'" Rose further opines that once this ambitious, world-creating self is established as the norm, the *abnormal* is correlative: "the shape and incidence of the pathology of depression in western developed nations can only be understood in relation to contemporary conceptions of the self."[12] People who are not up to the Herculean task of creating their own world of meaning are evidently in some peril of being diagnosed as ill.

It is easy to see that this whole complex of ideas spells great trouble for personal and familial well-being. Individual choice possesses little punch as a rallying point when efficient pursuit of collective goals threatens to diminish families and to impede persons' access to virtue. As Justice Bosson and Lord Justice Law both declared, the enlarged "public" realm has its own algorithm of value; all else is subordinate private opinion. The "personal life" of uninhibited assertion *begins* where the needs of collective objectives and writ of "nondiscrimination" *leave off*. "Freedom" in the workplace means cross-dressing to work at the law firm. "Injustice" pertains to anyone who offers less than a full-throated welcome.

The impotence of subjectivity is supported by the correlative view that no particular form of human flourishing or of the family is intrinsically better than another. The only common metric is authenticity of choice, which is more or less invisible to the eye. The lesbian "wedding" (and Everywoman's access to free contraception, for that matter), which in truth should inhabit a limited right of "privacy" or noninterference by the state, are not only elevated to the status of public goods, but in a perverse jiu-jitsu move, they require the privatization of religion.

Now, the law does not shape us only by setting up green lights and red lights. It does that sometimes, by prohibiting some acts and requiring others. The law also shapes us by creating incentives and disincentives. Permitted acts can be discouraged by taxes and burdensome regulations. Others can be encouraged and even subsidized. But the law can and does shape us more powerfully, yet more subtly, by shaping the *culture* in which we live. The law today powerfully shapes the social understandings, practices, and meanings of the good life that constitute our *culture*.

This is not a necessary truth about law. It is not an axiom of social theory or political science. The relationship between civil law and culture in any society is rather a contingent matter. In some places, the law has little or no purchase upon the local culture. Sometimes the government is too weak to matter. (Think of failing states in the Third World.) Sometimes the government is too remote to matter. ("God bless the czar and keep him . . . far away from us!" was the rabbi's prayer in *Fiddler on the Roof.*) Sometimes the government has no moral authority. (Consider the Communist regime in Poland before 1989.) Sometimes folk customs, tribal ways, and religious norms of conduct are enough to keep a community on track. Civil law might then be an afterthought. (Think of all of the above.)

Not so in the United States in the second decade of the twenty-first century. Francis George has argued that the "law has peculiar and unique cultural functions in American society":

> The many components of our culture are largely united by law, not by blood, not by race, not by religion, not even by language, but by law. It's the one principal cultural component we all have in common. . . . [L]aw is more important in teaching or instructing us than it is in directing us. . . . [O]ne must therefore ask how it is that law functions as a cultural carrier in [this country], and what does that mean for cultural institutions that are universal [i.e., objective, natural] but that are qualified by law: marriage, family [and others].[13]

Even so, culture does not determine anyone's life. In a debased culture, it is possible for at least some people—the morally heroic, perhaps, or those who migrate to a healthy subcultural setting—to live genuinely good lives. But all of us are captives of a social world we do not make, more or less constrained by it. And just about everything we have learned about the influence of family law upon culture since around 1963—starting with FDA approval of the pill and winding through the no-fault-divorce legal revolution, the utter destigmatization (first in law and then in culture) of "illegitimacy" and hard-core pornography, and the progressive decoupling of marriage and procreation by legal recognition of same-sex "marriages"—testifies to the *mighty* effect of law upon our culture when it comes to matters of the family.

After the divorce-law revolution of 1968–1973, it became difficult to believe that marriage really lasts "unto death us do part," especially if one's own marriage was breaking down. After the same-sex "marriage" revolution runs its course, it will be almost impossible to believe that marriage is what the entire culture thought it was before 1963: the legally enforced, morally normative context for having sex and having kids. Even people who welcome today's permissiveness do not deny that changes in *law* were indispensable to the arrival of this new understanding.

WHAT THEN SHOULD BE DONE?

The unfortunate situation described in the first two paragraphs of this essay is not beyond recall. It is, however, deeply embedded in law, culture, and consciousness. Undoing it will therefore require brilliant strategy, sustained effort, pluck, and the blessings of Divine Providence. This essay depicts a broad (as well as deep) front behind which the zeitgeist marches. This array can be intimidating and even discouraging. But it also means that opportunities to push back are plentiful and various.

The success of any reform campaign depends upon invigorating the people's power over both government and culture. Any such populist insurgency could be freestanding and political; think of the Tea Party or the Occupy Movement. But religion and religious institutions have an essential role in this reclamation project. Their importance can scarcely be overstated. Although religion is, to be sure, *not* principally concerned with temporal affairs and even less so with political arrangements as such, America's still robust religiosity is an irreplaceable asset in any campaign to reestablish government as an important but still secondary promoter of the genuine flourishing of persons and families.

One reason is that our constitutional tradition remains committed to the doctrinal and institutional autonomy of the churches. This means at a minimum that the government cannot tell believers and churches what it is they in fact believe. This minimum was resoundingly affirmed by a unanimous Supreme Court in early 2012 in the *Hosanna Tabor* case, where the Justices affirmed and found a constitutional home for the so-called ministerial exception to employment discrimination laws, and they did so on the basis of a constitutionally rooted, broad prerogative of the church leaders over the doctrine and message of their religion.[14] This is why the prevailing legal strategy (if you will) is not to commandeer the spirit but to prevent it from blowing where it wills. It is why, in other words, the government seeks to fence in religion, to pen it up in an innocuous personal or private realm.

Ground zero of the coming struggle is very likely to be therefore right here, where churches and believers *insist* upon their proper contributions to the shape of our culture, law, and government. The ground which they seek will not be conceded. Any forward progress will have to wrested from the powers that be.

There is good news to report, some formidable assets to assay. Some of the currents that have carried us thus far have probably crested. I shall conclude by describing two of them. Nikolas Rose writes persuasively that the deep psychological self, which was invented in the twentieth century, is dying: "The deep interior that inhabits each of us, the repository of our life history, the seat of our desires, the locus of our pleasures, the target of knowledge, intervention, management and therapy, the basis of our ethics—this deep space is flattening out."[15]

It is a good bet that, before too much longer, most people will come to see that seeking an authentic self way down deep inside is like chasing the rabbit down into its hole. The labyrinth of desire, subconscious urges, and noncognitive experience within each of us may have some explanatory power. But it is normatively bankrupt. The narcissist whom it has produced is neither good nor happy. Nikolas Rose worries (as does his co-author, Joelle M. Abi-Rached) that the twenty-first century might be the era of the brain and the neurochemical self.[16] Maybe so. But the demise of the deep self is going to be an opportunity to reinvigorate the lapsed moral person.

Starting at the turn of the century, the "gay" insurgency congealed around marriage equality. It did so for purely instrumental reasons. Matrimony was linchpin of and gateway to, not some bundle of material benefits (which was never the real issue), but social acceptance and legal equality, which was the end in view. It may not be long before it becomes manifest that the numbers of same-sex couples who wish to enter into something like marriage (a sexually exclusive and more-or-less permanent relationship) is very small indeed. If and when that happens, there will be a valuable opportunity to try to reinstall procreative marriage as the dominant social norm.

When that time comes, it will help to describe marriage (and the family rooted in it) as the answer to so many persons' questions about identity—who they are by dint of where they came from (really, who their mother and father were). It will help, too, to describe marriage as society's cradle of equality.

All the married couple's children come to be in and through the *same* act—separated only by time. This is the mother and father's marital love. Each child is equally and wholly the image of their parents' unique union. The siblings' family identity is just that: a matter of *identity*. All the children are, one compared to the others, equally and wholly the offspring of the same parents; mother and father are equally and wholly parents of each child, in whom they see (literally) so many unique but familiar expressions of their own union. For each child is *their* flesh, their marriage.

This matrix of familial equality, mutuality, and common identity is the wellspring and ground of love, duty, loyalty, caregiving—the whole moral culture of family life. The lifelong and unbreakable cords of fealty and relatedness that family members possess, one for the others, and that even distance and alienation never quite erase, depend upon it.

No other "family" form is anything like it. None could possibly replace it.

NOTES

1. Justinian, *Institutes, 1. 2. 12.*
2. *West Virginia State Board of Education v. Barnette*, 319 U.S. 624, 642 (1943).
3. Michael J. Sandel, *Democracy's Discontent: America in Search of a Public Philosophy* (Cambridge, MA: Belknap, 1996), 54.
4. See ibid., 4–5.
5. Yves R. Simon, "Beyond the Crisis of Liberalism," in Robert Edward Brennan, ed., *Essays in Thomism* (New York: Sheed & Ward, 1942).
6. *McFarlane v. Relate Avon, Ltd.*, EWCA Civ. 77 sect. 23 (2010).
7. *United States v. Windsor*, 570 U.S. _, 133 S. Ct. 2675, 2689–90 (2013).
8. *Michael H. v. Gerald D.*, 491 U.S. 110, 141 (1989) (Brennan, J., dissenting).
9. John Finnis, "Religion and State," in *Collected Essays*, vol. 5 (Oxford, England: Oxford University Press, 2011), 86.
10. Richard John Neuhaus, "Philip Rieff Has Died at Age 83," web exclusive, *First Things*, firstthings.com/web-exclusives/2006/07/rjn-philip-rieff-has-die.
11. *Elane Photography v. Willock* (August 22, 2013).
12. Nikolas Rose, *Inventing Our Selves: Psychology, Power, and Personhood* (Cambridge, England: Campbridge University Press, 1999), 151.
13. F. George, "Law and Culture in the United States," 48 *American Journal of Jurisprudence* 131, 135 (2003).
14. *Hosanna Tabor Evangelical Lutheran Church and School v. EEOC*, 565 U.S. _, 132 S. Ct. 694 (2012).
15. Nikolas Rose, *The Politics of Life Itself: Biomedicine, Power, and Subjectivity in the Twenty-First Century* (Princeton, NJ: Princeton University Press, 2007), 26.
16. Nikolas Rose and Joelle M. Abi-Rached, *Neuro: The New Brain Sciences and the Management of the Mind* (Princeton, NJ: Princeton University Press, 2013).

14

A Way Forward: The University

Steven Justice

Let's begin by considering the major challenges faced by any university that might wish to do its job. I don't mean the long-term demographic and social pressures on North American universities or the short-term fiscal crises that have made those pressures more visible. Relevant as both are, I refer to two challenges that higher education has created for itself.

The first is the disappearance of serious debate, the reduction of academic discourse to a bland, homogeneous consumer liberalism.[1] Robert P. George's gradation of decent societies and dynamic ones, in the essay to which this volume responds, reflects a conservative's explanation of how desirable robust and precise debate on fundamental questions should be. But the narrowness and insipidity of American universities is deplored by thinking leftists and thinking conservatives alike, not to mention those who simply care about thinking; it betrays the vision of the medieval founders of the university and of its Enlightenment refounders, and it betrays the calling of the university that Candace Vogler describes in Chapter 9. All these voices recognize how an increase in scholarly expertise should make debates over fundamental questions wider and more informed. Instead they have grown narrow at our universities, and that narrowness has become coercive as well as constraining. And it has intensified itself: as conservatives and leftists are excluded from serious discourse, they have increasingly left the university to itself.

The second challenge is the nearly universal failure of the institution to educate its students. This is the problem Vogler identifies in a devastating footnote at the end of her essay: "When students can satisfy their general-education requirements by taking a grab bag of courses in different fields of the arts and sciences, utter incoherence in the course of study at its very base is virtually inevitable." In North America, this "grab bag" is the almost unrivaled model of the undergraduate curriculum. Her footnote is devastating in part because it understates the case: not only do students not receive the direction required for assembling a coherent education, they ordinarily do not come to know enough what an education should be to know when they are cheated of it or about the conditions of university discourse to diagnose why.

This chapter will make three arguments: (1) that these two failures emerge as much from the academy's successes as from its defects, (2) that they are connected, and (3) that they are remediable. And it will make three suggestions: how (1) students, (2) donors, and (3) faculty can help remedy the two failures. These suggestions do not amount to a program of reform. The title assigned to this chapter, "A Way Forward," is well-chosen, for that is all it can offer. The university is a historical creation subject to historical logic; it is not a work of nature, and there is no guarantee that its present form can be indefinitely sustained. So: a way forward, nothing more. But nothing less also, because even if the university cannot sustain itself indefinitely, it will not disappear immediately either, and its importance will not be soon diminished. I will explain later why we can trust that a way forward does lie open.

It is now commonplace to say that the adoption in the United States of the German model of the research university, which began in the late nineteenth century with the founding of Johns Hopkins, decisively changed the course of its history.[2] It was this that led to the organization of universities into departments, their disposition into colleges and graduate schools, their emphasis on the discovery of knowledge and not just its transmission, the requirement of the PhD to enter the professoriate, and the expectation that those who enter would be published intellectuals teaching as specialists. The extraordinary expansion of knowledge this past century and a half has taken place largely in universities or in close connection with them, and by these means. Scientific and technological discovery gives us the most obvious example, and the proliferation of science departments, research centers, science programs, and medical schools gives a concrete emblem. Other areas of extraordinary growth, though less iconic, are almost as dramatic. The statistical social sciences analyze information about populations large and small that was unattainable a century and a half ago; many of the methods (and motives) of its collection and the means of its analysis have emerged from the universities. Even historiography, an art practiced since antiquity and massively refined in the seventeenth and eighteenth centuries, and literary criticism, in some sense the central subject of education for twenty-five centuries, saw refinement in analytic precision during this period greater than either had known before.

This is a great record of accomplishment, ennobling to recall, and it has been inseparable from the development of the research university. And so that development is often celebrated by commentators on education.[3] But it also is sometimes regretted, as the source from which narrow specialization, fragmentation, and politicization have grown metastatically.[4] This regret is only partly wrong. The rapid geometrical expansion of knowledge has been accompanied by a riot of specialization in university faculties, and this specialization (as I will say in a moment) does have unhappy effects. The narrowness of academic expertise is a routine object of fun, first of all among academics, and sometimes it is criticized as the vice produced by a grubbing and pedantic ambition. But it is not clear that there is any alternative to it besides the abandonment of research altogether, nor clear how it could be or why it should be avoided. Serious inquiry seeks precision; precision entails (though of course it is not limited to) the finest possible granularity, the clear distinction of details; and this proliferation of details changes the scale upon which ordinary inquiry can be conducted. As more detail is accumulated, the area of possible mastery becomes small; as a discipline grows, a single researcher, however tireless and brilliant, can have an active grasp of only smaller and smaller parts of it. A consequence less obvious, but just as important, is that productive and interesting questions tend to occupy an ever smaller scale. In the nineteenth century, one could make discoveries about the broad history of medieval Western monasticism; now discoveries are likely to concern scribal practices in the double monasteries of twelfth-century Bavaria. The broad history now will be altered only incrementally and by the continuing impact of many narrower inquiries such as this one. That is not how research has *happened* to develop; that is how it *must* develop if it is to be successful. Specialization is not a defect.

But though not a defect, it is still a problem, and because it is built into the logic of successful research, it is a problem without an easy solution. Two aspects of this problem are important to mention.

The first is that no one wields this knowledge. We regularly say, "We know more than we ever did," but this does not mean that any person or group possesses the body of that knowledge, or can manipulate it. Certainly there are more individuals involved in the act of knowing things with greater specificity. The truer thing to say is that more *has been known*—that more thought to higher degrees of granularity has passed through more minds and been recorded on more pages. But that is a predicament as well as a boast. The bulk of those past publications, past discoveries and clarifications, itself becomes a part of the burden of mastery, of what the next generation of scholars must know. "Lost knowledge"—the phenomenon of discoveries made, forgotten, and made again—threatens to become a feature of some disciplines. Increasingly, therefore, the rapidly growing archive of scholarly inquiries and their results does not organize the chaos of the world before inquiry; it reproduces it.

The chaos does not offer a clear way through. Sometimes people speak as though the rapid searchability of data coded digitally will alleviate the problem, but the central question is the mastery that would know what to look for and what to do with what is found. On the other hand, to propose that we should try to know *less* would be backward to the point of self-parody. And even if we tried it, the attempt would suffer from the same problem: less of what? The cuts would have to be distributed on the basis of some judgment.

The second aspect of the problem of the prolific specialization of research is that no one can evaluate this knowledge, for the multiplication of things known is not merely a multiplying of objects, and the specialization that attends it is not merely a cutting of the field of knowledge into ever smaller pieces. Cultivating that knowledge derives from, requires, and reinforces the differences among disciplines, and it prompts subdifferentiation into disciplinary units ever smaller and ever more incommensurate. This is an important point worth explaining.

Disciplines are areas of study conventionally stipulated, with conventional procedures: procedures for defining the objects of study, devising meaningful questions about them, answering those questions, and evaluating competing answers. The research university would be impossible without disciplines. The value of a discipline—its ability to offer a systematic way of building up and evaluating knowledge about its object—depends on self-imposed limitations: each one must limit the kinds of questions it can pose, the kinds of evidence it can consider, and the kinds of answers it can entertain. Within the protocols of each discipline, there are certain possibilities that cannot be useful, because they cannot be demonstrated or falsified by disciplinary methods. It is no use in suggesting to a literary critic that Shakespeare meant nothing at all by "This too too solid flesh," or to a historian that the so-called prophecies of Merlin really were fifth-century prophecies of twelfth-century events, rather than a twelfth-century forgery of fifth-century prophecies. Those suggestions would get nowhere—not because they are impossible (they are not), not because they are vanishingly improbable (they are, but improbability has been no barrier to many other literary-critical and historiographical suggestions), but because they disregard the constraints these disciplines must assume in order to allow any kind of systematic assessment and argument. Each discipline has systematic preferences, ways of thought, that are naturally at home in it, but not necessarily in other disciplines, even apparently adjacent ones. Heavily statistical disciplines, like some forms of social science, tend naturally to depreciate the importance of the outlier, the eccentric instance; heavily interpretative disciplines, like other forms of social science or literary criticism, tend naturally to seize on the outlier, the incongruous detail, as the precious clue to the design of the artifact being interpreted. Which approach is more right? Put without some definite conceptual framework, the question is simply unmeaning. But a definite conceptual framework is precisely what two such disciplines do not share.

One consequence of this organization of intellectual work is that no discipline can claim that it reliably tells the truth about its object. It is entirely possible that the history of the composition of the *Canterbury Tales* is utterly different from what the fragmentary evidence might allow us to discern; but we can only use what we've got and based on that, draw the best conclusions that the evidence and the discipline's protocols will underwrite. We assume, and have good reason to assume, that these conclusions are reasonable; and given the great advances in the dating of medieval manuscripts and the knowledge of their construction, their production, and the patronage that produced them, they probably are. But we cannot know for sure.

At the end of the last paragraph, I slipped in some details from the recent history of my own field: the huge increase in our knowledge of the late-medieval book trade, a real advance that has depended on the careful work of many scholars over several generations. What has happened with it has happened numberless times in numberless sub-branches of all the disciplines. As this knowledge grows, it is not merely that the number of objects known grows. At the same time, new ways of approaching them are elaborated and refined—new questions, new techniques, new specialized vocabularies, new conventions for the presentation of evidence. The discipline thus generates fields, which generate subfields, which then do the same. The more successful each is, the less confidence workers even in closely related subfields can feel in approaching it. When I was in graduate school, all literary critics needed to know something about textual criticism, and all of us could read technical introductions to scholarly editions with some ability to judge or at least to contextualize the arguments offered there. Now textual criticism has so refined itself that many of its arguments are simply unmanageable to most literary critics (as, apparently, is literary criticism to most textual editors).

Now in theory, the university within which all these disciplines are located provides a governing framework that should guarantee some commensurability among them. Two elements that are crucial to all universities and important in the lives of all its citizens come to mind as occasions for understanding how all the fields of knowledge are related to each other: the evaluation of the research of faculty members (such as that conducted when tenure and promotion are considered) and the definition and implementation of curricula and of requirements for undergraduate degrees. But in fact, neither really serves this function; neither could.

Evaluation of professors' research when they are considered for tenure, promotion, or merit increases is conducted almost entirely by those who work within the candidates' fields, and even by those who work within their subfields. It is disciplinary readers who accept or reject books submitted to presses and articles sent to journals, disciplinary external evaluators who are called in on tenure and promotion cases, and disciplinary colleagues who cast decisive votes. This is right and inevitable, for who else could? Though every research university has some mechanism above the level of the department for offering positions and awarding promotions, these disproportionately measure the various disciplinary judgments against each other (Was the departmental vote clear or close? Were the external reviewers from prestigious departments and known well in their fields?).

The same thing is true of curricula: the requirements for undergraduate majors are set almost entirely within the relevant departments (and those for PhDs are set [in practice] within the individual fields within departments). Again, this is both right and inevitable, but its rightness and inevitability cannot avert the incoherence that it creates in those requirements. There is in the university no framework of rational answerability by which the work of these disciplines could be measured against each other, placed in a meaningful set of evaluative relationships. Of course many will say that there is no such framework possible. That is a plausible argument, though it is not a slam dunk and must be defended. But to leave to the side the theoretical question, there are practical observations to make.

One is that when our universities describe the education they offer their undergraduates, they routinely speak as if such a rational framework is possible and gives shape to the study of undergraduates. They tend to speak this way only in very specific contexts—when trying to attract applicants with a vision of a broad liberal-arts education, for instance. I will come back to this.

A second is that the current patchwork of standards which cannot be made answerable to any overarching rationality brings with it severe inutilities *even for the health of continued research*. For instance, Vogler rightly warns that universities, as their financial needs become more acute, become more vulnerable to having their expertise and prestige "bought" by commercial and state interests that will offer funding in return for influence on the direction of research. The prospect will make most of us gag. But if we cannot give a programmatic *rational* account why the disciplines should be free of such influence, we can have only sentimental reasons for opposing such appropriations. The same goes for financial influences on allocations of personnel: on what grounds can you object to pouring massive funds into a new Center for Intelligence and Security Studies (if funds for such a thing are on offer), unless you can offer reasons why it is more important that students study (say) Tocqueville and Marx, or physics and history? And on what grounds can you call those things more important if you don't acknowledge standards across disciplines for judging importance? A skeptical reader might observe that universities' vulnerability to high market forces has more to do with their financial deficits than with the absence of shared intellectual standards. But the absence of those standards hurts us when we try to address the financial deficits. When the funding crisis hit the University of California, the constant discussion among Berkeley faculty was the awareness that we needed to make the case for higher education to the voting public. It was a cheering moment of shared purpose in the face of possible disaster, but the cheer dissipated as it became clear that we had no shared understandings that would let us even discuss how to do so; it was not just that we could not agree on how to make the case or on what case to make, but we could not marshal any set of standards (apart from guesses about political effectiveness) for discriminating between better and worse arguments.

It should be obvious what relation this situation bears to the incoherence of students' educations, briefly but devastatingly mentioned at the end of Vogler's essay. The way we do our business is such that we leave ourselves no grounds on which we could say that there are certain things every student must know. Nor do we leave grounds for saying that there are certain *kinds* of things that every student must know. That is, we give ourselves no *substantial or formal* criteria for awarding degrees. And so virtually all research universities use merely *procedural* criteria, requiring (say) humanities students to take a certain number of courses in the physical and social sciences. To say, as we often do, that such requirements expose students to multiple forms of reasoning is, strictly, correct. But it is disingenuous, because we offer them no obvious way of learning what the limits of these ways of thinking are, what purposes each can and cannot serve, and what relation each has to the others and to the array of reasonings on offer at the university. And we do not offer students that because most of us have no sense of these things ourselves. Nothing in our training especially encourages us to develop that sense, nothing in the requirements for professional advancement requires us to cultivate it, and nothing in our curricula puts anyone in the position of helping students develop it.

I also think, though it's a harder case to substantiate, that the narrow and insipid quality of intellectual debate in American universities (remarked earlier in this essay) has come all the more easily as, and because, they have given over the emphasis on a standard of rational accountability in the face of disciplinary proliferation and subdifferentiation. This would happen if only because there is less and less room to make large issues of principle the subject of reasoned discussion—these will usually fall into the cracks between disciplinary norms. So when large issues, moral or political issues, do arise, they typically do so in one of two ways: as presuppositions of a disciplinary discussion—in which case the politics coded into the discipline do most of the work that otherwise would require argument—or as matters of preexisting commitment or communal identity rather than of reasoned defense. The bland lifestyle-liberal consensus on our campuses may not be attractive, but it fits there.

Those who value inquiry and education, who embrace the ideals of the university and deplore the blandness and entropy, cannot but want to fix these problems. As I said before, I have not heard anyone suggest a plausible remedy, and I am skeptical that any permanent one is even possible. But there can be amelioration: some conditions inherent in the pursuit of higher education suggest clear means to making it better.

One of these conditions is that institutions—and the faculty and administrators that do much to determine their character—have long and consistently committed themselves to the goals of robust intellectual discourse and liberal education. From evidence admittedly anecdotal, my sense is that most administrators and most faculty truly want intellectual diversity, trenchant and engaged debate, and a rich liberal education for their students. But whether they truly want it or not, they say they do, and that means something. It means they have a sense that people who fund education (and people who are paying for theirs or their children's) expect to hear things like this; they have a sense that the integrity of the university's mission requires that a meaningful order give coherence to the great diversity of things that teachers teach, researchers research, and students study. Such statements of mission cannot be dismissed as the smug luxuries of universities in their days of ease, for they have been asserted all the more volubly since 2008, when the institution came to seem besieged by threats to its funding and by attacks on its usefulness. This suggests that administrators know that the credibility of the whole enterprise depends on showing that it has a rationale and an order. This is an opportunity for those willing to work to make the goods real.

But it is an opportunity that must be seized, and that must be done the hard way, through patient, slow work that concentrates on the only factor that can make serious change possible: the composition and the conduct of the permanent, full-time faculty of research institutions. Paper reforms and new programs cannot do much. If you want to reintroduce serious debate, you need to debate seriously, and that means having faculty in place who have the commitment, talent, and learning to conduct debate on first principles seriously and responsibly. If you want to reintroduce coherence to university curricula, you need to teach coherently, and that means having faculty in place whose courses both responsibly train students in their disciplines and also show where those disciplines point back to first principles. The kind of faculty needed are those who do well what good faculty must do: master their fields, produce outstanding work, participate reasonably in debates and discussions—but who also are willing to take unpopular positions and advance them with integrity, train and mentor students in the major intellectual traditions, and find what is good and useful in contemporary thought and research while being willing to submit it (and to submit their own work) to rigorous question. The experience of several universities has shown how the presence of even a very few permanent faculty who take this aspect of the calling seriously can change the atmosphere of a campus.

Above all this means fostering the careers of those who can become such faculty: those students and younger scholars who understand the importance of reason, tradition, and liberal education and who will insist on tough and rational debate about major issues and not be absorbed into the dull uniformity of sentiment around them. This will not come merely through funding programs for such students, and it will not come from merely encouraging them in their convictions. They need training and mentoring, practical and intellectual, in the skills they will need to succeed. It also means supporting them through the PhD process and after. As with any task of amelioration, greater success leads to greater opportunities. So sympathetic administrators, faculty, and donors must invite all interested students to discover the principles that underlie rational inquiry and to profit from the traditions that have given us those principles. And they also need to offer practical and intellectual help to those particular students who show interest and promise for exercising this kind of leadership themselves.

Students who want to have a crack at carrying out this vocation, at pursuing their careers in service to the recovery of the intellectual life, need to know that it will be tough work. We should not try to make it look otherwise. The academic career is a gamble for everyone. And those students who want to take that gamble while also bucking its fashions—especially if they bring unfashionable religious, moral, or political convictions—should be told frankly that they will need to work twice as hard and be twice as good as their peers, even while committing themselves to learn more than their peers must learn. We must frankly own that we are inviting them to the noble challenge of taking up a hard task for a public good. And then those who respond to that appeal will need to develop the canniness and the discipline to seek out the best intellectual and professional guidance from faculty, to develop real intellectual efficiency (using their time in the most effective ways to make conceptual progress in their disciplines), and to negotiate the challenge of remaining faithful to their convictions and commitments without wearing a chip on their shoulder or a target on their back. These are practical challenges; they require dedication. But they have practical solutions, and those who teach and sponsor teaching can find ways to offer those solutions.

And all those who do want to invite the best students to rise to such a challenge must consider themselves bound to a quite solemn obligation: If we encourage gifted students to make these sacrifices, we had better be willing to help them along and watch their backs; we had better work hard to give them the resources their success will require.

Those with the resources to offer financial support can do much to assist these students. The needs are specific and targeted. Imagine undergraduate students with the gifts to excel in academic work and the ambition to contribute to the effort of reinstituting the intellectual life—what will they need? They will first of all need faculty mentors during and after their undergraduate years who can offer them (both in groups and individually) the intellectual tools for understanding the disciplinary system, its opportunities and its limits, and the best paths to negotiate success within it. Programs at or near major universities offering such guidance are proving to be among the most effective ways of helping students achieve influential positions within the academy, all the while retaining their integrity; in ten years, the Witherspoon Institute has assembled an impressive roster of its alumni now placed in major PhD programs and in tenure-track jobs. These programs are likely to work at universities where there are permanent faculty already sympathetic to their aims. But not all universities have such faculty, and few have very many; undergraduate and graduate students at many universities will not have access to faculty who are sympathetic *and* secure enough professionally to offer support *and* accomplished and savvy enough to offer useful counsel. So at the same time, one of the most effective ways of advancing a cohort of aspiring scholars is to help them form networks that include both students and faculty from *other* universities. Intensive summer seminars for students from many universities—with colloquia and workshops led by such faculty and targeted to such students—can be a very cost-efficient way of fostering these networks and advancing the influence they can have on the various disciplines.

Finally, donors with large resources should be aware that the present moment is an especially propitious one for influencing the course of instruction and the intellectual life at universities. This is the other side of Vogler's just and powerful complaint that universities seem too often to be up for sale. The fact is that only a very few of them can feel the confidence both in their endowments and in the circumstances they will be facing in the next couple decades to be cavalier about sources of money. Universities that are prestigious but cash-strapped—these include the best public universities but also a surprising number of the most elite private institutions in the United States—simply cannot afford to disregard gifts, especially gifts that allow them to offer that most pressing of needs, funds for instruction. It is a maxim among development professionals at universities that it is vain to ask donors to support instruction, since they will regard that as the *normal* responsibility of the school. But precisely because instruction is costly, with enormous financial overhead, it is becoming something that at many schools the donor looking to have real influence on the future may consider. Grants targeted at establishing (say) a Western civilization course, if offered in the right terms and designed in the right way, may find ears readier to hear than they did ten and twenty years ago. Such gifts need to be carefully designed to ensure that the universities receiving them cannot merely do with them as they like, and there are innovative ways of achieving this.

But inevitably the most important duties for supporting the students who respond to the challenge of rescuing the intellectual life of universities devolve upon faculty; they are the ones in a position to make a difference from week to week and month to month in the careers of these students. And, like the students, they must face the fact that undertaking the task demands of them a double labor:

they will be of no use unless they are actively publishing as scholars and taking their duties in the classroom and in the conference room seriously—that is, unless they do what is required of all faculty who truly do their jobs. But they must work at a different set of challenges at the same time.

Trite as it may sound, practicing as completely as possible the virtues their roles call for is one important contribution they can make. Crucial is their willingness to model the intellectual rigor and candor that they want to promote. For those who hold religious or political commitments that vary from the easy menu of consensus found on most universities, this means resisting the temptation to dissemble those commitments. But it means also resisting the temptation, equally real and often more satisfying, merely to dismiss the claims, assumptions, and intellectual fashions around them and to assume an air of caustic disaffection. These faculty need to assume the intelligence and good faith of their colleagues, especially those whose views differ most from theirs; in most cases, the intelligence and good faith are pretty palpable to the fair-minded. They need to assume also the seriousness of these colleagues' work and bring to their engagement with that work the same rigor and the same charity they would want to see brought to their own. It is important that they not claim the role of a persecuted minority and claim attention and representation on that ground; true or not (and honestly, how badly persecuted can most tenured faculty be?), their only interesting claim is not that they have been treated badly but that they have better arguments. This requires some artfulness, some knowledge of what is useful to say and what is not. But far more, it requires that determination that Aristotle and Thomas Aquinas exemplify—to find what is true and useful even in the most unsympathetic positions.

What *practically* can such faculty do? First, they can ask whether the courses they are offering are the courses their students most need. In most disciplines, courses that teach basic principles of reason instantiated in disciplinary questions, that note and explain the limits of the discipline, and that introduce the classic sources of academic intellectual life are utterly legitimate. These courses, sustained over time, can draw the attention of serious students to the possibilities that the intellectual life holds. Faculty can also be alert for occasions to introduce academic programs and sequences at their universities that can accomplish these intellectual goals on a larger scale. Since the most alert administrators know that the continued prestige (or continued survival) of their institutions can depend on cutting loose from the lemming charge of universities toward automated instruction and utilitarian programs, some will recognize programs like this—when well-conceived and introduced with intellectual seriousness and generosity—as a real opportunity. They can be institutionally very successful; the voluntary core curriculum in great works of the Western tradition at Emory University is a good example.

Courses and programs, however, will not make even the best and most committed students into intellectual leaders; they can only attract students who have the talent and the interest to try. That is when the faculty's real work begins: the sustained, intense, hard work of mentoring students. They have to spend real time with students who seem interested in rising to the challenge and to accompany them intellectually in the way good teachers will do with protégés: guiding their reading, talking to them about their other coursework, reading paper drafts when asked, and so on. They need also to offer the practical guidance that, again, good teachers will offer: show them some of the professional tradecraft by which young scholars can state scholarly interests without sounding naive, can address faculty they have never met, and can know when and how to ask the right questions. But in addition to these things, mentors need to help students develop skills that are especially necessary for those who will bring to their intellectual careers a commitment to convictions (moral, religious, political) that do not routinely enjoy respect on university campuses. Students must learn how to look for what is reasonable and defensible in arguments and in fields of study that may seem (and may be) hostile to their convictions, how to discuss these sharply and courteously, how to call attention to fallacies and mistakes generously and without trying to close down discussion, how to own the presence of their convictions without expecting others to be interested in hearing about them, and how to avoid being classed as (indeed how to avoid being) a "special interest" scholar with an agenda. Students will need to know how to read the conventions of their fields and the scholarship in their fields, and how to place these in context. Mentors must think hard about the skills—skills in research, in note-taking, in reading, in writing, in professional rhetoric—that they have developed in their careers and about how to pass these on to the students they mentor.

This notion of "a way forward"—the amelioration of the state of the university through the fostering of the careers of those students who, one by one, can make a contribution to it—may seem tortuously prolonged, unambitious, anticlimactic. But the world of the university is lousy with paper reforms. Amelioration may transpire, or it may not; but if it does, it will be only slowly and patiently, and by means like this.

NOTES

1. See Louis Menand, *The Marketplace of Ideas: Reform and Resistance in the American University* (New York: W. W. Norton & Company, 2010), 134–41.
2. The story has been often told and often recalled. An important history is Laurence R. Veysey, *The Emergence of the American University* (Chicago, IL: University of Chicago

Press, 1965), 180 and following. A moving account of the episode at one major university is Lionel Trilling, "The Van Amringe and Keppel Eras," pp. 14–47 in *A History of Columbia College on Morningside* (New York: Columbia University Press, 1954).
3. See, for instance, Jaroslav Pelikan, *The Idea of the University: A Reexamination* (New Haven, CT: Yale University Press, 1992), ch. 8; Gerald Graff, *Professing Literature: An Institutional History* (Chicago, IL: University of Chicago Press, 1987), chs. 7–8.
4. One such complaint, much reviewed, is Anthony T. Kronman, *Education's End: Why Our Colleges and Universities Have Given Up on the Meaning of Life* (New Haven, CT: Yale University Press, 2007). There is a thoughtful discussion of the research-university model, with a critical edge, in Bill Readings, *The University in Ruins* (Cambridge, MA: Harvard University Press, 1996).

15

Healthcare

Jesús Fernández-Villaverde

Few tribulations are worse than illness. The torment in our bodies and the turmoil in our souls darken even the most resilient characters. When the sick person is a relative or friend, our impotence in the face of his suffering can hurt as much as physical pain. That is why all religions praise the comfort of the sick as a work of mercy. And that is why medical doctors are, in every society, among the most esteemed professionals.[1] In movies, marrying the doctor is the perfect happy ending. I have yet to see a movie where the hero or heroine ends up marrying the economist.

Similarly, healthcare is a crucial thread in the tapestry of social conditions that allows us, either individually or as communities, to fulfill our goals in life and attend to matters of ultimate concern. It is not by accident that John Finnis starts his celebrated enumeration of the basic forms of human good with life and the conditions for health.[2] It stands to reason that the common good requires the best healthcare possible given the current state of medical knowledge and the practical concerns of material resources.

Note that I chose the words healthcare, not health insurance. A distinction between these two terms is the basis of a sound analysis of the topic. The goal of healthcare is patient-centered, high-quality, innovative care for all. Health insurance is a means to achieve this goal. As I will argue below, an efficient and fair healthcare system will consist of parts that involve health insurance (coverage against large, unforeseen events) and parts that do not (preventive and routine care).

Confusion about the ends of healthcare has often led us astray. For example, sometimes costs containment seems to be an end in itself. Even worse, on occasion, positions that reflect personal values—perfectly respectable in a free society but not intuitively true to some of us—are presented as self-evident healthcare imperatives that government regulation should impose. When Aristotle stated that we deliberate not about ends but about means, he quickly added, "For a doctor does not deliberate whether he shall heal."[3] Unfortunately, in the modern world, what Aristotle thought was beyond dispute is no longer a safe bet.

But let's abandon these foundational issues and dive into the matter at hand. There is much material to cover.

HEALTH EXPENDITURES: HIGH AND GROWING

If it seems that we talk more than ever about healthcare, it is because health expenditures are high and growing fast. Every year, the Organisation for Economic Co-operation and Development (OECD), a group of representatives from democratic market economies, compiles key indicators of health across its members and when possible, for key emerging economies (such as Russia and Brazil). In the 2013 release of these indicators, we learn that health expenditure per capita in all OECD countries in 2011 (or nearest year available) was $3,322. From 2000 to 2011, the rate of growth on health expenditure per capita was 3.7 percent. That is, 44 percent of the total had accumulated in one decade.[4]

The figures for the United States are striking. The nation spent, in 2011, $8,508 per capita on health (with a growth rate of 3 percent from 2000 to 2011). As a share of gross domestic product (GDP), health expenditure is 17.7 percent: more than one-sixth of all the goods and services produced in a year by the U.S. economy. Of the $8,508, the government spends $4,066 (basically through Medicare and Medicaid), and families and firms spend $4,442. The U.S. government spends more on health per capita than the government of any other OECD country, except Norway. In fact, the United States spends more on healthcare than on Social Security or national defense.

The OECD data also tell us that health expenditure is uniformly high among rich countries (with the United States's health expenditure being very high). This is despite the different ways in which health systems are organized—from a more market-oriented system in Switzerland (11 percent of GDP) to the single-payer system of Canada (11.2 percent of GDP) to the national health system of the United Kingdom (9.4 percent of GDP).[5] A similar statement holds for the *growth* in health expenditure. Why do we spend so much on healthcare? And why is expenditure growing so fast? Many economists emphasize four reasons:

1. **Technological progress.** As medical technology improves, we develop better treatments. However, these treatments are often increasingly costly, as we run out of inexpensive innovations.[6] Take coronary heart disease, where death rates have fallen by more than two-thirds over the past four decades. In the early 1970s, after a patient had a heart attack, hospitals could do

little. Nowadays, hospitals offer an array of highly effective yet costly treatments to deal with heart attacks, and pharmaceutical companies sell an impressive set of expensive drugs to prevent relapses.

2. **Aging.** Health expenditure is linked with age. Most eighteen-year-olds are healthy. Except for checkups and perhaps glasses and the occasional prescription, they do not spend much on health. But even the healthiest ninety-year-olds require a fair amount of medical attention. Thanks to better medical knowledge, better behavior (mainly, less smoking), and higher income, life expectancy has increased dramatically. I could present dozens of statistics, but my favorite one comes from Angus Deaton:[7] Only one out of 2,500 girls born in 1910 in the United States celebrated her one-hundredth birthday in 2010. But it is a reasonable guess that one of two girls born in the United States in 2010 to a white, middle-class family will celebrate her one-hundredth birthday in 2110. Indeed, by 2050, 8 percent of the U.S. population will be eighty years or older.

3. **Economic growth.** As we become richer, we demand more health services. There are many goods of which, once we reach a certain level of income, we do not demand additional quantities. I drink the same amount of milk—and of the same quality—as when I was a poor graduate student. If my income were to triple tomorrow, I would still consume exactly the same amount of milk as I do today. But as our material needs (food, housing, transportation) are easier to meet thanks to economic growth, our demand for *other* goods (culture, amenities, health) increases. For example, health expenditures in South Korea have been growing a hard-to-believe 8.7 percent per year since 2000. As South Koreans have become well-off, they have started asking for more healthcare. Few things are more precious for a wealthy person than an extra year of life.

4. **Cost disease.** There are many goods and services where technological improvements do not easily translate into higher productivity. If you want to have a thirty-minute conversation with your doctor about treatment options, it takes the same thirty minutes that it took fifty years ago. However, as the general level of productivity in the economy increases, the opportunity cost of those thirty minutes for the doctor (and hence, her wage in a competitive market) has grown as well. This phenomenon is called by economists the "cost disease."

While the first three causes (technological progress, aging, and economic growth) raise challenges for societies (How will we finance Medicare when an older, richer population demands the latest oncological treatment?), they are also reasons to celebrate human ingenuity. For instance, according to Mark McClellan and Daniel Kessler, each dollar spent on cardiovascular care has brought four dollars in benefits.[8]

More problematic is the cost disease. However, there is no consensus about how important it is in practical terms: technologies, such as the internet, allow for a better use of doctors' time, which can compensate for the negative consequences of activities such as personal consultations that are harder to mechanize. In fact, other service industries, such as restaurants and retail, have experienced large productivity improvements that seemed unlikely in the 1980s. Amitabh Chandra and Jonathan Skinner have argued that similar improvements in productivity are possible in the health sector.[9]

Interestingly, the growth in health expenditures in the United States has slowed down in the last few years (even after controlling for the effect of the financial crisis).[10] The consequences of such a slowdown, if maintained, are considerable. For example, the sustainability of the federal budget hinges on the growth rate of Medicare and Medicaid (in comparison, the expected growth in Social Security benefits as a percentage of GDP is rather small). The literature is still discussing the reasons for this slowdown and whether it will be permanent. While there are some reasons to be optimistic (such as the adoption of information technology across the medical sector), one must remain cautious. A similar slowdown in the second half of the 1990s turned out to be short-lived.

In this section, I have argued that healthcare is expensive and likely to get more so over time. Our next task is to ask how we can provide it to all in a way that is both efficient and fair.

THE MARKET IN HEALTH SERVICES

Every morning, I can drive to Le Petit Mitron, a patisserie close to where I live, outside Philadelphia. For a few dollars, I can buy some of the shop's outstanding baguettes. Patrick, the owner of the shop, is a small-business owner. The market provides him with incentives to ensure that his costumers have a reliable supply of high-quality bread. Yes, there are health regulations, and yes, the price of the ingredients that go into the baguettes are distorted by agricultural subsidies. But, by and large, the government plays a minor role in guaranteeing that I can have my morning toast. Indeed, most people would find odd the idea of a public bread system. Similarly, most voters would respond with outrage to the idea of being forced into buying a bread-insurance plan.

The reason is simple: many markets work well. There is bread in the bakeries, there are cars at the car dealer, and there are books at bookstores, because the price system provides economic agents with incentives to ensure these results. Of course, markets are never perfect outside economics textbooks. More often than not, we face inefficiencies such as limited competition or externalities. The intelligent case for markets has never been that they are flawless, a proposition so obviously untrue that it is not even worth discussing.[11] The case for markets is that they *usually* work *better* than *feasible* alternatives.

Note that I italicized three words: usually, better, and feasible. The word *usually* tells us that sometimes, markets fail. A market for national defense is unlikely to work, because it is impossible for a private air force to defend my house but not that of my neighbor, who refuses to buy the service. The word *better* reminds us that, even when markets do not work well, the alternatives may be worse. Flying with a private airline can be a ticket to an unpleasantness experience. But those of us who have flown in government-run airlines understand that service can be considerably worse. The final word, *feasible*, emphasizes that one should not judge market behavior against an idealized public service staffed by angels. Alternatives to market systems are run by humans—with their greatness, their shortcomings, and in particular, without the incentives provided by the profit motive.

Do markets for health work like the market for bread or like the market for national defense? There is no widespread consensus among economists. Few economists would deny that the market for bread works well, and even fewer would claim that a market for national defense would work satisfactorily. But there is less agreement about the market for healthcare.

Why this divergence of opinion? The answer comes from a seminal article by Kenneth Arrow, who pointed out that markets for healthcare suffer from a few peculiarities.[12] I highlight four of them here.

First, the demand for healthcare is irregular and unpredictable. I never know when I will be diagnosed with cancer. The costs associated with these unforeseeable contingencies may run into hundreds of thousands of dollars. Except for the very rich, a healthcare system exclusively based on one's wealth implies too much risk-bearing. We need a mechanism for sharing these risks. Some of us will never have major healthcare costs and will die peacefully in our sleep; others will be less fortunate and will use millions of dollars of care. But it is difficult to tell today who will be in each group over forty years.

Unfortunately, insurance markets are plagued by what economists call moral hazard and adverse selection. Moral hazard means that I change my behavior when I know I am covered by insurance. I once went without health insurance for a week. During that week, I was really careful going down the stairs in my apartment building. Now that I am covered, I pay less attention. Moral hazard does not require that everyone start misbehaving (I still do not jump down the stairs!), only that some people will be a bit less careful. Adverse selection means that I will only enroll in insurance when, in my assessment, the probable benefits

I will get out of it are higher than the costs. Many young people enroll in the cheapest low-services insurance plan they can find. Later, as they age or they marry, they switch their insurance to a more expensive, high-services plan. While this behavior is rational at an individual level, it presents problems for a society. The high-services plans only pool bad risks, raising their costs and hence their prices. A higher price will induce even more people not to take up good insurance, making the pool of risks worse and worse. In fact, there can even be a complete breakdown of the insurance market.

Second, healthcare is a market where information is highly asymmetric between the seller (the hospital or the doctor) and the buyer. In addition, the buyer often cannot test or value the product. In nearly all markets, the seller of a good knows more than the buyer. Patrick, the owner of Le Petit Mitron, knows better than I do the ingredients he uses for bread. But I can easily taste the bread and assess its quality—perhaps not perfectly, but to a fair degree. Also, I know that I prefer an almond croissant to a regular croissant. In comparison, it is much harder for me to assess the quality of an oncological treatment or to decide which of the different treatment options I "prefer." Markets work better when the difference in information between seller and buyer is small than when it is large. Consider the problems of taking your car to the mechanic or hiring a contractor at your house: Do you really need that new transmission fluid or that new roof insulation? Few people rank dealing with car mechanics or with contractors as thrilling experiences.

Often, these problems are solved through reputation, established either by repeated interaction with the seller or through social knowledge, such as online reviews. However that leads us to the third peculiarity of the market: Purchases of health services are often urgent and nonrepeated. If my car breaks down tomorrow morning, I can always rent a car for a couple of days and search for a good mechanic. On the other hand, if I suffer a heart attack, I need immediate attention, and I cannot carefully consider the merits of different hospitals. Also, I will not likely have repeated heart attacks, so I can't really compare several hospitals in that regard.

Finally, many improvements in medical technologies are derived from research that has little immediate "market value." Without research in fundamental mathematics, your cellphone would not work. However, phone companies would have never financed mathematicians in the 1960s who were developing those algorithms, because nobody knew at the time that their discoveries would be crucial for a product that had not been invented yet. Without public subsidies for research, technological innovation is bound to slow to a crawl.

Of course, many of these arguments lie in a gray area: Yes, there are asymmetries of information, but the internet has lessened them. Yes, the need for many health services is unexpected, but many other services, such as checkups or maintenance treatments, are routine. Yes, we need subsidies for research, but the products that come from it also need to get to consumers. It is a matter of degree, and we lack a perfect index to assess whether we are closer to the situation in which markets work well or the situation in which they do not.

My assessment of the theoretical arguments and my reading of the empirical evidence is that when all considerations have been weighed, a carefully designed market for healthcare that includes vouchers for basic insurance (taking into account the needs of lower-income families and the chronically ill) plus public subsidies for research and development in basic medical sciences is the best way to organize our health system.

But before I can outline how such a market would work, I need to discuss how healthcare is, right now, not working well in the United States. Those failures, however, cannot fully be blamed on the market system: Distortions and regulations are so pervasive in the system that it is hard to even call it market-based.

HEALTHCARE IN THE UNITED STATES: PROBLEMS

I have already pointed out that the United States spends considerably more on healthcare than does any other country. That fact, by itself, is neither positive nor negative. The problem comes when we realize that we do not get a good return on our investment.

First, let us consider the investment in terms of outcomes. In 2011, the life expectancy at birth in the United States was 78.7 years, lower than the average of the OECD (80.1 years) and more than fours years below the leader (Switzerland, with 82.8 years). A child born in Slovenia, Portugal, or Greece will live longer, on average, than a person born in the United States. Part of the difference comes from a high homicide rate, a high traffic-accident rate, a high suicide rate, and rampant obesity (all areas where the United States does poorly—particularly in the area of weight, where the United States defeats all competitors by several pant sizes). While all of those statistics are deplorable, they are largely beyond the scope of the healthcare system. However, part of the difference comes from a healthcare system that falls short for many.

This can be seen, for example, in the fatality rate of adults age forty-five and over within thirty days of hospital admission for ischemic stroke, in the rate of surgical complications, in the life expectancy of cancer patients, and in vaccination rates. While in most cases, the United States does better than the average OECD country along those dimensions, it never reaches the tops of the table, and often, it is outclassed by countries that spend much less on healthcare.

Second, consider fairness. In 2009, 26.2 percent of the poorest Americans visited their dentist, while 56.9 percent of the richest ones did. In France, 63.9 percent of the poorest French visited their dentist, and 82.3 percent of the richest ones did. The United States ranked second in terms of inequality in access to dental care in a sample of sixteen OECD countries (after Canada, although Canada has a much higher level of *overall* access). Poor Americans go less often to the dentist than do the poor in any of the other countries in the sample.

Obviously, not everything is bleak: Some of the leading hospitals in the world are in the United States, and U.S. universities, clinics, and firms are world leaders in medical innovation. When potentates around the world fall ill, they quickly forget their virulent anti-Americanism and find their way to the Mayo Clinic. Every year, when the Nobel prizes in medicine and physiology are announced, U.S.-based researchers receive a disproportionate share of them.[13]

Where do the problems come from? Why is the United States not getting a good return for its money? Because a number of misguided policies undercut cost control, competition, and efficiency. Let's investigate some of them.

1. The Tax Deductibility of Employer-Paid Health Insurance

In 1942, in an effort to curb war-related inflation, Congress authorized and directed the president to impose widespread price and wage controls. Firms, suffering from shortages of labor and searching to lure employees, started to offer health insurance as an alternative to the temporarily unavailable wage increases. The Internal Revenue Service sanctioned the practice when, one year later, it determined that some forms of employer-based health insurance would be tax-free. In 1954, a new IRS code solidified and extended the ruling.[14]

This tax deductibility generates important distortions:

1. **It changes the relative prices of goods and services.** Once you add up my federal, state, and local income tax, my marginal income tax rate[15] is close to 50 percent: All the goods I pay for with pretax money are effectively half as cheap as the goods I pay for after tax.[16] Thus, I bias my consumption toward pretax goods, even when it is not socially efficient to do so. This is why economists are suspicious of tax deductions for health, education, or pretty much any other good.
2. **It induces individuals to purchase low-deductible, low-copay insurance** instead of more efficient high-deductible, high-copay plans (a similar problem occurs with Medicare's low-deductible limits). Since the marginal decision about whether to use healthcare is not determined by price,

patients demand extra services, such as redundant tests or luxurious hospital amenities.
3. **It triggers the inclusion in health insurance of goods and services that do not have an insurance component.** A large share of health insurance premiums are, right now, prepaid healthcare plans. Imagine that my health insurance could include toothpaste (after all, it is related to dental health). Since health-insurance payments are pretax, I would choose to add toothpaste to it. Given that the insurance company would need to spend some administrative effort handling the reimbursement of toothpaste, resources are used. At the same time, if my insurance pays for the toothpaste, I would be less careful about its use. The health insurance company will respond by setting up standards for the use of toothpaste (three tubes per year per person!). Before I realize it, I will be spending hours on the phone fighting with a representative of the company about my latest toothpaste reimbursement.

Also, the tax deductibility of employer-paid health insurance means that most employees would not get their health insurance through the individual market but through their employer. This choice has several important drawbacks:

1. **It reduces the options of individuals.** Most employees are offered only a small set of health-insurance options, and they cannot search for those insurance plans that are more convenient for them.
2. **It limits labor mobility and entrepreneurship.** Workers are "locked" into jobs that are not a good fit for them but that offer good health benefits. Individuals are reluctant to create their own small businesses, because they would lose their health insurance.
3. **Finally, it increases the risk associated with unemployment.** Not only does the worker lose her job, but she also loses her insurance.

2. Prices Negotiated by Third Parties

Since most healthcare is paid through third parties (insurance companies, Medicare, etc.), the prices of medical services (and the reimbursement formulas) reflect negotiation tactics, complicated contractual arrangements, sharing of profits across different providers, and other factors that have little to do with the marginal cost of a service. Individuals cannot purchase goods directly at a reasonable price, and this limits the incentives for cost control. Some services are oversupplied, others are rationed, and considerable effort is spent gaming the system. The cross effects among all of these different arrangements are nearly impossible to understand, making the consequences of reform unpredictable.

3. Restriction in Supply

Several important restrictions to the supply of healthcare raise prices and lower service. The most salient is the limited number of medical doctors. There are 2.5 practicing doctors in the United States per 1,000 people. The average in the OECD is 3.2. The reason is that there are 6.6 medical graduates in the United States per 100,000 people, while the average in the OECD is 10.6. This lower supply means, as any textbook in microeconomics would predict, that medical doctors' wages are higher than what they could be. The average U.S. physician makes 5.5 as much as the average worker, while the average Swiss doctor makes only 2.1 times as much. While there are other reasons to account for these differences in relative wages, the limited supply of doctors is a prominent one.[17] American medical schools could train a substantially larger number of students without a significant reduction in quality.

Other important limitations to the supply of healthcare include these:

1. **Around thirty-six states have certificate-of-need programs** that impose regulatory approval for the expansion of medical facilities or major capital projects.
2. **Insurance regulations at the state level have precluded the appearance of a national insurance market, reducing competition.** This problem is particularly serious in small states and in rural areas.
3. **The government has not enforced antitrust legislation vigorously enough in the healthcare sector.** In particular, the McCarran-Ferguson Act shields insurance companies from antitrust litigation.
4. **Abusive malpractice suits have led to defensive practice and excessive litigation costs.** For example, Daniel Kessler and Mark McClellan have calculated that defensive treatments with minimal health benefits have increased the costs of heart disease among elderly Medicare beneficiaries from 3 to 7 percent.[18]

HEALTHCARE IN THE UNITED STATES: CURRENT REFORMS

Not surprisingly, the problems of the U.S. healthcare system (outlined in the previous section) have led to a major reform: the Patient Protection and Affordable Care Act (PPACA) of 2010. The PPACA is not totally without merit. It imposes an excise tax on high-cost health plans that compensates for some of the worst consequences of the tax deductions, it creates health exchanges that are supposed to increase competition, and it advances the idea that cost must be controlled and adverse selection in the insurance market reduced. However, the PPACA has failed at addressing important problems and will probably exacerbate many others, increasing the danger of a move to a single-payer, government-run system in the middle run.

While I would not try to analyze the shortcomings of the reform (which would require a whole chapter by itself), I will note the following:

1. **The cost-control measures in the PPACA are insufficient,** because the underlying problem of misaligned incentives has not changed. In fact, by lowering out-of-pocket payments in some cases, it may worsen it. The actual cost-control measures, based on administrative decisions, are bound to be resented by the public and create strong political forces against their enforcement.
2. **The phasing out of private insurance subsidies will generate effective marginal taxes as high as 80 percent for some families,** with large negative consequences for labor supply and human capital accumulation.
3. **Additional regulation will create the demand for additional regulation,** as the problems of the former are likely to be interpreted as failures of the remaining market aspects of the system.
4. **The dependence of some healthcare regulation on the size of the firm's workforce will create distortions in the size distribution of firms and in their growth.** This phenomenon is well-known in Europe, where collective-bargaining regulations also depend on the firm size.[19]

HEALTHCARE IN THE UNITED STATES: PROPOSALS

Given the problems with the PPACA, what *can* we do about the healthcare system in the United States? The word *can* could be understood in two ways: as in what one could do given control of the presidency and both houses of Congress, or as in what is feasible given the actual structure of the U.S. electorate, the two political parties we have, and the interest groups we endure. I will focus on the first meaning of *can*; I will not worry about whether or not the proposals would ever get sixty votes in the Senate to break a filibuster. I am an economist, not a politician, and I will leave that concern to someone else. (I will not propose, however, ideas so far away from the mainstream that there is no course of events whereby they could be enacted.)

Among the main proposals—and skipping many of the technical details in the interest of concision—I would highlight the following twelve ideas:

1. **The elimination of the tax deductibility of health insurance and the move toward a system of individual portable insurance for unforeseeable contingencies plus health savings accounts (HSAs).** The government should not discourage employer-sponsored health coverage (once, of course, its tax treatment is put on a common ground with other health insurances). It may be the case that the market, on its own, will discover that this is an efficient way to provide healthcare, and we should not prevent this discovery from happening (although I do not think this will be the case; few employees get car insurance through their firm).
2. **The introduction of vouchers for the purchase of health insurance.** The federal government would define a minimum health-insurance package that includes catastrophic coverage, high deductibles (possibly capped by income levels), transferability, and guaranteed renewal. Health-insurance companies would be certified to offer such a package at an actuarially fair price and at the national level. The federal government would offer a voucher to each individual to purchase such insurance.[20] Such a voucher, while respecting individual freedom (nobody would be forced to buy health insurance), would induce a nearly universal take-up rate and eliminate the worst consequences of adverse selection in the insurance market.[21] The basic voucher could be complemented by special additions in cases where extra care is required (such as chronic conditions). It is better to separate these conditions to allow for a cleaner pricing system.
3. **Enhancing the role of HSAs,** which should be the normal way to pay for preventive and routine healthcare.
4. **The voucher system plus additional credits to top off the HSAs of lower-income households** as a substitute for Medicaid and similar programs.
5. **More cost-control measures added to Medicare,** including higher (means-tested) copayments.[22] Also, Medicare should move, when appropriate, toward results-based payments (hospitals and doctors would be paid according to their results in improving patient health) and away from input-based payments (where hospitals and doctors are paid for services they provide). This would be particularly useful in improving preventive care.
6. **The deregulation of the insurance markets to increase competition and technology adoption.** In particular, insurance markets should become national, and in addition to the minimum health-insurance package, insurance companies should have as much freedom as possible to offer individual plans.

7. **The enforcement of antitrust regulation** for all participants in the market, while allowing for mergers of hospitals when economies of scale are at stake.
8. **Increasing the number of medical doctors,** both through a higher number of medical-school graduates and through targeted immigration. The Accreditation Council for Graduate Medical Education should limit itself to quality control and not engage in quantity control.
9. **The modification of malpractice regulation to return to a system that ensures liability but prevents abuse.** In particular, caps on noneconomic damages and widespread (and enforceable) mediation outside the courts are promising avenues of reform.
10. **The acceleration of the adoption of new technologies that save costs,** through a number of regulatory changes. Among these changes, we could mention the repeal of the certificate-of-need program, the elimination of barriers-to-entry in the healthcare sector, and the relaxation of medical-practice restrictions on how to organize healthcare provision (for example, allowing a better management and coordination of specialist care). In particular, specialized providers should face fewer restrictions on their activities.
11. **The distribution of information among patients about healthcare options, treatments, and the quality of providers.** Healthcare providers should also have access to better clinical guidelines, success rates, and rates of medical errors through integrated databases. These databases should be protected from abuse by plaintiffs in medical-malpractice suits who would like to use them as discovery tools. Also, the use of "big data" may help in identifying and correcting hot spots of medical expenditure and high-cost patients.
12. **A redesign of the support for basic research and development** to maximize its impact in the long run.

This long list of proposals must be completed with a note of humility. Designing a better and fairer health system is a daunting challenge. When faced with this challenge, I cannot but remember what F.A. Hayek wrote in his final book, *The Fatal Conceit*: "The curious task of economics is to demonstrate to men how little they really know about what they imagine they can design."[23] Even though I am more sanguine than was Hayek about our prospects for reform, I know we may err and have to adjust our policies along the way. Or simply, as society and technology change, we may need to let institutions respond.

I am not the bearer of good news for those who have tired of the debate about healthcare reform over the past five years. The healthcare system is bound to become a permanent focus of policy discussion. Demographics and technological improvements will ensure that.

Economics tells us that we can do better. Distributive justice demands from us that we do better. A judicious combination of market forces, regulation, and transfers can provide us with more efficient healthcare for all at a cheaper price. More important, the failure to fix the current problems and the refusal to accept the existence of those problems (shown by many who claim to defend freedom) means that we risk a backlash against markets in the near future. In particular, the move to a universal single-payer system looms on the horizon. Because, as Edmund Burke reminded us in 1790, "A state without the means of some change is without the means of its conservation."[24]

NOTES

1. In the United States, "physician" scored highest in occupational prestige in the 1989 General Social Survey.
2. We can quote from John Finnis, *Natural Law and Natural Rights* (Oxford, England: Oxford University Press, 1980), 86: "A first basic value, corresponding to the drive for self-preservation, is the value of life. The term 'life' here signifies every aspect of the vitality (*vita*, life) which puts a human being in good shape for self-determination. Hence, life here includes bodily (including cerebral) health, and freedom from the pain that betokens organic malfunctioning or injury. And the recognition, pursuit, and realization of this basic human purpose (or internally related group of purposes) are as various as the crafty struggle and prayer of someone fallen overboard seeking to stay afloat until the ship turns round; the teamwork of surgeons and the whole network of supporting staff, ancillary services, medical schools, etc." It is most interesting that Finnis explicitly mentions mental health, an area of growing concern in contemporary societies.
3. *Nicomachean Ethics, Book III*.
4. There are three technical details to note here. First, all the numbers are in what economists call purchasing power parity. That is, they already control for the fact that goods have different prices in different countries. Second, all changes in expenditure over time are in real terms—that is, after controlling for inflation. Third, unless otherwise noted, numbers include both public and private expenditures on health.
5. In a single-payer system, health providers are private but they are paid by the government (Medicare is effectively a single-payer system for the elderly in the United States). In a national health system, the government directly provides most of the health services (this is similar to what the Veterans Health Administration does in the United States).
6. Much of the gains in health in the first decades of the twentieth century came from improvements in hygiene, vaccination, and drugs triggered by the discovery of the

germ theory of disease. These advances, such as washing one's hands regularly, were relatively cheap to implement.

7. See Angus Deaton, *The Great Escape: Health, Wealth, and the Origins of Inequality* (Princeton, NJ: Princeton University Press, 2013).
8. See Mark B. McClellan and Daniel P. Kessler, eds., *Technological Change in Health Care: A Global Analysis of Heart Attack* (Ann Arbor, MI: University of Michigan Press, 2002).
9. See Amitabh Chandra and Jonathan Skinner, "Technology Growth and Expenditure Growth in Health Care," *Journal of Economic Literature* 50 (September 2012): 645–80.
10. See Amitabh Chandra, Jonathan Holmes, and Jonathan Skinner, "Is This Time Different? The Slowdown in Healthcare Spending," National Bureau of Economic Research working paper 19700 (December 2013).
11. Many enemies of the market system in academia and the media love to draw caricatures of economists so in love with markets that they cannot see their flaws. These caricatures may make for amusing fiction, but they are a rather mediocre sociological observation of my profession.
12. See Kenneth J. Arrow, "Uncertainty and the Welfare Economics of Medical Care," *American Economic Review* 53 (December 1963): 941–973.
13. There is a subtle point here. Canada can afford to squeeze drug companies and obtain better prices from them, because Canadians understand that by doing so, they change little the incentives of those companies to innovate at the world level. If the United States were to do the same, the incentives would change, and innovation would slow down. There is a compelling case that Europe and Canada enjoy a cheaper healthcare system because they free ride (or at least they do not contribute their fair share) on U.S. medical innovation. It also shows that those who propose that we copy the Canadian system may not be fully aware of what economists call the general equilibrium effects of policy reform.
14. See Melissa A. Thomasson, "The Importance of Group Coverage: How Tax Policy Shaped U.S. Health Insurance," *American Economic Review* 93 (September 2003): 1373–1384. There is also a deductibility of out-of-pocket health expenditures, but only for large expenses (currently, 10 percent of adjusted gross income).
15. The marginal tax rate is the tax I pay on my last earned dollar. More generally, economists use the word "marginal" to refer to a quantity or a price at the border (i.e., the marginal tax is the tax paid on the last earned dollar, the marginal cost is the cost of the final good produced, etc.).
16. This difference is also true, although smaller, for lower-income households, where in addition to the income tax, their marginal dollar is also subject to the payroll tax.
17. See Uwe E. Reinhardt, Peter S. Hussey, and Gerard F. Anderson, "Cross-National Comparisons of Health Systems Using OECD Data, 1999," *Health Affairs* 21 (May 2002): 169–181.
18. See Daniel Kessler and Mark McClellan, "Malpractice Law and Health Care Reform: Optimal Liability Policy in an Era of Managed Care," *Journal of Public Economics* 84 (May 2002): 175–197.

19. See Luis Garicano, Claire LeLarge, and John Van Reenen, "Firm Size Distortions and the Productivity Distribution: Evidence from France," National Bureau of Economic Research working paper 18841 (February 2013).
20. Technically, the voucher could be a refundable credit in the income tax. For example, if the voucher is for $1,000 and the household's tax liability was $2,500, the household would pay $1,500. If the tax liability was only $400, the household would receive $600 from the federal government.
21. The government would need, in the short run, to educate the public about the system. Low take-up rates are already a problem in Medicaid and the State Children's Health Insurance Program. Also, some financial adjustments would be required to equilibrate the ex-post different pools of consumers across insurance providers.
22. A mean-tested copayment is one where the monetary cost to be covered by the patient depends on his income and/or wealth.
23. F.A. Hayek, *The Fatal Conceit: The Errors of Socialism* (Chicago, IL: University of Chicago Press, 1988), 76.
24. Edmund Burke, "Reflections on the Revolution in France," in *Select Works of Edmund Burke: A New Imprint of the Payne Edition* (Indianapolis, IN: Liberty Fund, 1999), v. 2, p. 108.

ABOUT THE AUTHORS

Michael D. Bordo is the Board of Governors Professor of Economics and director of the Center for Monetary and Financial History at Rutgers University. He has held previous academic positions at the University of South Carolina and Carleton University in Ottawa, Canada. Bordo has been a visiting professor at UCLA, Carnegie Mellon University, Princeton University, Harvard University, and Cambridge University (where he was the Pitt Professor of American History and Institutions) and a visiting scholar at the International Monetary Fund, Federal Reserve Banks of St. Louis and Cleveland, the Federal Reserve Board of Governors, the Bank of Canada, the Bank of England, and the Bank for International Settlement. He also is a research associate of the National Bureau of Economic Research in Cambridge, Massachusetts. Bordo has a BA from McGill University and an MS in economics from the London School of Economics. He received his PhD from the University of Chicago in 1972. Bordo has published many articles in leading journals and fifteen books on monetary economics and monetary history. He is the editor of a series of books for Cambridge University Press, titled *Studies in Macroeconomic History*.

Gerard V. Bradley has been a professor of law at the University of Notre Dame since 1992, having taught at the University of Illinois from 1983 to 1992. He earned his BA from Cornell University in 1976 and his JD from Cornell Law School in 1980, graduating *summa cum laude*. Bradley practiced law as an assistant district attorney with the New York County District Attorney's Office until 1983. He participates in numerous professional organizations that involve the study of law and religion and related constitutional issues. With John Finnis, Bradley serves as director of Notre Dame's Natural Law Institute and as coeditor of the institute's *American Journal of Jurisprudence*. He has been a visiting fellow of the Hoover Institution at Stanford University, and is a senior fellow of the Witherspoon Institute. Bradley served for many years as president of the Fellowship of Catholic Scholars.

About the Authors

Paul O. Carrese is professor of political science at the U.S. Air Force Academy, and cofounder and former director of its honors program. He holds a doctorate from Boston College in political science, and masters' degrees from Oxford University in theology and in philosophy and politics. Carrese has been a Rhodes scholar, a research fellow at Harvard, a Fulbright scholar at the University of Delhi, and a visiting fellow in the James Madison Program in American Ideals and Institutions in the politics department at Princeton University. He teaches and publishes in political philosophy, constitutionalism, American political thought and constitutional law, and American foreign policy and grand strategy. Carrese is author of *The Cloaking of Power: Montesquieu, Blackstone, and the Rise of Judicial Activism* (University of Chicago Press, 2003), and *Democracy in Moderation: Montesquieu, Tocqueville, and Sustainable Liberalism* (Cambridge, forthcoming 2016). He is coeditor of John Marshall's *The Life of George Washington: Special Edition* (Liberty Fund, 2001); of *Constitutionalism, Executive Power, and Popular Enlightenment* (SUNY Press, forthcoming 2015); and, of *American Grand Strategy: War, Justice, and Peace in American Political Thought* (Johns Hopkins University Press, forthcoming).

Michael Doran is a senior fellow at the Hudson Institute, where he specializes in Middle East security issues. He has been a visiting professor at the Robert F. Wagner Graduate School for Public Service at New York University. Prior to that, Doran was an assistant professor of Near Eastern studies at Princeton University and taught at the University of Central Florida. He served as a deputy assistant secretary of defense and a senior director of the National Security Council under the second Bush administration. Doran currently serves on the advisory boards for the Alexander Hamilton Society and the Foreign Policy Research Institute and is a member of the Council on Foreign Relations. His 2002 article, "Somebody Else's Civil War" (*Foreign Affairs*, January/February 2002) was the first to advance the thesis that Osama bin Laden used the attacks of 9/11 as a tool to foment a conflict among Muslims.

Michael O. Emerson is the Allyn R. and Gladys M. Cline Professor of Sociology and academic director of the Kinder Institute for Urban Research at Rice University. He earned his PhD in sociology from the University of North Carolina, Chapel Hill, in 1991. Emerson currently teaches courses in race and ethnic relations, religion, urban sociology, poverty and justice, and research methods. His main research interests lie in these areas as well. Emerson has focused most closely on the role of race in shaping social action in the United States, recently by focusing on health, residential segregation, and the institution of religion. Considered one of the leading scholars on race and religion, his work in this area began with *Divided by Faith: Evangelical Religion and the Problem of Race in America* (Oxford University Press, 2000), which was named the 2001 Distinguished Book of the Year by the Society for the Scientific Study of Religion. In addition to several other books on the topic, he also published *People of the Dream: Multiracial Congregations in the United States* (Princeton University Press, 2006). This award-winning book serves as a seminal work on multiracial religious congregations.

Jesús Fernández-Villaverde is a professor of economics at the University of Pennsylvania, where he has taught since 2001. He is also a research associate for the National Bureau of Economic Research and the University of Pennsylvania's Population Studies Center and a research affiliate for the Center for Economic Policy Research. Fernández-Villaverde's research agenda is in macroeconomics and econometrics, with a focus on the computation and estimation of dynamic macroeconomic models. He holds a PhD in economics from the University of Minnesota.

Robert P. George is McCormick Professor of Jurisprudence and founder and director of the James Madison Program in American Ideals and Institutions at Princeton University. He has served as chairman of the U.S. Commission on International Religious Freedom and as a presidential appointee to the U.S. Commission on Civil Rights. George also has been a member of the President's Council on Bioethics and UNESCO's World Commission on the Ethics of Science and Technology. He was a judicial fellow at the Supreme Court of the United States, where he received the Justice Tom C. Clark Award. George has been a visiting fellow at Oxford University and a visiting professor at Harvard Law School. A Phi Beta Kappa graduate of Swarthmore College, he holds degrees in law and theology from Harvard and a doctorate in philosophy of law from Oxford University, in addition to fifteen honorary degrees. George is a recipient of the U.S. Presidential Citizens Medal and the Honorific Medal for the Defense of Human Rights of the Republic of Poland, and is a member of the Council on Foreign Relations. He has given the John Dewey Lecture in Philosophy of Law at Harvard, the Judge Guido Calabresi Lecture in Law and Religion at Yale, and the Sir Malcolm Knox Lecture in Philosophy at the University of St. Andrews. George's books include *Making Men Moral: Civil Liberties and Public Morality* (Clarendon Press, 1993), *In Defense of Natural Law* (Clarendon Press, 1999), *The Clash of Orthodoxies* (Intercollegiate Studies Institute, 2002), and *Conscience and Its Enemies* (ISI Books, 2013). He is co-author of *Body-Self Dualism in Contemporary Ethics and Politics* (Cambridge University Press, 2008), *Embryo: A Defense of Human Life* (Witherspoon Institute, 2nd edition, 2011), *What Is Marriage? Man and Woman: A Defense* (Encounter Books, 2012), and *Conjugal Union: What Marriage Is and Why It Matters* (Cambridge University Press, 2014).

John Haldane is the first holder of the J. Newton Rayzor Sr. Distinguished Professorship of Philosophy at Baylor University and professor of moral philosophy in the department of philosophy at the University of St Andrews, Scotland, where

About the Authors

he is also the director of the Centre for Ethics, Philosophy, and Public Affairs. His research interests include central issues in philosophy of mind; the history of philosophy; theoretical and normative issues in social and political philosophy, ethics, and aesthetics; and artistic, educational, and theological issues approached through the methods of those disciplines rather than through philosophy. Haldane has received numerous awards and grants, as well as fellowships from the Universities of Oxford, Cambridge, Aberdeen, Edinburgh, and Pittsburgh. His recent publications include *Reasonable Faith* (Routledge, 2010), *Practical Philosophy* (Imprint Academic, 2009), *The Church and the World: Essays Catholic and Contemporary* (Gracewing, 2008), and *Seeking Meaning and Making Sense* (Imprint Academic, 2008). Haldane has served as an editor of several academic journals and also has written numerous articles for such journals. Prior to his career in academic philosophy, he studied and taught art, and he continues to contribute to the study of art and art history. Haldane completed both his bachelor's degree (1980) and his doctorate (1984) in philosophy at the University of London.

Harold James is the Claude and Lore Kelly Professor in European Studies, professor of history and international affairs, and director of the Program in Contemporary European Politics and Society at Princeton University. He also holds a joint appointment as professor of international affairs in the Woodrow Wilson School of Public and International Affairs at Princeton University. James was educated at Cambridge University (PhD, 1982) and was a fellow of Peterhouse for eight years before coming to Princeton University in 1986. His books include a study of the interwar depression in Germany, *The German Slump: Politics and Economics 1924–1936* (Oxford University Press, 1986); an analysis of the changing character of national identity in Germany, *A German Identity 1770–1990* (Routledge, 1989); and *International Monetary Cooperation Since Bretton Woods* (International Monetary Fund, 1996). James's most recent works include *The End of Globalization: Lessons from the Great Depression* (Harvard University Press, 2001), *The Roman Predicament: How the Rules of International Order Create the Politics of Empire* (Princeton University Press, 2006), and *Making the European Monetary Union* (Belknap, 2012). In 2004, he was awarded the Helmut Schmidt Prize for Economic History, and in 2005, the Ludwig Erhard Prize for writing about economics. James was Marie-Curie Professor at the European University Institute, and is an adjunct professor at the Norwegian Business School.

Steven Justice is Chancellor's Professor of English at the University of California, Berkeley, where he teaches topics in English and medieval literature and in medieval religious thought, classical literary traditions, and literary criticism. He has held major fellowships from the Stanford Humanities Center, the Princeton University Council of the Humanities, the National Endowment for the Humanities, and the University of California. Justice is the author of *Writing* *and Rebellion: England in 1381* (University of California Press, 1994) and *Adam Usk's Secret* (University of Pennsylvania Press, 2015) and numerous essays. He holds a BA in English from Yale and a PhD in English from Princeton.

Sanjeev R. Kulkarni holds a PhD from the Massachusetts Institute of Technology, masters' degrees in electrical engineering (Stanford University) and mathematics (Clarkson University), and bachelors' degrees in electrical engineering and mathematics (Clarkson University). From 1985 to 1991 he was a member of the technical staff at M.I.T. Lincoln Laboratory. Since 1991 he has been with Princeton University, where he is currently professor of electrical engineering and dean of the graduate school. Kulkarni also is an affiliated faculty member in the department of operations research and financial engineering and the department of philosophy. He spent January 1996 as a research fellow at the Australian National University, 1998 with Susquehanna International Group, and summer 2001 with Flarion Technologies. Kulkarni received an ARO Young Investigator Award in 1992, an NSF Young Investigator Award in 1994, and a number of teaching awards at Princeton. He has served as an associate editor for the *IEEE Transactions on Information Theory*. Kulkarni's research interests include statistical pattern recognition, nonparametric estimation, learning and adaptive systems, information theory, wireless networks, and image/video processing.

Donald W. Landry is the Samuel Bard Professor and chair of the department of medicine at Columbia University. He completed his PhD in organic chemistry under R.B. Woodward at Harvard University in 1979 and his MD degree at Columbia University in 1983. After residency in internal medicine at the Massachusetts General Hospital, Landry returned to Columbia for training as an NIH physician-scientist (1985–1990). He has remained at Columbia, focusing on intractable health challenges. Landry also has advanced an alternative, embryo-sparing method for the production of human embryonic stem cells. He was a member of the President's Council on Bioethics (2008–2009) and, in 2008, received the Presidential Citizens Medal, the nation's second highest civilian honor.

Harvey C. Mansfield is the William R. Kenan, Jr., Professor of Government at Harvard University and a senior fellow at the Hoover Institution at Stanford University. He has held a Guggenheim fellowship and been a fellow at the National Humanities Center. Mansfield received the National Humanities Medal in 2004 and delivered the Jefferson Lecture in 2007. He is the author of books on Edmund Burke, Machiavelli, and Tocqueville, and of studies of liberalism, constitutional government, and executive power. Mansfield has translated books of Machiavelli and Tocqueville, and is the author of *Manliness* (Yale University Press, 2006). In interviews, he counts himself in the school of Leo Strauss and politically as a conservative. He has been at Harvard since arriving as a freshman in 1949, with a BA in 1953 and a PhD in 1961; he joined the faculty in 1962.

About the Authors

Mark Regnerus is an associate professor of sociology at the University of Texas at Austin and a research associate with the university's Population Research Center. His areas of research are sexual behavior and family formation. Regnerus is the author of *Forbidden Fruit: Sex and Religion in the Lives of American Teenagers* and *Premarital Sex in America: How Young Americans Meet, Mate, and Think about Marriage* (Oxford University Press, 2007 and 2011). His research on the adult children of parents who have had same-sex sexual relationships was published in the July 2012 issue of *Social Science Research*.

Roger Scruton is an English philosopher who specializes in aesthetics. He has written more than thirty books, including *Art and Imagination: A Study in the Philosophy of Mind* (Methuen, 1974), *The Meaning of Conservatism* (St. Augustine's Press, 1980), *Sexual Desire: A Philosophical Investigation* (Weidenfeld and Nicolson, 1986), *The Philosopher on Dover Beach* (Continuum, 1990), *The Aesthetics of Music* (Oxford University Press, 1997), *Beauty* (Oxford University Press, 2009), *Our Church: A Personal History of the Church of England* (Atlantic Books, 2012), and *Notes from Underground* (Beaufort Books, 2014). Scruton has written five works of fiction, created a number of general textbooks on philosophy and culture, and composed two operas. He was a lecturer and professor of aesthetics at Birkbeck College of the University of London from 1971 to 1992. Since then, Scruton has held part-time positions at Boston University, the American Enterprise Institute, and the University of St Andrews. In 1982, he helped found *The Salisbury Review*, a conservative political journal that he edited for eighteen years, and he founded the Claridge Press in 1987. Scruton sits on the editorial board of the *British Journal of Aesthetics* and is a senior fellow at the Ethics and Public Policy Center.

James R. Stoner, Jr., is Hermann Moyse, Jr., Professor of Political Science and director of the Eric Voegelin Institute at Louisiana State University. He is the author of *Common-Law Liberty: Rethinking American Constitutionalism* (University Press of Kansas, 2003) and *Common Law and Liberal Theory: Coke, Hobbes, and the Origins of American Constitutionalism* (University Press of Kansas, 1992), as well as a number of articles and essays. A senior fellow of the Witherspoon Institute, Stoner has coedited two other books the Institute self-published, *The Social Costs of Pornography: A Collection of Papers* (with Donna M. Hughes, 2010), and *Rethinking Business Management: Examining the Foundations of Business Education* (with Samuel Gregg, 2008). In 2013–2014 he was Garwood Visiting Professor and visiting fellow in the James Madison Program in American Ideals and Institutions at Princeton University. Stoner served on the National Council on the Humanities 2002–2006, chaired his department at LSU 2007–2013, and served as acting dean of the LSU Honors College in Fall 2010. He earned a BA from Middlebury College and a MA and PhD in political science from Harvard University.

Candace Vogler is the David B. and Clara E. Stern Professor of Philosophy at the University of Chicago. She received her PhD in philosophy from the University of Pittsburgh. Vogler's specific fields of interest are ethics, action theory, and social and political philosophy, as well as sexuality and gender studies. She has special interests in English literature and literary theory and did doctoral work in cultural studies with an emphasis on twentieth-century French thought. Vogler's recent work centers on Immanuel Kant, Karl Marx, Thomas Aquinas, and Elizabeth Anscombe. She has emphasized in various lectures the importance of a liberal arts education at the undergraduate level. From 2004 to 2007, Vogler was codirector of the Master of Arts Program in the Humanities at the University of Chicago. She is the author of *John Stuart Mill's Deliberative Landscape: An Essay in Moral Psychology* (Routledge, 2001) and *Reasonably Vicious* (Harvard University Press, 2002). Vogler has coedited two special issues for the journal *Public Culture: Critical Limits of Embodiment* (with Carol Breckenridge, 2002) and *Violence and Redemption* (with Patchen Markell, 2003). She has just begun writing a monograph on Elizabeth Anscombe.

INDEX

Abi-Rached, Joelle M., 172
abortion, 1, 5, 55, 56, 92, 123, 162, 165
Abraham, 15, 17
academia, 9, 22, 124
  See also university
academics, 23
accountability, 40–41, 42, 44, 181
Adams, John, 89, 156
Adams, John Quincy, 151
Affordable Care Act. *See* Patient Protection and Affordable Care Act (PPACA)
Afghanistan, 145, 147, 152
African Americans, 5–6
aged. *See* elderly
agnosticism, 21, 99, 163, 164
aletheism, Greek, viii, 15, 17, 19
alienation, 15, 21, 173
alliances, 145, 146, 150, 158
American Cancer Society, 124
American Community Survey, 51
American exceptionalism, 145, 146, 147, 149, 162, 165
Ammerman, Nancy, 103
anthropology, 19
anti-Americanism, 196
Aquinas, St. Thomas, 12, 37, 185
Arendt, Hannah, 87–88
aristocracy, 75, 86, 88
Aristotle, 10, 11, 12, 17, 18, 43, 46, 87, 137, 185, 189–90
Arnold, Mathew, 23
Arrow, Kenneth, 192–95

atheism, atheists, 18, 89, 99
An Atheist Defends Religion: Why Humanity Is Better Off with Religion than without It (Sheiman), 98
authoritarianism, 77, 86
autonomy, 169
  family and, 6–7
  individual, 28, 39, 40, 42, 53, 55
  university and, 111, 115

Becker, Penny Edgell, 104
Ben Ali, Zine El Abidine, 147
Benda, Julien, 23–24
Bentham, Jeremy, 1, 19
Berger, Peter, 98
bias, ix, 122–25, 127
Bible, 33, 165
Boethius, 37
Bordo, Michael, ix
Bradley, Gerard V., ix–x
Brennan, William, 167
Brown v. Board of Education, 92
Buber, Martin, 40
Buddhism, 100
Burke, Edmund, 12, 13–14, 24, 32, 202
Bush, George W., 147
business, 3, 4
  dynamism and, 9
  family and, 5–6
  government and, 7
  human good and, 9
  university and, 4, 22
  See also economy

Canada, 190
capitalism, 39
capital punishment, 78
caritas. *See* compassion
Carrese, Paul O., ix
Catholic Charities, 102
Chandra, Amitabh, 191
character, viii, 2, 7, 8, 8n1, 20, 37, 83, 110
chastity, 12, 42, 165
children
    abuse of, 45, 49
    care of, 5, 11
    family and, 11, 50, 51, 64
    marriage and, 53
    sex education and, 42–43, 45
    socialization of, 50, 51, 64
China, 101, 102, 162
Christianity, 15–17, 18, 23, 27, 29, 40, 88, 157
church, ix, 18, 40, 88, 107
    state and, 100, 105, 162
Churchill, Winston, 27, 157
Cicero, 18–19, 19
civility, 2, 113
civil rights, 91, 92
Civil Rights Movement, 91
climate change, 126
Climategate, 126
Cnaan, Ram, 102
Cold War, 89–92, 145, 147, 158
collectivism, 45, 46
Collini, Stefan, 111
Common Era, 18
common good, 3, 11, 90, 162, 163, 189, 215
communism, 1, 170
communitarianism, 39, 40
community
    Christianity and, 40
    family and, 64, 161
    freedom and, 39, 41
    marriage and, 161
    moral, 14
    person and, ix, 1, 38, 42, 45
    political, 39
    religion and, 98
    university and, 107, 114–15

Community Reinvestment Act, 135
compassion, viii, 2, 64
    competition and, 28–34
    economy and, 29–30
    family and, 33
competition, viii
    compassion and, 28–34
    family and, 33–34, 63
    free market and, 31
    religion and, 29
    tradition and, 31
    virtue and, 30
congregational life, 100–104
conscience, 5
consensus, 39, 126, 130, 133, 146, 153, 154, 158, 167, 181
consent, 44, 92, 146
consequentialism, 20
conservatism, conservatives, 3, 23
    competition and, 31
    decency and, 14
    neo-, 146, 147
    social, 13
Constantine, 18
constitutional law, ix–x
consumerism, 3, 14
contraception, 53, 55, 56
Contribution to the Critique of Political Economy (Marx), 23
Copernicus, 125, 126, 127
corruption, 3, 10, 81–82, 93
courage, 43–44
covenant, 15–16
Critique of Hegel's Philosophy of Right (Marx), 13, 23
culture, 43
    family and, 2, 55, 64–65
    Greek, 17
    law and, 167, 169–71
    marriage and, 51
    Western civilization and, 10, 15–19

Darwall, Stephen, 40
Dà Xué (The Great Learning) (Confucius), 33
Decalogue, 16–17, 164

decency
  dynamism and, viii, 3, 9, 14, 21
  family and, viii, 2, 9
  government and, 2–3
  law and, 2–3
  morality and, vii
  person, respect for and, 9, 20–21
  person and, viii
  pillars of, 9–10, 14, 19, 20–21, 33
  society and, vii, 1–3, 9
  sources of, 15–19
  threats to, 9–10
Declaration of Independence, 74, 91, 153
democracy, x, 2, 42, 67, 74, 81, 104, 147
Democracy in America (Tocqueville), 157
deontology, 20
De Re Publica (Cicero), 18–19, 19
dignity, ix, 1–2, 10, 15, 28, 31, 38
divorce, 39, 51, 165, 170
Don Giovanni (Mozart), 32
Doran, Michael, ix
Dred Scott, 92
duty, 20, 29, 43, 68, 81, 93, 155, 172
dynamism
  business and, 9
  decency and, viii, 3, 9, 14, 21
  economy and, 34
  free market and, vii
  morality and, 3
  pillars of, 3–4, 9–10, 33
  social mobility and, vii, 6
  society and, 9
  threats to, 9–10
  university and, vii, viii, 9

economic crisis. *See* Great Recession
economic freedom, 4, 5, 7
economy, 3, 147
  compassion and, 29–30
  dynamism and, 34
  family and, 5–6, 50
  financial policy and, 139–40
  fundamentals of, 132–34
  government and, 133, 134–37, 141
  Great Recession and, 130–32
  healthcare and, 191

  law and, 11, 133
  learning from crises and, 130–32
  monetary policy and, 137–39
  policy and, 133–34
  politics and, 138–39
  reform and, 129
  society and, 129, 132
  sustainability and, 133–34, 139, 141
  university and, 108–10
  See also business; policy
education, 38
  democracy and, x
  moral, 46
  obedience to law and, 76, 77
  rejection of, 3
  religious, 42
  research and, 125
  sex, 42–43, 45
  See also university
Egypt, 147
Einstein, Albert, 113–14
Eisenhower, Dwight D., 153, 154, 155, 156, 157, 158
elderly, 11, 31, 50
Elements of the Philosophy of Right (Hegel), 10–11, 11
Eliot, T.S., 13–14, 14
Emerson, Michael O., ix
Enlightenment, 5, 32, 37, 157, 175
entitlement mentality, 7
European Union, 148
euthanasia, 5
exceptionalism, American, 145, 146, 149, 162
existentialism, 38
Exodus, 15

Fairbank, William, 114
family, vii, ix, 10, 14
  autonomy of, 6–7
  business and, 5–6
  character and, 7, 8n1
  children and, 9, 11, 50, 51, 57–63, 64
  community and, 64, 161
  competition and, 63
  culture and, 2, 55

family *(cont.)*
  decency and, 2, 9
  economy and, 5–6
  erosion of, 2
  failure of formation of, 5–6, 7
  functions of, 50–51
  government and, 6–7, 161–73
  institutions and, 2, 8n1
  kinship and, 62
  law and, ix–x, 11, 55, 65, 162
  love and, 63
  marriage and, 9, 49, 51, 165, 172
  monopoly and, 33–34
  out-of-wedlock birthrates and, 5–6
  person and, 2
  sex and, 50
  social change and, 52–57
  as social construction, 50–52, 53
  society and, 7, 49
  stability in, 49, 58, 59–61fig
  state and, 63–65
  threats to, 4, 9
  university and, 4
  virtue and, viii, 2, 7, 8n1, 33
fanaticism, 2, 9
Fannie Mae, 135
fascism, 1
The Fatal Conceit (Hayek), 201
federalism, 89, 91, 162
The Federalist, 147
Fernández-Villaverde, Jesús, viii
Fichte, Johann, 38
financial policy, ix, 130, 139–40
Finnis, John, 167, 189
fiscal policy, ix, 34, 132, 133
Five Pillars. *See* business; family; law; person; university
"Five Pillars of a Decent and Dynamic Society" (George), vii–ix, 9–10
foreign policy, ix
  alliances and, 145, 146
  democracy promotion and, 147
  disentanglement and, 149–52
  faction and, 155–56
  liberal internationalism and, 146, 148–49
  military readiness and, 154–55
  nation building and, 147
  natural rights and, 154
  neoconservatism and, 146–49
  principles for, 152–58
  realism and, 146–47
  religion and, 154
  schools of thought on, 146–49
  statesmanship and, 153, 157–58
  Washington, George and, ix, 150, 151, 152–58
Founders, 87, 91, 149–52, 156, 159, 162, 164
Francis, Pope, 34
Freddie Mac, 135
freedom
  accountability and, 40–41
  community and, 39, 41
  economic, 4, 5, 7
  individual, 7, 39, 41, 52
  law and, 11
  marriage and, 52
  person and, 28, 37
  philosophy and, 38
  political, ix, 86–89, 89–92, 94–95
  religious, ix, 4–5, 55, 57, 91, 105, 165, 166
  responsibility and, 28
  transcendental, 37, 40
  university and, 107
  virtue and, 164
free market, vii, viii, 4, 8, 31–32
  See also economy
Friedman, Milton, 132

Gaddis, John Lewis, 152
Galileo Galilei, 125
gay marriage. *See* same-sex marriage
Genesis, 15
gentility, 41, 42
George, Francis, 170
George, Robert P., vii–ix, 9–10, 11, 13–14, 33, 67, 175
Germany, 138
Giddens, Anthony, 53, 55, 57
globalization, ix, 34
God, 2, 16–17, 34, 103, 105, 164, 165, 167
  law and, 70, 74

love of, 39
purgation from political language of, 27–28
religious education and, 42
Trinity and, 37
good, 9, 12, 20, 24
family and, 21
law and, 17
state and, 85
university and, 115
government
authority of, 83
business and, 7
constitutional, 89–92
debt and, 131
economy and, 133, 134–37, 141
family and, 6–7, 161–73
intervention by, 28–29
law and, 2, 28
limited, 6–7, 10, 89
marriage and, 7
person and, 161–73
research and, 120–21
self-, 81, 90
subsidiarity and, 6–7
Great Depression, 131–32
Great Recession, ix, 34, 57, 129, 130–32, 135–136
Greeks, 10, 15, 17, 18, 19, 86

habits, 45, 46
Haldane, John, viii
Hamilton, Alexander, 89, 147, 151, 152, 156
happiness, vii, 19, 27, 99
Hardy, Thomas, 30
hate speech, 40
Hauser, Marc, 121
Havel, Vaclav, 28
Hayek, F.A., 201
healthcare, 38, 56, 57, 70, 162
economy and, 191
goal of, 189
health expenditures and, 190–92
health insurance and, 189
markets in, 192–95
problems in, 195–98

proposals for, 199–202
reform and, x, 198–99
taxation and, 196–97
Hegel, Georg Wilhelm Friedrich, viii, 10–13, 15, 38, 40
Herberg, Will, 104
higher education. *See* university
historicism, 11
history, 23, 38–39, 53
homosexuality, 55, 168–69
See also same-sex marriage
honesty, 2
honor, 43–44
Hosanna Tabor case, 171
Hughes, Charles Evans, 93–94
Hugo, Victor, 27
human good. *See* good
human rights, 2, 38, 39
humility, 28
Hunter, James, 55
Hussein, Saddam, 147

Ich und Du (Buber), 40
idealism, 38, 68, 150
Idea of a University (Newman), 22
Imanishi-Kari, Thereza, 121
immigration, 6, 76, 100, 103–4, 150, 163, 201
incarnationalism, viii, 15, 16, 19
individualism, 2, 39, 45, 85, 100
industrialism, 3
industrialization, 21, 134
inequality, 34, 131, 196
innovation, 32, 34, 119
institutions, 27
family and, 2, 8n1
governmental, 2
legal, 2
person and, 1–2
political, ix, 2
reform and, x
religious, ix, 7, 97–105
research, 120–21
social, 10
Interfaith Ministries, 102
Internal Revenue Service (IRS), 196
internationalism, liberal, ix, 146, 148–49

international law, 145, 148–49
Iran, 145
Iraq, 147, 152
Ireland, 100
IRS. *See* Internal Revenue Service
Isaac, 15
Isaiah, 16
Islam, 34, 162
Islamic Society of Greater Houston, 101
isolationism, 148, 149–52
Israel, 15
I-You dialogue, 40–41, 44

Jackson, Andrew, 151
Jacob, 15
James, Harold, viii, ix
Jay, John, 156
Jefferson, Thomas, 150–51, 152, 156
Jehovah's Witnesses, 164
Jesus, 16, 29, 137
Jewish Family Service, 102
Jewish Federation of Greater Houston, 102
John Paul II, Pope. *See* Wojtyla, Karol
Johnson, Lyndon B., 5
Judaism, 16–17
justice, vii, 2, 3, 9, 10, 12, 19, 21, 38, 39, 84, 145
    See also law
Justice, Steven, x

Kant, Immanuel, viii, 20, 32, 37–38, 39, 40, 41, 77, 98
Kennedy, Anthony, 166
Kessler, Daniel, 191, 198
Keynesianism, 131
kinship, 62
Klinenberg, Eric, 57
knowledge
    human good and, 12
    practical, 12
    research and, 107, 119
    science and, 98
    university and, viii, 3–4, 22, 24, 107, 109, 176–79
Kulkarni, Sanjeev R., ix

Landry, Donald W., ix
Lasswell, Harold, 84
La Trahison des Clercs (The Treason of the Learned) (Benda), 23–24
law, 164
    authority of, 28, 68
    consistency and, 71–72, 76
    constitutional, ix–x, 74
    contract and, 11
    culture and, 167, 169–71
    economy and, 11, 133
    family and, 11, 55, 65
    freedom and, 11
    God and, 70, 74
    good and, 17
    government and, 2, 28
    hate-crime, 5
    as instrumental, ix
    international, 145, 148–49
    majesty of, ix, 67–69, 70–71, 73, 74, 77, 79, 92
    marriage and, 52
    natural, 10, 18, 69–71
    necessity of, 67–79
    obedience to, 2, 68, 76–77
    person and, 162
    politics and, 11, 81
    positive, 11, 69–71
    privilege and, 28
    property and, 11
    realism and, 67–69, 73, 76–77, 78
    reason and, 74
    responsibility and, 77–79
    rule of, 38, 90, 133, 155
    society and, 28
    source of, 73–75
    universal, 28–29
    virtue and, 3
Lawrence v. Texas, 92
legalism, viii, 15, 19
liberalism, liberals, 31, 85, 164, 167, 175
libertarianism, libertarians, 7, 38, 39–40, 42
liberty. *See* freedom
Lincoln, Abraham, 92, 149, 153, 157, 164
Lister, Joseph, 125
Little, William, 114

localisation, 14
localism, 14
Locke, John, 37
love, 31, 32, 42
　family and, 63
　of God, 39
　marriage and, 53
　romantic, 29
Luke, St., 16
Lutheran Social Services, 101

Machiavelli, Niccolò, 73, 76, 157
Madison, James, 89, 90, 91, 151, 152, 156
Manent, Pierre, 88
Mansfield, Harvey C., ix
Mantega, Guido, 131
marriage, vii, 8, 21
　attacks on, 4
　children and, 53
　community and, 161
　culture and, 51
　defense of, 4, 10
　equality and, 172
　erosion of, 34
　family and, 9, 49, 51, 165, 172
　freedom and, 52
　government and, 7
　heterosexual, 9
　identity and, 172
　law and, 52
　love and, 53
　meaning of, 54fig
　monogamy and, 14, 58
　nature of, 21
　rates of, 51–52
　redefinition of, 5
　rights and, 56
　same-sex, 39, 52, 55–56, 57, 166, 168
　sex and, 52, 55, 56
　social change and, 53
　as social construction, 52, 53
　tradition and, 14, 52
　university and, 4
Marx, Karl, 13, 21, 23, 180
Marxism, Marxists, 4, 39
materialism, 3, 14, 22, 23, 31

Mayor of Casterbridge (Hardy), 30
McCarran-Ferguson Act, 198
McClellan, Mark, 191–92, 198
Medicaid, 190, 191, 200
Medicare, 190, 191, 196–97, 200
me-generation, 1, 2
Michael H. case, 166–67
Middle East, 147
Mill, John Stuart, 19–21, 39
Miller, Donald, 103
monetary policy, ix, 129, 130, 131, 137–39, 142
monogamy, 15, 58
monopoly, 33
monotheism, viii, 15–17, 19
moralism, viii
morality, vii, 3, 11, 165
moral reasoning, 10, 13, 19–21
Morris, William, 21
Moynihan, Daniel Patrick, 5–6
Mozart, Wolfgang Amadeus, 32
Mubarak, Hosni, 147

Napoleon, 150
narcissism, 42
national security, 154, 155, 162
natural law, 10, 18
neoconservatism, 146–49
neo-Kantianism, 20
Neuhaus, Richard John, 167
New Family Structures Study (NFSS), 58, 62, 63
Newman, John Henry, 22, 23, 24, 32–33, 107
Newton, Isaac, 125
NFSS. *See* New Family Structures Study
Nichomachean Ethics (Aristotle), 137
nihilism, 22
nostalgia, 14
Nozick, Robert, 39

Obama, Barack, 164
Obamacare. *See* Patient Protection and Affordable Care Act (PPACA)
O'Connor, Sandra Day, 67

Index

Organisation for Economic Co-operation and Development (OECD), 190, 195, 196, 198

parenting. *See* family
parson, 40, 42–43
partisanship, 83, 93–94
Pasteur, Louis, 125
paternalism, 20
Patient Protection and Affordable Care Act (PPACA), viii, 70, 198–99
Paul, Rand, 147
Pelikan, Jaroslav, 108–9
person, vii
  autonomy and, 28
  becoming and, 42
  community and, ix, 38, 42, 45
  decency and, 9
  dignity of, 10, 15, 19, 28, 31, 38
  duty and, 37
  family and, 2
  freedom and, 28, 37
  government and, 161–73
  history and, 38–39
  institutions and, 1–2
  law and, 162
  philosophy and, 37–38
  reason and, 37
  religion and, ix
  respect for, 1–2, 7, 9, 15, 20–21, 31
  rights and, 37
  society and, 1–2
  theory of, 39–46
  threats to, 9
  utilitarianism and, 1
  virtue and, viii, 46
  Western civilization and, 38
personalism, 38
personal responsibility, 7
Peterson, Scott, 166
Phenomenology of Spirit (Hegel), 40
Philip Neri, St., 33
philosophy
  freedom and, 38
  Greek, 17, 18
  justice and, 38
  moral, 10, 11
  moral reasoning and, 13

  normative, 12
  person and, 37–38
  political, 1, 10, 84–86
  practical, 17, 18
  reality and, 17
  reflective, 12
  Roman, 18
  social, 10
  of social critique, 10–14
  speculation and, 17, 18
Piketty, Thomas, 34
pillars of decency. *See* family; law; person
pillars of dynamism. *See* business; university
Piltdown Man, 121
Plato, 10, 17, 18
pleasure, 19, 45
Plessy v. Ferguson, 92
pluralism, 68
Poehlman, Eric, 121
policy, 10
  economy and, 133–34
  financial, ix, 139–40
  fiscal, ix, 132, 133
  foreign, ix, 145–59
  interactions of, 140–41
  monetary, ix, 129, 131
  trade, 129, 132
  See also economy
political institutions, ix
Political Liberalism (Rawls), 84
politics
  constitutional government and, 89–92
  corruption and, 81–82, 93
  dignity of, ix, 81–85
  economy and, 138–39
  financial, 130
  freedom and, 86–89, 89–92, 94–95
  justice and, 84
  law and, 81
  monetary, 130, 142
  partisanship and, 83, 93–94
  philosophy and, 84–86
  politicians and, 82–83
  research and, ix, 125–27
  society and, 81
  virtue and, 89
Politics (Aristotle), 137

polytheism, 18
pornography, 39, 40, 45, 165
positive law, 11
positivism, 69–71
poverty, 8
PPACA. *See* Patient Protection and Affordable Care Act
pragmatism, 73
pre-Socratics, 17
prisoner's dilemma, 68
private property, 21
progressivism, 31–32, 68, 73, 74, 76
promiscuity, 39, 40
property, 11, 21
Protestant Ethic and the Spirit of Capitalism (Weber), 30
prudence, ix, 30, 149
Prusiner, Stanley, 125–26
psychology, 28
"The Puzzle of Monogamous Marriage," 58

Qadhafi, Muammar, 147
Quran, 29

racism, 5
Rawls, John, 39, 84–86
realism
  foreign policy and, 146–47
  legal, 67–69, 73, 76–77, 78
  political, ix
reason, 5
  freedom and, 74
  law and, 74
  person and, 37
  reality and, 17
reasoning
  moral, 10, 13, 19–21
  philosophy and, 13
  right, 18–19
redemption, 14
redistribution, 34, 39, 40
reform, vii
  economy and, 129
  healthcare, x
  healthcare and, 198–99
  institutions and, x
  threats to, 4–5
  university and, 110, 176

Regnerus, Mark, ix
religion, 165
  community and, 98
  competition and, 29
  fanaticism and, 2, 9
  freedom and, 55, 57, 91, 105, 165, 166
  institutions of, 97–105
  neutrality in, 28
  person and, ix
  purpose of, 97–100
  religious expression and, 28
  sex education and, 42
  state and, 100
  truth and, 99, 167
  volunteering and, 102–3
Religion Matters (Emerson, Monahan, and Mirola), 104
republicanism, 91, 93, 154
Republican Party, Republicans, 146
Rerum Novarum (Leo XIII), 21
research
  applied, 108–9, 120, 124
  basic, 120, 124–25
  bias and, ix, 127
  bias in, 122–25, 126–27
  categories of, 119–20
  demand-side view of, 120
  and development, 119–20
  dynamism and, 9
  education and, 125
  funding of, 120–21, 124–25
  government and, 120–21, 124–25
  human good and, 9
  institutions of, 120–21
  integrity of, 121–22, 126–27
  knowledge and, 107, 119
  misconduct in, 121–22
  politics and, ix, 125–27
  society and, 120, 121
  specialization of, 178
  truth and, 123, 126
  university and, viii, 22, 110, 113, 176, 178
  virtue and, 23
responsibility, 2, 7, 28, 40, 42, 77–79
Rieff, Philip, 167
rights, 53
  civil, 91, 92
  human, 2, 38, 39

rights *(cont.)*
  individual, 57
  marriage and, 56
  natural, 1, 153
  person and, 37
  political, 91–92
  property, 133
  respect for, 19
  of the unborn, 5
  voting, 84, 86
Roe v. Wade, 92, 166
Romans, 86
  law and government, 18
  legalism and, 15, 19
  philosophy and, 18
  religion and, 18
Roosevelt, Franklin D., 73, 152, 153, 158
Röpke, Wilhelm, 14
Rose, Nikolas, 169, 172
Rousseau, Jean-Jacques, 39, 42, 43
rule of law, 38, 90, 133, 155
Ruskin, John, 21
Russia, 145, 162
Ryan, Paul, 7–8

salvation, 16
same-sex marriage, 39, 52, 55–56, 57, 166, 168
Sandel, Michael, 164, 165
Sartre, Jean-Paul, 38
Savanarola, Girolamo, 33
Schattschneider, E.E., 132
Scheler, Max, 38
Schelling, Friedrich, 38
Schiff, Leonard, 114
Schiller, Friedrich, 38, 41, 42
Schomburg, Harald, 109–10, 113
Schön, Hendrik, 121
science, ix, 22, 164
  human behavior and, 12
  knowledge and, 98
  person, dignity of and, 169
  tasks of, 12
Scripture, 164
Scruton, Roger, ix, 13–14, 14
The Second Person Standpoint (Darwall), 40

secularism, 28
secularization, 27
Semmelwis, Ignaz, 125
sentimentality, 13
sex, 39, 40, 42, 44–45
  family and, 50
  marriage and, 52, 55, 56
  virtue and, 42
sex education, 45
sexual desire, 44–45
sexuality, 43, 53
shame, 42, 43, 45
Sheiman, Bruce, 98
Simeon, 16
Simmel, Georg, 52, 53
Simon, Yves, 164, 165
skepticism, 22
Skinner, Jonathan, 191
Smidt, Corwin, 103
Smith, Adam, 30, 32
Smith, Christian, 52, 55, 97
Snowden, Edward, 154–55
social critique, philosophy, 10–14
social mobility, vii, 6
Social Science Research, 62
Social Security, 190, 191
society
  bourgeois, 39
  civic engagement and, ix
  commercial, 3
  decency and, vii, 9, 14
  disintegration of, 34
  dynamism and, 9
  dynamism in, vii, 14
  economy and, 129, 132
  family and, 7, 49
  international dimension of, ix
  modern, 14
  perfection of, x
  person and, 1–2
  politics and, 81
  religious institutions and, ix
  research and, 120, 121
  state and, 63–64
  university and, 107, 110–11, 115
Socrates, 17, 68, 78
solidarity, 31

Sophists, 17
sovereignty, 38, 39, 70
speculation, 17, 18
speech, freedom of, 39, 40
spirit (*geist*), 11
Stalinism, 134
state
   church and, 105, 162
   good and, 85
   religion and, 100
   society and, 63–64
   See also government
statesmanship, 153, 157–58
statism, 7, 8, 9
Stoner, James R., ix
subsidiarity, 6–7, 63, 64
suffering, 31, 169, 189
Supplemental Security Income, 135
sustainability, 129, 130, 131, 133–34, 139, 140, 141, 192
sympathy. *See* compassion
syncretism, 18

taxation, 34, 40, 135, 137, 141
   family and, 7
   healthcare and, 196–97, 200
technology, 28, 53, 190–91
Teichler, Ulrich, 109–10, 113
Ten Commandments, 162
theism, 39
theology, 14, 16
Theory of Justice (Rawls), 84, 85
Theory of Moral Sentiments (Smith), 32
Theses on Feuerbach (Marx), 13
Thomas Aquinas, St., 12, 37, 185
Tocqueville, Alexis de, 157, 158, 180
totalitarianism, 1, 86, 89
trade policy, 129, 132
tradition, 13
   apostolic, 14
   Catholic, 14
   Christian, 29
   competition and, 31
   marriage and, 14, 52
   progress and, vii
traditionalism, 14
Trinity, 37

Trotsky, Leon, 152
Truman, Harry S., 158
truth, 17, 42, 164
   religion and, 99, 167
   research and, 123, 126

United Nations, 146, 148
United States, 27, 28, 102
   foreign policy of, 145–59
Universal Declaration of Human Rights, 86
universalism, 23
university, vii, ix, 22–24
   academic careers and, 183–86
   autonomy and, 115
   business and, 4, 22
   campuses, role of and, 113–15
   community and, 107, 114–15
   dynamism and, vii, viii, 9
   economic life and, 108–10
   economy and, 22
   education and, 175–76
   family and, 4
   freedom and, 107
   funding and, 182–83
   good and, 115
   humanities and, 112–13
   independence and, 111
   international dimension of, ix
   knowledge and, viii, 3–4, 22, 24, 107, 109, 176–79
   learning and, 113–14
   marriage and, 4
   mission of, 110–13
   reform and, 110, 176
   research, 22
   research and, viii, 110, 113, 119–27, 176, 178
   society and, 107, 110–11, 115
   specialization in, 177–79
   virtue and, 23
U.S. Census Group, 58
U.S. Constitution, 82, 88, 90, 91, 92, 150, 166
U.S. Federal Reserve, 142
U.S. Supreme Court, 85, 92, 162, 164, 171

utilitarianism, viii, 1, 2, 19–20
utopia, viii, 1

virtue, viii, 17
  acquisition of, 12, 43
  competition and, 30
  family and, 2, 7, 8n1, 33
  freedom and, 164
  function of, 44
  law and, 3
  moral reasoning and, 20
  person and, 46
  political, 89
  research and, 23
  sex and, 42
  university and, 23
Vogler, Candace, ix, 175, 180, 181
voting rights, 84, 86

Warner, R. Stephen, 100
Washington, George, ix, 150, 151, 152–58
Wealth of Nations (Smith), 30, 32
Weber, Max, 30, 76
welfare, 19–20
Wesley, John, 30
Western civilization
  cultural foundations of, 10, 15–19
  person and, 38
West Virginia v. Barnette, 164
Whittier, John Greenleaf, 33
Wilson, James Q., 71
Wilson, Woodrow, 6
wisdom, 12, 87, 93, 98
Wojtyla, Karol. *See* John Paul II, Pope
World War II, 145

Zimbabwe, 138

A NOTE ON THE WITHERSPOON INSTITUTE

The Witherspoon Institute works to enhance public understanding of the political, moral, and philosophical principles of free and democratic societies. It promotes the application of these principles to contemporary problems.

The Institute is named for John Witherspoon (1723–1794), a leading member of the Continental Congress, a signer of the Declaration of Independence, the sixth president of Princeton University, and a mentor to James Madison. As important as these and his other notable accomplishments are, however, it is Witherspoon's commitment to liberal education and his recognition of the dignity of human freedom, whether it be personal, political, or religious, that inspire the Institute's name.

In furtherance of its educational mission, the Witherspoon Institute supports a variety of scholarly activities. It sponsors the research and teaching of its fellows; organizes consultations, lectures, and colloquia on contemporary issues and problems; and encourages and assists scholarly collaboration among individuals sharing the Institute's interest in the foundations of a free society. The Witherspoon Institute also serves as a resource for the media and other organizations seeking comment on matters of concern to the Institute and its associated scholars.

For more information about the work of the Witherspoon Institute, please visit www.winst.org.

A NOTE ON THE SOCIAL TRENDS INSTITUTE

The Social Trends Institute is a nonprofit research center that offers institutional and financial support to academics of all fields who seek to make sense of emerging social trends and their effects on human communities.

STI focuses its research on four subject areas: Family, Bioethics, Culture and Lifestyles, and Corporate Governance. Primarily it organizes Experts Meetings, which bring together various scholars to present and discuss each other's original research in an academic forum. These meetings are intended to foster open intellectual dialogue between scholars from all over the world, of various academic backgrounds, disciplines, and beliefs. At times, STI helps to publish a collection of the meeting papers in a single volume, revised and reviewed in light of the discussion.

STI promotes research and scholarship of the highest academic standards. In so doing, it aims to make a scholarly contribution toward fostering understanding the varying and complex social trends that are intertwined with the modern world. STI is committed, then, to that which makes such scholarship possible: intellectual freedom, openness to a diversity of viewpoints, and a shared commitment to serve the common good.

Carlos Cavallé is president of the Social Trends Institute. Founded in New York City, STI also has a delegation in Barcelona, Spain. For more information about the Social Trends Institute, please visit www.socialtrendsinstitute.org.

ABOUT THE TYPE

This book was set in Caslon, the first original typeface of English origin, designed by William Caslon I (1692–1766). Its design was influenced by Dutch type and its characteristics and legibility are the reason it remains a typography standard and one of the most popular typefaces today.